COSMETOLOGY HAIRSTYLING TEACHER-TRAINING MANUAL

BY JACOB J. YAHM

Consultant
PAULINE GRIPALDI

MILADY PUBLISHING CORPORATION
3839 WHITE PLAINS ROAD
BRONX, NEW YORK 10467

ISBN 0-87350-069-5

Revised 1977

©Copyright 1971—1977—1983
MILADY PUBLISHING CORP.
Bronx, N.Y.

Printed in the United States of America

All Rights Reserved.

1988 Printing

FOREWORD

The forward movement in cosmetology education becomes possible only through correct teaching. Beauty culture training advances in accordance with the quality of its teaching staff. The influence of the competent teacher extends through school and far into the professional service in the salon. It far transcends the student's period of formal schooling and continues for many years after graduation.

The most valuable asset of any school of cosmetology is its teaching staff. Providing suitable teachers for all schools of cosmetology is a task so colossal as to challenge the ingenuity of the entire profession in its effort to meet the demand. The ability or inability to provide competent teachers will determine the success or failure of professional education in cosmetology.

The teacher is certainly the most influential factor in cosmetology education. Curriculum, organization, equipment, important as they are, count for little or nothing except as they are vitalized by the living personality of the teacher.

Cosmetology teachers are often recruited from among the most capable practitioners in the salons. These individuals have proven their manual skills and their technical knowledge. They may possess very pleasing personalities and have the ability to express themselves well. However, before these craftsmen can teach satisfactorily they need other types of skills; namely, those associated with teaching.

Although actual work experience in cosmetology is necessary to good teaching, it does not by itself insure good instruction. Teachers must be trained also in the art and practice of teaching if they are to be expected to properly perform their duties.

This text has been prepared to assist in the training of new teachers, and as an aid to practicing teachers in reviewing teaching theories and practices.

Its purpose is to provide teacher educators with well-planned basic course material to train competent individuals to teach in schools of cosmetology.

This publication is not intended to lay down specific guidelines and definite terms for teaching. Its intent is to suggest practical procedures, to identify resources and to stimulate thought processes by which teaching can be made effective and stimulating. It graphically presents ideas that deal with the live, vital problems of teaching and provides suggestions helpful to the planning of practical programs of teaching. It sets forth an outline of ideas that will assist teachers to develop the skills, techniques and understanding required to deal effectively with the many problems of teaching.

Since many teachers of cosmetology are not professionally trained in the profession of teaching, this material should prove helpful as an introduction, a reminder, a reference and as a stimulant for those persons engaged in cosmetology instruction. A special effort has been made to help the teacher to communicate and transfer his skills, knowledge and ideas to his students.

The information contained herein is derived from the experiences of many teachers extending over long periods of time. We are indeed indebted to many State Board officials and progressive beauty school owners and cosmetology teachers for their valuable suggestions in the preparation of this text,

The cosmetology instructor should not feel that he must slavishly follow all of the teaching practicas or procedures set forth in this text. However, it is reasonable to expect potential teachers to be familiar with the careful use of them in their teaching work.

THE AUTHOR

JACOB J. YAHM

Jacob J. Yahm is a graduate of the College of the City of New York, with a Bachelor of Business Administration degree and a Secondary School Teacher's Certificate.

He became a member of the Department of State of New York in 1939, and in 1948 was appointed Examination Technician in charge of all examinations conducted by the Department of State, and served in that capacity until his retirement at the end of 1975.

Nationally, Mr. Yahm played a major role in effecting the merger of the National Council of State Boards of Cosmetology and the Interstate Council of State Boards into what now is the National-Interstate Council of State Boards of Cosmetology. He was especially active in negotiations leading to the merger of the National Association of Cosmetology Schools and the All American Beauty Culture Schools Associated — now operating as the National Association of Cosmetology Schools, Inc.

Mr. Yahm's extensive beauty industry activities are further reflected in the fact that he was chairman of the Allied Cosmetology Council for three years and editor of the National-Interstate Council Bulletin for five years.

For four years he served as Executive Commissioner and Chairman for the National Accrediting Commission for Cosmetology Schools, Inc. In these positions he acquired an extensive knowledge and understanding of cosmetology schools and teaching problems.

Mr. Yahm served as a Commissioner of the Cosmetology Accrediting Commission 1969-1974 and in 1975 served as the 1st Vice-Chairman of the Commission.

In July, 1975 he was made an Honorary Member of the National-Interstate Council of State Boards of Cosmetology.

It is from this wide and varied background and experience that he has compiled the information contained in this text and also for the text titled "325 Teaching Hints for Professional Cosmetology Instruction" and other texts now in process.

PAULINE GRIPALDI

PAULINE GRIPALDI ... Cosmetologist - Teacher - Director - Writer

Mrs. Gripaldi has been actively engaged in the cosmetology educational field for many years.

Starting as an operator in New Jersey beauty salons, her deep interest in education—especially cosmetology education—led her back to school. She continued her cosmetology and teaching education and obtained a teacher's license.

Mrs. Gripaldi's vast interest in cosmetology education continued unabated, and she served as teacher, director of teachers and director of her own beauty school.

On a national level, Mrs. Gripaldi joined and became a very valuable member of the Teachers' Educational Council. As a result of hard work while serving on many national education committees, she was elected to the Executive Board of TEC. She has served as vice-president, president (two terms) and editor of that organization's publication.

Mrs. Gripaldi brought to her task as textbook consultant an impressive background of teaching knowledge, experience and talent. Her efforts in developing this textbook were simply a continuation of her many services to cosmetology education.

CONTENTS

OBJECTIVES OF THIS TEXT

1. **To develop the ability to:**

   a) Teach the theory and practice of cosmetology, using the four-step teaching plan.

   b) Use various teaching aids, such as textbooks, workbooks, audio-visual aids, tests, etc., to the best advantage in the classroom.

2. **To provide information about:**

   a) Specific teaching techniques to be used by the cosmetology teacher in the classroom.

   b) The principles of psychology as applied to teaching.

   c) Personal qualities of a good teacher.

3. **To develop an appreciation of:**

   a) Achieving professional competency as a teacher.

   b) Those personal characteristics that contribute to success in teaching.

KEY TO TERMINOLOGY

In order that the teacher receive the utmost benefits from this text, the use of certain words must be explained.

1. The terms he, him, his, etc. are used instead of he/she, him/her, his/hers, etc. This is done to prevent cumbersome and sometimes ungrammatical language and **not** to denote the sex of the individual.

2. The terms "teacher" and "instructor" are used interchangeably. This is often done just to avoid repetition and sometimes for better phraseology.

3. Beauty culture is used interchangeably with cosmetology, whichever term is most descriptive or suitable.

4. Theory and science in cosmetology are also used interchangeably. Whichever term is being used, reference is made to the textbook or the "why" a thing is done rather than physical performance.

CHAPTER 1

FUNDAMENTAL PRINCIPLES OF TEACHING

FUNCTIONS OF A COSMETOLOGY TEACHER

The basic function of a cosmetology teacher is to provide effective instruction to his students. He should present learning situations that are up-to-date, accurate and based upon currently acceptable practices in cosmetology.

Classroom instruction must be sufficiently flexible to allow the instructor to adjust readily to the varied backgrounds and individual differences of his students. He must understand the methods, limitations and possibilities of individual and group instruction in order to cope with the problems that may arise in the classroom.

The fact that a teacher is an outstanding cosmetologist provides no assurance that he will be successful in his efforts to teach others. In order to teach, it is necessary to be familiar with and know how to use a great many materials, techniques, ideas and special skills, which are referred to as teaching methods.

Teaching is not a routine process; it is truly an intellectual experience. It demands the ability to invent, to adapt and to create new techniques and procedures to meet the everchanging demands of teaching-learning situations.

Although cosmetologists may know **what** to teach, it is important to learn **how** to teach. This in no way reflects upon their skill or knowledge as artisans. It merely means that they must prepare for a new occupation, that of teaching, and will require instruction in how to help others learn what the cosmetologist already knows.

This text deals largely with the methods that teachers must learn to use if they are to have reasonable success in teaching others. The material presented is primarily confined to those methods that are basic in the teaching of cosmetology.

THE ART OF TEACHING

Teaching is an art. It requires dynamic, conscious effort on the part of the instructor and close, personal relationship between instructor and student. Instructors must be able to communicate ideas effectively. At the same time, they must be conscious of each student as an individual and have the insight and understanding necessary to establish a teaching climate which will assist learning.

The successful cosmetology teacher must possess habits of orderly and constructive thinking and analysis in order to help guide the educational processes in the classroom, on the clinic floor and in teacher-student relations.

Good cosmetology instructors must be competent in three general areas. They must:

1. Have a complete mastery of their subject.
2. Know how to organize their material in order to present it most effectively.
3. Possess an attractive teaching personality. Other factors, such as good training facilities, imaginative use of visual aids and periodic evaluation, will make the program even more effective. However, the basic need is for competency on the part of the instructor.

In addition to teaching the basic skills, theories and sciences, the cosmetology teacher must:

1. Develop in students the habit of following an orderly procedure and an appreciation of good workmanship.
2. Emphasize sanitation and safety rules by teaching the safe and sanitary way to do the job.
3. Help build good grooming habits, personality and character in students.
4. Develop wholesome attitudes toward the public.

The basic elements involved in a comprehensive training program for cosmetology teachers are as follows:

1. Teacher's Personality.
2. Technical Knowledge.
3. Manipulative Skill.
4. Intelligence.
5. Good Judgment in Teaching.
6. Efficiency in Teaching.
7. High Teaching Morale.
8. Desire for Self-Improvement.
9. Leadership.
10. Motivation.

1. Teacher's Personality. An instructor may have knowledge and extensive training but for various reasons fails to become a qualified teacher because of a "defect in his or her personality."

More cosmetology teachers fail because of personality deficiencies than because of lack of knowledge. Good moral character, health, intelligence and general education are all necessary for the successful teacher. Other important personality qualities include initiative, industry, tact, good grooming, poise, honesty and loyalty.

To maintain a balanced temperament in the classroom, a teacher should possess the following qualities:

1. An even disposition.
2. A fair, firm and friendly manner.
3. Patience.
4. Sympathetic understanding.
5. Sense of humor.

Good grooming, posture and manners are very evident in the appearance and bearing of the teacher. Furthermore, oral instruction requires clarity, good enunciation, proper pronunciation, effective speech, good tone and proper voice pitch. In addition, other human traits such as enthusiasm, a sense of responsibility, interest, curiosity, and an appreciation of other intangible personal characteristics are also essential to good teaching.

2. **Technical Knowledge.** It is almost axiomatic to say that we cannot teach what we do not ourselves know. In order that the instructor be prepared to devote the proper time to technical instruction he must possess a thorough knowledge of the subject matter. Any plan for effective instruction can succeed only if the teacher has a complete understanding of his material, plans carefully and prepares a meaningful interpretation for presentation to his students.

3. **Manipulative Skills.** The effective cosmetology instructor must use every tool at his command in order to advance the learning process. The demonstration of beauty culture techniques is a most useful teaching device. However, this method of instruction requires that the teacher possess a high degree of manual skills, finger dexterity and coordination of movements. It also requires extensive experience and a thorough understanding of the teaching process.

4. **Teaching Intelligence.** This teaching essential cannot be easily defined. However, it is easily recognized in the successful instructor. It is clearly discernible in the teacher's ability to deal with unusual and unexpected problems. Teaching intelligence becomes evident in the handling of classroom emergencies and even in everyday student-teacher relations.

5. **Good Teaching Judgment.** Good judgment can be developed through experience and conscientious effort by the teacher. Confidence in one's own ability, resulting from a thorough knowledge of the teaching process, contributes to the growth of good teaching judgment.

6. **Teaching Efficiency.** An efficient instructor starts classroom activities without delay. He will inaugurate and develop new ideas without supervision. He will look for and discover weaknesses in his instruction and seek ways to correct them. He will solve problems with a minimum of assistance from superiors and does not expect others to perform his duties.

7. **Teaching Morale.** The instructor's morale is reflected in his attitude toward his duties. He develops a pride in his work which is quickly evident to both students and fellow teachers. He shows an **enthusiasm** for teaching which sets the pace for his students. Enthusiasm is contagious and spreads quickly to the entire classroom.

8. **Self-Improvement.** A good instructor will constantly strive for improvement in professional attitude, approach and teaching proficiency. He constantly keeps up with new trends, new techniques and new developments in order to keep his teaching material up to date.

9. **Leadership.** The instructor must provide the leadership required for directing the student's path to acquiring professional skills, knowledge and technique.

10. **Motivation.** The most perplexing problem confronting the teacher is to find and utilize the motives and incentives for effective learning. The progressive instructor must develop and provide the enthusiasm, interest and desire for creative learning.

Over the years, educators have developed methods for teaching the students who come under their supervision. These methods are the subject of constant examination and study. The progressive teacher strives constantly to improve these methods in order that he may transmit to his students, in the most effective way, the skills, knowledge and characteristics which make for success in the practice of cosmetology.

R E V I E W

1. **In providing effective instruction to his students, the cosmetology teacher must present learning situations of a special type. Name three qualifications for these situations.**
    1. They should be up-to-date.
    2. They should be accurate.
    3. They should be based upon currently accepted practices in cosmetology.

2. **Classroom instruction must be flexible enough to allow the instructor to adjust to the needs of his students. What two factors must be considered?**
    1. The varied backgrounds of his students.
    2. The individual differences of his students.

3. **In addition to being an outstanding cosmetologist, name another qualification that is essential if the teacher is to be successful in his efforts to teach others.**

    The instructor must be familiar with and know how to use a great many materials, techniques, ideas and special skills, which are referred to as teaching methods.

4. **The art of teaching cosmetology requires that instructors be competent in three general areas. List them.**
    1. Have complete mastery of their subject.
    2. Know how to organize their material for effective presentation.
    3. Possess an attractive teaching personality.

5. **List four other teaching areas which the good cosmetology instructor should cover, in addition to teaching the basic skills and sciences.**
    1. Develop orderly procedures and an appreciation of good workmanship in the student.
    2. Teach sanitation and safety rules.
    3. Build good grooming habits, personality and character.
    4. Develop wholesome attitudes toward the public.

6. **Name the ten basic elements in a comprehensive training program for cosmetology teachers.**
    1. Teacher's personality.
    2. Technical knowledge.
    3. Manipulative skill.
    4. Intelligence.
    5. Good judgment in teaching.
    6. Efficiency in teaching.
    7. High teaching morale.
    8. Desire for self-improvement.
    9. Leadership.
    10. Motivation.

7. **More cosmetology teachers fail because of personality defects than because of lack of knowledge. List ten qualities required for a good personality.**
    1. Good moral character.
    2. Health.
    3. Intelligence.
    4. General education.
    5. Initiative.
    6. Industry.
    7. Tact.
    8. Good grooming.
    9. Poise.
    10. Loyalty.

8. **For a balanced temperament in the classroom, name the five qualities which the teacher should possess.**
    1. Even disposition.
    2. Fair, firm and friendly manner.

3. Patience.
4. Sympathetic understanding.
5. Sense of humor.

9. **For good oral instruction, specify six qualities which are important for the instructor.**
   1. Clarity.
   2. Good enunciation.
   3. Proper pronunciation.
   4. Effective speech.
   5. Good tone.
   6. Proper voice pitch.

10. **The instructor must have a thorough technical knowledge of his subject matter for effective instruction. List three important steps for the successful teaching of technical knowledge.**
    1. The teacher must have a complete understanding of his material.
    2. He must plan carefully.
    3. He must prepare a meaningful interpretation.

11. **The demonstration of beauty culture techniques is a useful teaching device. Name three qualifications required for this method of instruction.**
    1. The teacher must have a high degree of manual skills.
    2. He must have finger dexterity.
    3. He must have good coordination of movements.

12. **To prove teacher intelligence is difficult, since it is intangible. Name three ways in which this trait is shown.**
    1. By the teacher's ability in dealing with unusual and unexpected problems.
    2. By his handling of classroom emergencies.
    3. By everyday teacher-student relations.

13. **Good teaching judgment can be developed in what way?**
    By experience and conscientious effort of the teacher. Confidence will result from teaching experiences and contribute to the growth of good teaching judgment.

14. **Name six ways in which teaching efficiency is demonstrated.**
    1. The instructor starts classroom activities without delay.
    2. New ideas are inaugurated and developed without supervision.
    3. He will look for and discover weaknesses in his instruction.
    4. He will seek ways to correct them.
    5. He will solve problems with a minimum of assistance from supervisors.
    6. He does not expect others to perform his duties.

15. **Teaching morale is important. Name two ways in which an instructor Maintains his morale.**
    1. He develops pride in his work.
    2. He shows enthusiasm for teaching which spreads to his students.

16. **How does a good instructor work for self-improvement?**
    He keeps up with new trends, techniques and developments.

17. **Why is the teacher's leadership very important with relation to students?**
    It is essential for directing the students path to acquiring professional skills, knowledge and technique.

18. **What is the most perplexing problem confronting the teacher?**
    To find and utilize the motives and incentives for effective learning.

CREATING A PROFESSIONAL IMAGE

(The Endless Public Relations Task)

It is the responsibility of the cosmetology instructor to create a professional image for the:

1. Teaching profession
2. Student
3. School
4. Beauty industry
5. Public

This goal is enhanced through the use of textbooks, companion workbooks and exam reviews that are professionally illustrated and contain accurate information that all students can understand.

Textbooks that meet these requirements are the:

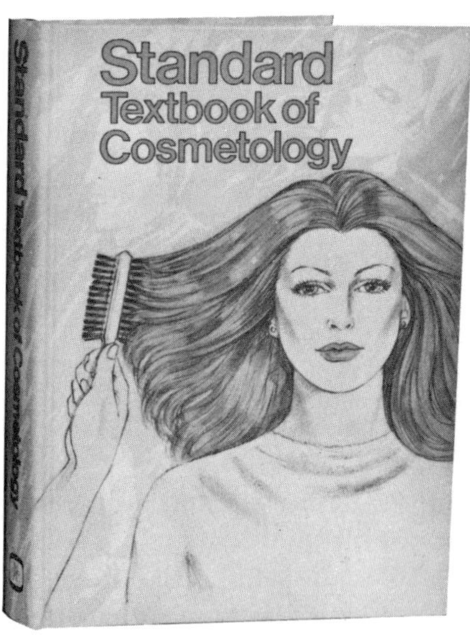

For the proper use of textbooks, consult page 106.

CHAPTER 2

TEACHER MATURITY

THE EFFECTIVE TEACHER

Shortly after the turn of the century, one of the leaders in education wrote as follows: "The teacher is, by all odds, the most influential factor in school education. Curriculum, organization, and equipment, as important as they are, count for little or nothing except as they are utilized by the living personality of the teacher." It would seem obvious from the above that the teaching staff of any educational institution is perhaps its most valuable asset, its most essential requirement for successful operation. As yet, no substitute has. been found for the impact of mind upon mind, personality upon personality.

Teaching is both an art and a science and involves many variables and intangibles which are extremely difficult to describe. For one thing, **there is no single best way to teach.** Effective teaching is a result of a combination of: favorable classroom climate; student desires, motivation and interest; teacher enthusiasm and comprehensive subject matter. All of these factors develop an atmosphere of great diversity and stimulate imagination and creativity on the part of the teacher. This is exactly why all good teachers are not the same nor is it desirable that they be the same.

The greatest value of a teacher lies not in the regular performance of routine duties, but rather in the ability to lead and inspire students to a sincere desire for learning. The instructor must provide the enthusiasm, interest and motivation for such learning. The major problem is to find and utilize the motives and adequate incentives for effective training.

GOOD TEACHING REQUIRES:
1. A teacher with a balanced personality.
2. The proper organization of the cosmetology curriculum and classroom.
3. The ability to recognize individual differences in students.
4. A thorough knowledge of, and experience with, effective teaching procedures.
5. Stimulating student participation in the learning process.
6. The ability to direct the mastery of proper skills and knowledge.
7. Teacher maturity.

IN TEACHING YOU MUST HAVE:

1. **Mastery of Material or Subject Matter.**

    a) Know more than the basic subject matter.

    b) Tie in what you teach with other experiences, needs or problems of students. Develop the importance of the work

    c) Keep up with the latest methods and techniques.

    d) Build a professional attitude toward your work and take pride in it.

2. **Executive Ability.** A classroom requires businesslike management. Besides knowing your subject, you require experience in:

    a) Course and lesson planning.

    b) Adjusting programs to individual students.

    c) Controlling supplies, equipment and operating efficiency.

    d) Preparing records and reports.

    e) How to break down a course into suitable lessons.

    f) How to prepare for the teaching of a lesson.

    g) How to present ideas, facts, theories, principles and information so they are interesting, and easy to understand.

    h) How to demonstrate trade techniques to students.

    i) How to develop practical problems for students to solve by applying cosmetology theory.

    j) How to choose suitable jobs for students to perform in order to learn cosmetology skills.

    k) How to test or measure the amount of learning that has taken place.

    l) How to maintain the interest of students throughout the course.

FOUR AREAS OF TEACHER MATURITY

A teacher indicates that he is mature and well adjusted by his activities in four general areas: (1) social maturity, (2) emotional maturity, (3) moral maturity, and (4) professional maturity.

1. **Social Maturity.** A teacher is socially mature when he can function easily, comfortably, and harmoniously with students. He must be free from the neurotic necessity to dominate and control students, to be unduly submissive to them, or to withdraw from direct contact with them.

2. **Emotional Maturity.** A teacher is emotionally mature when he is able to control his energies, and manage his fears, hates, resentments and loves. The teacher grows in emotional maturity as he learns to accept the realities of situations rather than thinking in terms of his own wishes, desires and prejudices. The teacher who is emotionally mature feels secure and has a healthy respect for himself and his objectives.

3. **Moral Maturity.** A teacher is morally mature when he is equipped to analyze situations and make his own decisions as to how to handle them. He has the mental capacity to make decisions on the basis of known facts or on the basis of his understanding. He has the capacity to make decisions with the full readiness to accept the responsibility for the results of such decisions.

4. **Professional Maturity.** A teacher is professionally mature when he has developed personally-satisfying and socially-acceptable educational objectives, and when he has learned to make constructive and knowledgeable choices from among a number of possible courses of action. He is capable of making such choices after careful consideration and not on the basis of whim, fancy or impulse. Neither are these choices made strictly on the basis of strict rules or rigid taboos handed down by narrow tradition.

The kind of behavior and emotional atmosphere developed in the classroom depends to a large extent upon the teacher's behavior patterns in the four areas of maturity.

STUDENT NEEDS FOR EFFECTIVE LEARNING

One very important element contributing to the success of a teacher is the complete cooperation of students. However, in order to obtain this cooperation it is first necessary to create a classroom atmosphere and tempo which is conducive to good training and a willingness to learn. This atmosphere requires the presence of the eight basic student needs which help to develop and maintain that frame of mind or student morale necessary for effective learning. These basic student needs are:

1. **The need for knowledge and understanding.**
   The teacher must create a classroom atmosphere in which students feel free to ask questions. Every question must be treated seriously and given the attention and respect required to clear up troublesome areas. No question should ever be laughed at or ridiculed.

2. **The need for freedom from guilt.**
   Students must not be made to feel guilty for the most innocent infractions. They should not be constantly reminded of past infractions and made to feel uncomfortable and uneasy. They should be helped to minimize past unpleasant actions and be given the opportunity for unmarred future activities.

3. **The need for freedom from embarrassment.**
   Students should not be made to feel embarrassed by any error in understanding or performance. If necessary, the instructor should assume some of the responsibility to relieve the student of embarrassment.

4. **The need for belonging — being part of the group.**
   Students should be made to feel that their presence is important. If they are absent, the instructor should make them feel that they were missed. Make him feel that he is an important member of the group.

5. **The need for a feeling of accomplishment.**
   Students must feel that they are achieving success. They should be made to feel that they are making progress, even if it is slow.

6. **The need for acceptance as an individual.**
   Students must be made to feel that they are recognized and accepted as individuals. They must feel and understand that the instructor is receptive to their personal hurts and sympathetic to their personal needs.

7. **The need for economic security.**

All students must be made to feel economically equal in every way. No student should ever be embarrassed or made to feel inferior, in any way, for lack of money or financial ability.

8. **The need for appreciation.**

The instructor must make every student feel that his contribution to the over-all learning situation, no matter how slight, is sincerely accepted and appreciated. Students should be encouraged to give of themselves, in every way, to improve and encourage learning.

Summary

To summarize briefly, the art and science of teaching requires a combination of many factors for successful performance.

There is no one trait, quality or personal characteristic which makes a good teacher. A good teacher is the result of a combination of a balanced personality, a well organized educational program, a knowledge and understanding of teaching principles, a complete mastery of the subject matter, business-like classroom management, and of extreme importance, the full cooperation of eager and interested students.

Whether the teacher createst these conditions or the conditions create the teacher is, unfortunately, an unknown factor. However, it is essential to understand that quality in teaching is the result of a well-coordinated combination of numerous educational factors.

ADVICE TO TEACHERS

If it is your ambition to be a great teacher you must:
1. Take an intense interest in your students.
2. Be professional in your relationship with school staff.
3. Be sensitive and understanding of the student's environment.
4. Be successful in maintaining your own life.

1. **Take an intense interest in your students.** The relationship between teacher and students must be one of genuine interest and affection. It is not sufficient that the teacher be interested in all students; each student must feel and be certain that the teacher is interested in him personally. Teachers who daily seek to recognize the needs of students and search for ways to meet those needs are on their way to teaching greatness. They are also on their way to savoring the real joy and thrill of teaching.

2. **Be serious and professional in your relationships to the other members of the school staff.** Teamwork is an essential in providing good education and training to cosmetology students. This does not mean the sacrifice of individual initiative, imagination, or of inventiveness. Teamwork recognizes and makes good use of the strengths of each teacher in the sharing and pooling of ideas and techniques. The professional attitude of a teacher can often be measured by his respect and admiration for other teachers and especially for those with whom he works. There is also a direct relationship between the professional growth and development of a teacher and his interest and participation in educational meetings and organizations.

3. **Be sensitive to and understanding of the environment from which your students come** before school and to which they return after school; in other words, home, parents and community. To understand a student, the teacher must have an insight into, and understanding of, the world from which the student comes. The teacher must be familiar with the patterns of the home and of the general environment, in order to strengthen the ties between the student and himself.

For teen age students, education in general, and cosmetology education in particular, must be accepted as an extension of home. This requires a close understanding and a single (mutual) objective of parents and teachers. The teacher must be able to understand the environment of the students if they are to satisfactorily train and equip those students to live and earn a living in that environment.

4. **Teachers must learn to be successful in maintaining their own personal lives** on a normal, even keel. They must live and maintain themselves as individuals, with their own personal likes, tastes, desires and loves.

Your objective, as a teacher, is to help shape the lives and destinies of your students. You cannot hope to function efficiently and effectively in shaping the lives of others if your own living patterns are filled with frustrations and unhappiness. You cannot expect to maintain high standards of enthusiasm and interest without a deep feeling of self-satisfaction and personal accomplishment.

As a teacher, you are part of the "teaching profession." However, you must not completely immerse yourself in that profession and lose your personal identity as a human being. You must at all times maintain yourself as an individual, with your own personal feelings.

There is no logical reason why your personal views of life and of living should conflict with what you teach. You should at all times live on a personal plane of normal human behavior. Primarily and basically you must remember that a successful teaching career can be built only on a foundation of personal self-respect, self-satisfaction, and happiness.

1. **Where does a teacher show his greatest value?**

    In his ability to inspire students to a sincere desire for learning.

2. **In addition to educational material, what important learning necessities must be provided by the teacher?**

    Interest, motivation and enthusiasm for learning.

3. **Name seven qualities demanded for good teaching.**
    1. A balanced personality.
    2. Organization of curriculum and classroom.
    3. Ability to recognize individual differences in students.
    4. Knowledge and experience in teaching procedures.
    5. Ability to stimulate student participation.
    6. Ability to direct the mastery of skills and knowledge.
    7. Teacher maturity.

4. **What are the four general areas of teacher maturity?**
    1. Social maturity
    2. Emotional maturity
    3. Moral maturity
    4. Professional maturity

5. **One way in which an instructor shows mastery of his material is to tie in what he teaches with other experiences of the students. Name another aspect of thorough mastery of your material.**

    The instructor keeps up with the latest methods and techniques in his field and has a professional attitude toward his work.

6. **Name three examples of executive ability, a requirement for good classroom management.**
    1. Course and lesson planning always ready ahead of time.
    2. Supplies, equipment and operating efficiency always under control.
    3. Suitable jobs selected for students to perform in order to learn cosmetology skills.

7. **What are the eight student needs for better learning?**
    The need for:
    1. Knowledge and understanding.
    2. Freedom from guilt.
    3. Freedom from embarrassment.
    4. Belonging
    5. A feeling of accomplishment.
    6. Acceptance as an individual.
    7. Economic security.
    8. Appreciation.

CHAPTER 3

PERSONALITY
AND
PROFESSIONAL CONDUCT

TEACHER'S PERSONALITY

One of the great educators of the twentieth century once said, "The supreme value of a teacher lies not in the regular performance of routine duties, but in his power to lead and inspire his students through the influence of his own mental and moral personality and example."

An instructor can never be a wholly efficient teacher, no matter how thoroughly he knows the cosmetology subject material or how completely he masters the technique of teaching, important as both are, unless he has a good personality. Many instructors have knowledge and training, but for various reasons they fail to become successful teachers because of defective personalities. They lack the "spark" or dynamic quality which marks the quality teacher.

One of the prerequisites all teacher training institutions consider as a basis for judging a promising teacher is personality. Most educational writers and school officials insist that personality is one of the important factors in evaluating the equipment of the successful teacher. During recent years there has been an ever increasing interest in those personal qualities which contribute to teaching success. It is becoming ever more apparent that the wise selection of individuals for teacher-training or employment depends upon the ability to identify those qualities which make for teaching success. If teacher misfits could be anticipated in the teacher-training programs, much disappointment, humiliation, and misdirected energy could be avoided. The schools, also, could select, with greater assurance, those individuals most likely to succeed.

Good personality in the teacher is just as important as complete mastery of the subject matter and the development of finger dexterity. Teachers must possess poise, tactfulness, self-reliance, social consciousness and optimism. Personality can be defined as the extent to which instructors develop habits and skills which interest and please other people. Personality embraces what you have and what other people think about you.

Teaching is one of the most exciting and stimulating of all professions. It requires extended preparation, continuing study, and sincere devotion to meet the demands of modern cosmetology education. The success of the instructor depends to a great extent upon his relations with his students. He must not only be skilled in his profession and possess fine personal qualities, but must also be able to develop and maintain proper teacher-student relations in the classroom. Success depends upon many small things that may mean the difference between good and poor learning results. A combination of a friendly attitude, a well-groomed appearance and a pleasant voice make for a successful teaching personality.

CLASSROOM ATMOSPHERE

The cosmetology teacher's personality will be reflected in the general atmosphere of the classroom. The atmosphere created in the room should be conducive to good teaching and learning.

The work attitude of the students should indicate a willingness and eagerness to learn, to solve and to execute the problems in which they are engaged. There is a need for mutual cooperation — to work harmoniously together in order to achieve the objectives of the cosmetology training program.

A competent instructor is not "one of the boys" or "one of the girls." He must command the respect of all students and must never let down the bars too far. Students look up to and admire a teacher who maintains the reserve required of his position, particularly during school hours.

The overall atmosphere should be one of quiet dignity, friendliness and consideration. The entire classroom should reflect the instructor's eagerness to do a good job and turn out properly trained students. Effective teaching requires the ability and willingness to inspire, guide, and direct the formation of good learning habits.

Create an atmosphere which is conducive to serious, thoughtful work.

TEACHER'S APPEARANCE

Your appearance creates the first impression your students will have of you. Be well groomed and appropriately dressed. It is wise to be a little conservative in your dress in the classroom.

Grooming, clothing and general appearance are among the most important factors in the impression teachers make on other people. They are judged to a large extent on their external appearance. At any rate, the first opinions and frequently the most lasting ones are created by appearance. The properly dressed instructor makes a better impression on students and the public.

Well-groomed instructor

Cleanliness Rules To Be Followed:

1. Bathe daily.
2. Use a deodorant.
3. Brush teeth at least twice a day.
4. Have your hair shampooed and properly styled as often as needed.
5. Keep your fingernails clean and well groomed.
6. Change your underclothes regularly.
7. Brush your outer garments daily.
8. Polish your shoes regularly and keep them in good repair.
9. Men teachers, shave daily. If beard or mustache is worn, trim or style it regularly.
10. Eyebrows should be properly cared for to avoid unruly bushiness.

Dress includes neatness, appropriateness, cleanliness and style.

MANNERS

Manners involve being courteous and applying the rules of etiquette that are considered to be universally and socially acceptable, such as:

1. Properly introducing people.
2. Proper table manners.
3. Using gestures appropriate to your sex
4. Courtesy and consideration of others.
5. Respect for the right of others.
6. Use of proper and dignified language.

SELF-CONTROL

Be cheerful and have
a ready smile.

As a cosmetology teacher, you must practice self-control if you expect to have control over others. Be cheerful, patient and understanding. You can distort your personality by being indifferent, snobbish or resorting to sarcasm or ridicule.

No instructor can afford to lose his temper with the class. The use of profane or obscene language in the classroom is inexcusable. At all times and at all costs the instructor must maintain his dignity and his self-control.

An instructor who "explodes" or "blows off" is likely to make statements he doesn't mean, and quite likely will regret his action later. Self-control is the first requisite in order to maintain proper control of the class and to create proper teaching-learning situations.

SELF-IMPROVEMENT

As a cosmetology teacher, you are expected to project a good image of yourself, the teaching profession, and the entire vocation of beauty culture. The good instructor will constantly strive for self-improvement in professional attitude, ethics, technical knowledge and teaching skills.

Professional Approach

A cosmetology teacher is a member of a highly respected professional group. As a member of this profession he has a definite responsibility to reflect credit upon himself and fellow educators. The professional attitude he maintains may be projected in various ways.

1. It is his duty to try, at all times, to improve instruction and to offer suggestions as to how this may be done.

2. He must be open-minded under all conditions and be willing to accept and appreciate constructive suggestions for improvement.

3. The professional teacher maintains his status by constant study; participates in teacher-training seminars and accepts eagerly every opportunity for improvement of his teaching ability. He must keep up with new teaching trends and learning techniques in order to perform honestly and efficiently.

4. Cosmetology is a rapidly changing field. New equipment, techniques and products are constantly being developed. It is mandatory that the instructor keep abreast of these changes.

5. Successful teachers are highly skilled and competent individuals. The person who practices the highly professional task of teaching makes a great contribution to the entire industry and to society. As an instructor he is responsible for developing the skill, knowledge and professional attitudes of all students. The only limitations placed upon his educational opportunities are his own interest, initiative, knowledge and technical skill.

6. The professional instructor is trying to teach every trade skill he possesses. He wants students to learn every technique, every skill and every bit of knowledge possible in the short time at his disposal. His status as a professional educator also requires that he does not hesitate to share new ideas and knowledge with fellow instructors.

7. The alert and progressive instructor makes it his business to join and support the professional organizations in his field. This is an important way of keeping up to date in his work. New teaching methods and techniques are presented at organization seminars and meetings, which should be attended by the teacher, for continuous improvement in teaching knowledge and ability.

8. Both the public and industry have the right to expect that a teacher should at all times conduct himself in a manner above reproach. The youth of the nation are being subjected to the influence of the teaching profession. The teachers must therefore set an example of personal conduct that students will be proud to follow.

9. An instructor who attempts to teach students technical skills without being able to do the job skillfully himself can only be an incompetent teacher. The confidence and respect of students will soon be lost if the teacher tries to bluff or performs in an inept manner. The teacher personally must be a master of each cosmetology technique before he can teach it effectively.

10. The teacher's time in school must not be spent in handling personal business problems. All school time should be devoted to the job of training or improving students' knowledge and techniques, and developing them into skilled artisans.

Professional Ethics

The hub of every classroom is the teacher. The one person whose dedication, understanding, knowledge, skill and personal effort will, to a large extent, determine the progress of students, is the teacher. It is the teacher's privilege and challenge to work with young adults at the moment in their lives when they are most in need of help and guidance.

However, the test of a teacher often comes in his relationship to the rest of the staff, rather than in the classroom. Teaching is a cooperative enterprise. It requires the effort of every teacher working with every other teacher and with the administration if the school is to succeed. The work of the school is closely interrelated. The teachers must necessarily work together if a unified educational effort is to be assured.

While elaborate works are available on professional ethics for teachers, with which every instructor should be familiar, a few items deserve special mention. Some of these appear so self-evident that their mention would seem unnecessary if their violation were not so frequent.

1. The teacher should give full and complete loyalty to the school and to fellow teachers. Whenever it is possible to give assistance, he should do so freely. Such an attitude is the essence of cooperation.

2. The policies of the school should be defended whenever necessary. The strength of the organization depends upon the actions and attitudes of its teaching staff.

3. Teachers should not gossip about fellow teachers or criticize them unfairly to other teachers, to students or to outsiders. The efficiency of the teacher himself may be greatly impaired if he has a habit of criticizing other teachers.

4. Teachers must refrain from talking disparagingly about one student to another. Students quickly lose respect for teachers who talk about other students.

5. A teacher who uses profane or foul language indicates that he lacks the ability to express himself correctly. Profanity is employed to cover up personal shortcomings.

6. The instructor who attempts to improve his own position by "backbiting" fellow teachers quickly loses the respect and confidence of all. Such action is soon recognized as a major violation of the teachers' code of ethics.

Speech and Voice Projection

The quality of an instructor's voice has a definite effect upon the success of his teaching. A voice which is pitched too high or has a harsh quality may be annoying to students. Class interest can soon be destroyed completely by a teacher speaking in a constant monotone. A cosmetology teacher must consider the tone, quality and volume of his voice. The voice is an essential tool in the learning process and great care in tonal projection must be exercised.

Words should be correctly and distinctly pronounced in order that they may be clearly heard and understood. Teachers must be careful to use good grammar, avoid profanity, speak clearly and distinctly, avoid slang and use words correctly. The abuse of the English language is a guaranteed method of destroying class interest and detracting from other teaching qualities.

Care must be exercised to speak clearly, slowly enough to be understood and loudly enough to be heard by all students. A teacher should watch his class very carefully. If students appear to be restless, falling asleep or straining to hear, the fault usually lies with the teacher's voice; perhaps you are not speaking loudly or clearly enough. If students look puzzled, the probability is that you are mumbling, talking too fast or are not being understood; speak more distinctly and slowly. If many students appear inattentive, perhaps you are not speaking to the entire class but are directing your attention to only a few students.

Remember, teachers must employ good diction, appropriate vocabulary and proper English construction to be effective.

CLASSROOM DISTRACTIONS

Peculiar mannerisms of any kind are detrimental to the teaching and learning process. Instructors must avoid such distractions as continually looking out of the window, using a finger as a pointer or tossing chalk in the air. If the teacher waves his arms wildly, plays with eyeglasses, continually drums with his fingers on his desk or performs similar actions, students will soon begin to concentrate on these antics instead of listening to the presentation.

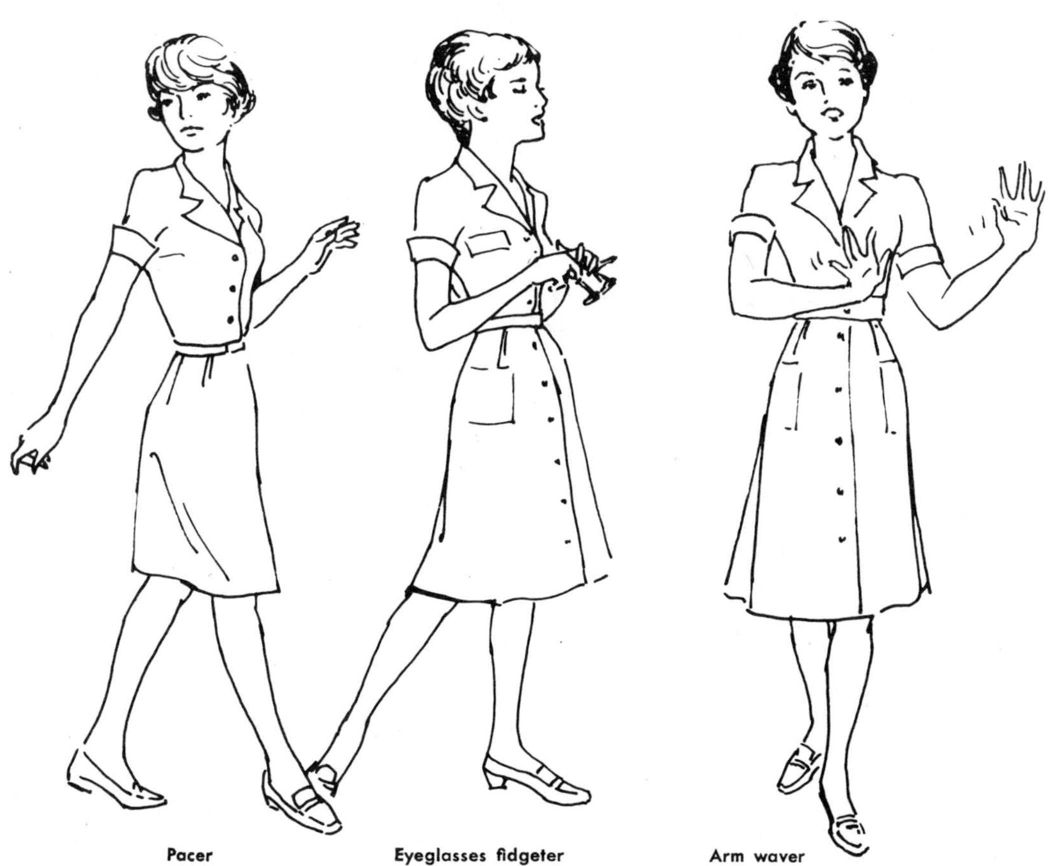

Pacer   Eyeglasses fidgeter   Arm waver

Pointer   Chalk tosser.   Window gazer

The instructor must exert every effort to eliminate distracting influences such as outside noises, chewing gum, students coming late to class, smoking, talking, whispering or similar interruptions.

Student attention may be easily diverted by objects displayed on the teacher's desk, by messages written on the chalkboard, or similar distracting items. These should either be covered until required, or completely removed.

While a teacher may employ a little showmanship to help drive home a point, the excessive use of gestures may detract rather than add to the effectiveness of the lesson.

> **The elimination of all outside distraction will add to teaching effectiveness and contribute materially to the learning process.**

Late students will distract from your lessons.

Writing on blackboard not pertaining to the
current lesson can often be distracting.

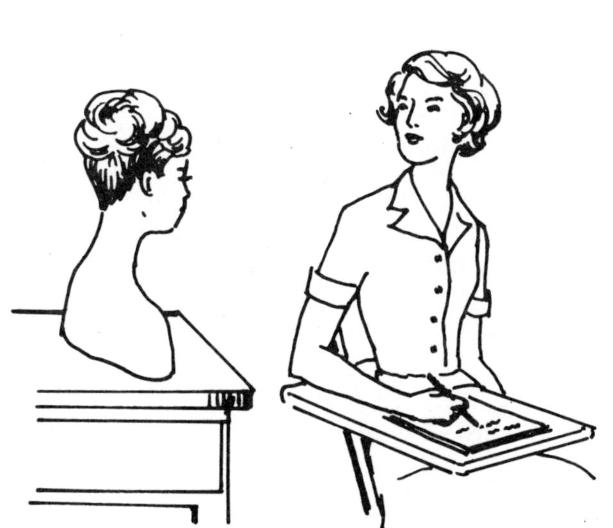

Remove all mannequins after use which might be distracting.

Outside noises can be distracting.

R E V I E W

1. **Define good personality in teaching.**
   Good personality in teaching can be defined as the extent to which instructors develop good habits and skills which interest and please other people.

2. **Name three essentials for a successful teaching personality.**
   1. A friendly attitude.
   2. A well-groomed appearance.
   3. A pleasant voice.

3. **Describe the proper attitude of the instructor toward all students.**
   The teacher must command the respect of all students and maintain the reserve required of his position.

4. **Name three aspects of good overall classroom atmosphere.**
   1. Quiet dignity.
   2. Friendliness.
   3. Consideration.

5. **The teacher's appearance should always be evaluated. Name three areas to consider.**
   1. Grooming.
   2. Clothing.
   3. General appearance.

6. **In creating the proper impression, in what direction should the teacher plan his clothing?**
   A conservative taste in dress is desirable in creating a good first impression in the classroom.

7. **List the ten rules of cleanliness which should be followed by all teachers.**
   1. Bathe daily
   2. Use a deodorant.
   3. Brush teeth at least twice daily.
   4. Have hair shampooed and styled when needed.
   5. Keep fingernails clean and well groomed.
   6. Change clothes regularly.
   7. Brush outer garments daily.
   8. Polish shoes regularly and keep in good repair.
   9. Men teachers shave daily.
   10. Eyebrows should be properly cared for to avoid unruly bushiness.

8. **Name six areas in the field of manners that must be mastered by the successful teacher.**
   1. Introductions.
   2. Table manners.
   3. Gestures appropriate to your sex.
   4. Courtesy and consideration for others.
   5. Respect for the rights of others.
   6. Use of proper and dignified language.

9. **If you expect to have control over others, as a cosmetology teacher you must practice self-control. What is the danger for an instructor who "blows off" in the classroom.**
   The instructor is likely to make statements he doesn't mean and which he might regret later on.

10. **List ten ways in which a cosmetology teacher proves a professional attitude toward his career.**
   1. He does his best to improve instruction.
   2. He is open-minded and willing to accept constructive criticism.
   3. He participates in teacher-training seminars and keeps up with new teaching methods.
   4. He learns about new equipment and products.
   5. He does his best to develop the skill, knowledge and professional attitudes of all students.
   6. He tries to teach every trade skill he possesses and shares new ideas with fellow instructors.
   7. He belongs to the professional organizations in his field.
   8. He conducts himself in a manner beyond reproach.
   9. The teacher makes certain he is a master of each cosmetology skill before teaching it.
   10. He devotes all time in school to the job of training students.

11. **Professional ethics demand that teaching be a cooperative enterprise. Name six points which illustrate a good code of professional ethics.**
   1. The teacher has complete loyalty to the school and fellow teachers.
   2. He defends the school policies.
   3. He does not gossip about fellow teachers.
   4. He refrains from criticizing one student to another.
   5. He avoids the use of profanity or foul language.
   6. He does not seek to improve his own position by "back-biting" fellow teachers.

12. **The instructor's voice has a definite effect upon the success of teaching. Name two voice problems which must be avoided.**
   1. A high-pitched or harsh voice is annoying.
   2. A constant monotone can put any student to sleep.

13. **The good instructor keeps watching the class. Name three situations which may cause problems.**
   1. Students appear to be falling asleep or restless; check if you are speaking loudly or clearly enough.
   2. Students look puzzled; check if you are mumbling or talking too fast.
   3. Students appear inattentive; check if you are directing your attention to only a few of them.

14. **The good teacher should avoid distractions. Name three which interfere with class attention.**
   1. Peculiar personal mannerisms such as gesturing, tapping, waving.
   2. Objects displayed on the teacher's desk.
   3. Messages left on the blackboard.

15. **The instructor should not permit students to cause distractions in the class. List four distractions caused by students.**
   1. Chewing gum.
   2. Coming late to class.
   3. Smoking.
   4. Talking or whispering.

THE COST
OF EDUCATION

The cost of education has risen so
sharply in recent years that cosmetology educators are being pressed
to obtain a value in training results
of 100% for every dollar spent.

CHAPTER 4

DEVELOPMENT
OF
A COSMETOLOGY COURSE

ORGANIZATION NECESSARY

The day is past when education in any field can be carried on in a hap-hazard manner. Experience in every field of human endeavor indicates the need and wisdom of careful organization of activities. Organization and careful planning make it possible for a school to provide a maximum educational and training effort at minimum cost. Knowing what the school intends to accomplish and how it intends to fulfill its objectives makes the difference between a mediocre educational program and a good, professional program.

CAREFUL PLANNING

Only careful planning can effectively eliminate economic waste in cosmetology education. This efficiency in the teaching and training program is an absolute necessity if cosmetology schools are to survive in today's economy.

Educational simplicity in cosmetology training programs is but a memory. Today the school plant is larger, the period of training is constantly being increased and the equipment required is becoming more complicated and costly. To conform with an ever-increasing expansion of cosmetology knowledge and to meet the needs of the beauty industry, which are rapidly becoming more complex, careful selection and organization of subject matter is required. Only vigorous planning will make possible the most intelligent selection and coordination of cosmetology knowledge to form a well-balanced training program.

Preliminary Analysis

The first step in the development of a cosmetology teaching program is to determine, as completely as possible, the areas of knowledge to be included. All that follows bears a direct relationship to this preliminary study. The general subject matter must be determined before we can undertake an accurate outlining of the details.

Since a good cosmetology teaching program must prepare students for future performance in the beauty salon, it must cover the important areas of knowledge and ability expected of the qualified cosmetologist. It should involve not merely a casual outlining of material, but rather a detailed dividing and subdividing of areas of knowledge. It requires a thorough study of the entire field of cosmetology. It should include a survey of the different subdivisions of the field to provide knowledge of the time to be devoted to each subject in the overall program construction. The completion of preliminary analysis of the entire subject matter leads to the next step in the development of the course: the detailed breakdown.

Detailed Breakdown

The study of the various subjects which compose a complete cosmetology course helps to determine the relative amount of time spent by cosmetologists on particular operations in the beauty salon. The detailed breakdown must indicate which are primary tasks and must distinguish between the major and minor duties performed. This determination will point the way to a breakdown of large areas of knowledge into smaller units and to the selection of components to facilitate teaching. In fact, the entire subject matter should be separated into its major elements and then into subdivisions. This will point the way toward placing greater emphasis upon the most important phases of work and devoting less time to minor operations.

The detailed subject breakdown also assists in the selection of actual jobs through which manual skills are developed. Whenever possible, selected tasks should include skills which are fundamental to a group of similar or related jobs. This enables the widest possible application of fundamental techniques in teaching. Jobs selected should be sufficiently broad and flexible to enable students with different capabilities to perform at their maximum abilities.

Selection of Related Subject Matter

The analysis of subjects to be covered in a cosmetology course points the way to the selection of required related information. Material for the teaching of necessary theoretical and technical knowledge may then be selected intelligently. Preparations must be made for the teaching of information concerning the required equipment, processes, materials and products necessary for successful cosmetology practice. Areas of information essential to complete instruction in the skills required and for the efficient development of manipulative techniques must be identified.

Suggested headings for presentation of related information:
1. Implements and Equipment.
   a) Proper usage.
   b) Function of each.
2. Materials.
   a) Various kinds in use.
   b) Their properties and qualities.
3. Processes.
   a) Cold Waving.
   b) Hair Coloring
   c) Hair Lightening.
   d) Hair Relaxing.

The ability to analyze and evaluate the subject matter of cosmetology will enable teachers to determine more clearly their instructional needs for both the manipulative skills and related subjects. To determine the instructional content requirements of any given technique, teachers must have a complete understanding of:

1. The manipulative skills involved.
2. The related knowledge required to effectively and efficiently perform these opeartions.

To determine its instructional content, a technique must be broken down into various manipulative operations. This includes all of the things which the student must do in order to efficiently complete the job and achieve the desired results. It is clearly evident therefore, that the teacher must develop a detailed analysis of the various areas of knowledge required, in order to be able to impart the necessary training.

Occupational Background

In order that students develop a thorough understanding and appreciation of the practice of cosmetology, they should receive training in many background and related fields.

This background knowledge may be developed by a study of:

1. Cosmetology history.
2. The economics of the practice of cosmetology.
3. Professional ethics.
4. Health and safety rules and practices.
5. Cosmetology state laws.
6. Working conditions in various areas of cosmetology practice.

The subjects should be taught at the most opportune periods in the development of the course. They may also become part of the introduction of individual new areas of training.

CURRICULUM

Professional cosmetology education is based on an organized and planned program, to assure complete training in every facet of beauty culture knowledge and practice. In order to properly develop an efficient and integrated teaching and learning program it is essential that each step in the overall planning structure be clearly understood and evaluated.

The first step in the development of a cosmetology training program is the creation of an organized curriculum.

A **curriculum** is defined as a body of selected subjects, **phrased in general terms,** indicating the time to be devoted to each general subject, which is designed to stimulate the development of cosmetologists, to acquaint them with necessary knowledge, to develop fundamental skills and to make clear the inter-relationships of **all phases** of cosmetology. (In cosmetology, the curriculum is usually prepared by the state licensing authorities.)

A professional curriculum can be prepared only after completion of the preliminary analysis of the subject matter to be covered, a determination of the various instructional and skill areas to be included and the relative importance, or weight, to be assigned to each area.

The next step in the planning structure is the development of a **course of study,** which must be in direct relationship, in every way, to the curriculum.

ILLUSTRATION OF CURRICULUM BREAK-DOWN

Note: Fill in time to conform with your State Board requirements

REQUIRED SUBJECTS	TOTAL TIME ALLOTTED	Classroom Lectures Time Allotted	Classroom Demonstrations Time Allotted	Practice Room & Clinic Time or Operations
SCIENCE SUBJECTS:				
Sanitation & Sterilization (including Bacteriology)				
Hygiene—(Personal & Public)				
Hair				
Skin, Scalp and Nails				
Cosmetic Chemistry				
Electricity — Light Therapy				
Anatomy				
Hair and Skin Disorders				
MANAGEMENT SUBJECTS:				
Personal Improvement				
License Law				
Business Ethics				
Telephone Techniques				
Receptionist Techniques				
PRACTICAL SUBJECTS:				
Manicuring & Hand Care				
Shampoos & Rinses				
Scalp Treatments				
Hair Shaping (Cutting)				
Permanent Waving				
Hair Coloring				
Hair Styling (Fingerwaving, Pin Curling, etc.)				
Theory of Massage				
Facial Treatments				
Facial Makeup				
Eyebrow Arching				
ELECTED SUBJECTS:				
Heat Permanent Waving				
Chemical Hair Straightening				
Hair Pressing				
Thermal Waving & Curling				
Customer Relations—Selling				
Pedicuring				
Wiggery				
Temporary Hair Removal				
Electrolysis				
Examinations & Review				
Unassigned				
TOTAL CURRICULUM				

COURSE OF STUDY

The complexity of cosmetology education requires wise general planning. If each cosmetology technique is taught as it comes up, teachers will never be prepared for proper instruction. The natural result of such a school policy is a completely haphazard and disorganized teaching program. It is impossible to check student progress or to determine whether or not the students have received a complete course of instruction and have been properly prepared for service in the beauty salon. On the other hand, a properly developed course of study would result in an orderly and systematic process of education.

A course of study is defined as a complete and detailed breakdown into their specific component parts of the general subjects listed in the state board curriculum. **The course of study is developed by the cosmetology school, and is based on the curriculum mandated by the state board.**

A unified approach to cosmetology education must be created which will integrate all of the curriculum areas with each other. This integrated learning or teaching situation is created when the program prepared draws upon and inter-relates the different curriculum areas.

In planning a course of study it is necessary to:

1. Arrange the subject matter in proper teaching order.

2. Include all facets of each curriculum area.

3. Plan the structure of training in terms of the time allotted for each curriculum area.

4. Indicate which teaching method is to be used with each part of the subject matter.

5. Indicate specific concepts, subject matter and technical skills to be taught.

6. Follow an orderly program of instruction, scheduling, and recording of student achievement.

7. Exclude all unnecessary subject matter.

8. Include plans for continuous evaluation of student progress and provide for follow-up, based on the needs of the class and of individual students.

The proper and complete course of study in cosmetology becomes a "blueprint" enabling the instructor to know:

(1) **What** is to be taught. (2) **When** it is to be taught. (3) **How** it is to be taught.

It is followed as a guide to advise both teachers and students of:

(1) **Where** they are going. (2) **How** they are to get there. (3) **Why** they are to arrive at this destination.

The subject matter and occupational analysis provide the material from which the course of study is to be prepared. This analysis also indicates the ultimate objectives of the course and the natural instructional units to be followed in reaching these objectives.

OBJECTIVES OR AIMS

The statement of objectives or aims is an expression of the purpose of the course. The determination of these aims and objectives is one of the first requirements of instructional planning. At this point, extreme care is necessary if confusion is to be avoided and correct procedures assured. The desirable goals to be attained should be very definite and they must be achievable.

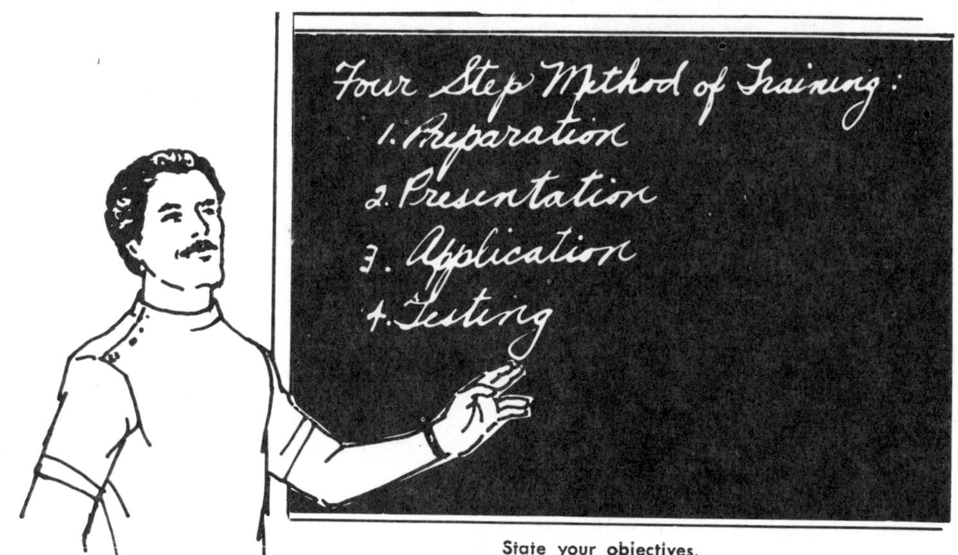

State your objectives.

Examples of Attainable Objectives

1. To develop a knowledge, understanding, skill and appreciation of the theory and practice of cosmetology.
2. To develop habits of doing things properly in the interest of safety and sanitation for one's self as well as others.
3. To develop habits of good workmanship and the orderly performance of the various tasks performed in a beauty salon.
4. To impart knowledge of and to develop the technical skills required in the practice of beauty culture in the salon.
5. To learn to select wisely, care for and use properly, the commercial products that are related to the application of cosmetic treatments.
6. To encourage growth and the desire to keep abreast of the new and unique developments in the practice of beauty culture.
7. To encourage the student to strive for the establishment of methodical habits of performance.
8. To impart ideals and attitudes of willingness to cooperate with employer and employees.
9. To foster an appreciation of the scientific contributions to the progress of cosmetology.
10. To help students to prepare for state board examinations in order to obtain a license to practice cosmetology.

CONTENTS AND FORMAT

The span of memory is too short and the span of attention is too brief, to expect extended teaching programs to be carried on in vigorous, orderly and developmental fashion without planning and organization. Too many possibilities must be taken into consideration in the anticipatory stages of teaching. Only as planning is committed to written form, with a carefully prepared course of study, with opportunity provided for revision and supplementation, can we be sure of the proper sequence in teaching and the proper training of tomorrow's cosmetologists.

The first step in the preparation of a course of study is to develop an inventory of the skills and fields of knowledge required in cosmetology.

Following the listing of essential skills and knowledge, a determination must be made of the order or sequence in which they are to be taught. A good rule to follow is to go **from the simple to the more complex.**

The course outline is actually being prepared in the process of establishing the instructional sequence.

The next step in this project is to consider the amount of time to be devoted to each area. Taking into consideration the proposed overall length of the course it becomes necessary to allocate sufficient time to each area of instruction. Great care must be exercised to avoid the allocation of excessive time in one area and the slighting of another, equally important, area.

The last section of the course of study should be a bibliography section in which all available teaching aids (films, slides, transparencies, charts, models, mock-ups) are listed. This section should also contain a ready list of additional reference materials such as technical books, trade journals and manufacturers' manuals.

SAMPLE (FOR ONE SUBJECT) OF A COURSE STUDY

Subject: **Care of the Scalp and Hair.**
1. Introduction
2. Disorders of the Scalp — Theory
   a) oil glands
   b) sweat glands
   c) dandruff
   d) inflammations
   e) alopecia
   f) parasitic infections
   g) non-contagious infections
3. Scalp Manipulations
   a) hand and vibrator
   b) hair brushing
4. Care of Normal Scalp
5. Dandruff Remedy Applications
6. Care of Dry Scalp
7. Care of Oily Scalp
8. Corrective Hair Treatments
9. Corrective Applications for Alopecia

Each general subject listed in the curriculum would be similarly broken down into its component parts.

COURSE OUTLINE

Purpose of Course Outline

A **course outline** may be defined as a comprehensive and organized series of class sessions, covering the entire course of study, as a coordinated and cohesive unit.

A properly prepared course outline is extremely valuable in the learning process. It plans each day's work to fulfill some specific function in the realization of the course objectives. It requires a complete and thorough analysis of the entire field of cosmetology in order to insure the best coverage. Educational study and psychology have forced the realization that not all materials or activities contribute to the achievement of the desired goals. There must be a judicious selection of material and activities that give reasonable hope of functioning efficiently in a real life situation. Learning tends to be more specific than general. Out of the mass of material available, a wise selection must be made. If learning of a competent nature is to take place, there must be a proper organization of classroom activities.

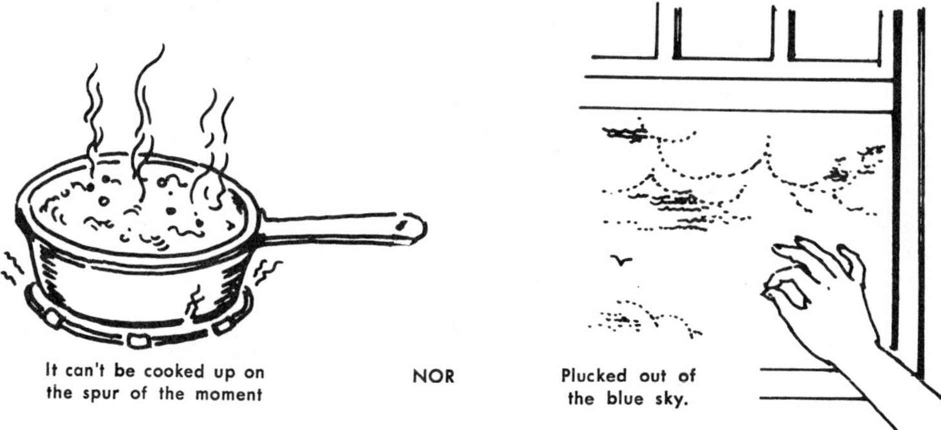

A course outline cannot be cooked up on the spur of the moment or plucked out of the sky. It is the result of considerable study and careful planning. If properly prepared it can eliminate much misunderstanding between teacher and students. It also serves as an important aid in improving the instructor's teaching techniques, the preparation and use of teaching aids, test preparation and the evaluation of student progress.

A cosmetology educational program can be successful only if it is well organized and functions as a cohesive unit. This means that the course outline must be coordinated with the course of study and a complete series of lesson plans. (The subject of Lesson Plans and Lesson Planning will be covered in a later chapter.)

Planning a course outline is an individualized project which must take into consideration the approved curriculum, the course of study, the school's facilities and the school's short and long range objectives. It must be flexible enough to be expanded or contracted in order to meet the educational requirements of the modern school of beauty culture and the practice in the salons. Basically and of primary importance is the demand that it present a planned and organized approach to a well-rounded cosmetology educational program.

The progressive teacher can prepare his teaching activities well in advance by referring to the course outline, which sets forth the entire program in detail. The program presents the subjects to be taught on an hourly basis and indicates the lesson plan required for each class by number. The teacher is thus in a position to prepare for each lesson far in advance. The proper lesson plan is selected and all required supplies and materials can be assembled. The entire educational program is scientifically organized and is thus conducive to good teaching and learning.

TIME	MONDAY	TUESDAY	WEDNESDAY	THURSDAY	FRIDAY
8:45 9:00	INSPECTION				
9:00 10:00	Review Cold Permanent Waving. LR	Semi-Perm. Tints Temporary Color Tints. LP-100 LR	Examination Permanent Waving.	Demonstration Lightening Virgin Hair Retouch. LP-102 LR	Lightener on Virgin Hair (Projector, Slides). LP-103 LR
10:00 11:00	Practice Permanent Waving. PR	Practice Tinting. PR	Review of Examination.	Practice Hair Lightening. PR	Practice Hair Lightening PR
11:00 11:15	REST PERIOD				
11:15 12:15	Continued. PR	Continued. PR	Hair Lightening. LP-101 LR	Continued. PR	Practice Hair Tinting. PR
12:15 1:00	LUNCH				
1:00 2:00	Demonstration DBL. Appl. Tints Virgin Hair Retouch. LP-99 PR	Practice Hair Styling. PR	Practice Hair Lightening. PR	Practice Permanent Waving. PR	Practice Permanent Waving. PR
2:00 3:00	Practice Tinting. PR	Continued. PR	Continued. PR	Continued. PR	Continued. PR
3:00 3:15	REST PERIOD				
3:15 4:15	Clinic Assistant.	Clinic Assistant.	Clinic Assistant.	Clinic Assistant.	Clinic Assistant.
4:15 5:15	Continued.	Continued.	Continued.	Continued.	Continued.
5:15 5:30	CLEAN UP				

INSTRUCTIONAL UNITS

The basic skills to be developed and the allied knowledge to be taught form the basis for the listing of instructional units and individual jobs. The difficulty in the learning process will decide the order in which these topics or units are to be arranged.

Consideration must be given to the entire content of the subject matter to be taught in the complete course of study. Each unit or topic must be considered in relation to the course objectives. The items selected must fulfill some real function in the overall teaching and learning program. Arranged in proper sequence, listed topics or units will aid in the achievement of the ultimate objective of the school.

An **instructional unit** may be defined as a unit of knowledge or information which is the teaching and learning objective of a class session.

(The instructional unit is developed as part of the course of study.)

EXAMPLE OF INSTRUCTIONAL UNIT IN TEACHING COSMETOLOGY

NOTE: Although more time may be allocated for various subjects, a good rule to follow is that "No lecture should be more than 30 minutes." Spend additional time in asking questions or demonstrating. The teacher loses the attention and interest of his class if lectures continue for more than a maximum of 30 minutes.

1. **Scalp Manipulations**

    a) Preparation
        1. Cosmetologist preparation
        2. Patron preparation

    b) Hair Brushing

    c) Technique — Manipulations
        1. Relaxing movement
        2. Sliding movement
        3. Sliding and rotating movement
        4. Forehead movement
        5. Moving the scalp
        6. Hairline movement
        7. Front scalp movement
        8. Back scalp movement
        9. Ear to ear movement
        10. Back movement
        11. Shoulder movement
        12. Spine movement

1. **What is the first step in planning the development of a cosmetology course?**
   Determine the areas of knowledge to be covered. The general subject matter must be determined before details can be accurately outlined.

2. **In a detailed breakdown, how do you determine the amount of study time for the various operations?**
   You must decide which are the primary tasks and then distinguish between the major and minor duties performed. Topics selected should be broad and flexible enough to enable students with different capabilities to perform at maximum ability.

3. **In selecting related subject matter, what factor must be considered?**
   The subjects to be covered in the cosmetology course will point the way to the selection of related subject matter.

4. **Name two areas which must be understood by the instructor before determining the instructional content requirements of any given technique.**
   1. The manipulative skills involved.
   2. The related knowledge required to perform the operations.

5. **Name six ways in which the student may develop a better occupational background in cosmetology.**
   1. Study of cosmetology history.
   2. The economics of cosmetology practice.
   3. Professional ethics.
   4. Health and safety rules and practices.
   5. Cosmetology state laws.
   6. Working conditions.

6. **What is a curriculum, as outlined by state boards of cosmetology?**
   A body of selected subjects, phrased in general terms, indicating the time to be devoted to each subject, which is designed to stimulate the development of cosmetologists, to acquaint them with necessary knowledge, to develop fundamental skills and to make clear the inter-relationships of all phases of cosmetology.

7. **What is a course of study?**
   A complete and detailed breakdown of the general subjects listed in the curriculum, into their specific component parts.

8. **In planning a course of study, list eight points to be considered.**
   1. Proper teaching order for the subject matter.
   2. Inclusion of all facets of each curriculum area.
   3. Time to be alloted to each area.
   4. Selection of method to teach each portion of subject matter.
   5. Indication of specific concepts and subject matter to be taught.
   6. Orderly program of instruction.
   7. Exclusion of unrelated subject matter.
   8. Plans for continuous evaluation of student progress.

9. **What does a properly constructed course of study tell the instructor?**
   1. What is to be taught
   2. When it is to be taught.
   3. How it is to be taught.

10. **What are the objectives of a good curriculum in cosmetology?**
To develop a knowledge, understanding, skill and appreciation of the theory and practice of cosmetology.

11. **What is a course outline?**
A comprehensive and organized series of class sessions, covering the entire course of study as a coordinated and cohesive unit.

12. **What is the purpose of the course outline?**
It plans each day's work to fulfill some specific function in the realization of the course.

13. **What is the first step in the development of the content and format of a course outline in cosmetology?**
Inventory the skills and fields of knowledge required in the practice of cosmetology.

14. **What is a good rule to follow in determining the sequence of teaching?**
Go from the simple to the more complex.

15. **How do you allocate the amount of time to be devoted to each area?**
Take into consideration the proposed overall length of the course and allocate sufficient time for instruction in each area of equal value.

16. **What should the last section of the course outline be?**
A bibliography in which all teaching aids are listed, as well as additional reference materials.

17. **In planning a lecture, what time schedule should be planned?**
Most lectures maintain class interest for no longer than thirty minutes, so plan on this time, with additional time spent in questioning and demonstrating.

18. **What is an instructional unit? Give an example.**
An instructional unit is a unit of knowledge or information which is the teaching and learning objective of a class session. Example: Teaching "Scalp Manipulation."

CHAPTER 5

TEACHING PRINCIPLES

INTRODUCTION
"Those who dare to teach must never cease to learn."

It is almost exiomatic to teaching logic to say that a new experience or technique is not learned until it begins to function as a habit.

It is also basic for cosmetology instructors to understand that students must always do their own learning. Such learning takes place in one of two ways:

1. Through the students' own experiences.
2. By interpreting the experiences of others.

The qualified teacher must know just how much knowledge students can acquire from their own discoveries and how much they can absorb from the experiences of others. The basic function of the cosmetology teacher, as of any teacher, is to provide effective direction, guidance and instruction to students in a learning atmosphere.

In cosmetology education it is essential that regardless of the method or methods employed, students must acquire all of the basic skills and techniques necessary for service in the beauty salon. It is the teacher's primary responsibility to make certain that they do acquire such skills.

It is a monumental task to mold the raw material first presented to the instructor into an able, competent artisan. It requires constant effort, planning and understanding on the part of the instructor. He must employ every possible teaching method, technique and teaching device in the various learning areas, in order to assure effective training. The teacher must take advantage of a knowledge of student habits, previous experience and proven aptitudes in order to develop and maintain student interest and learning attitudes. However, regardless of the teacher's efforts and application, in the final analysis the real acquisition of knowledge can be accomplished only through the student's own desires and efforts.

The primary responsibility in cosmetology teaching is to direct and assist students in the learning process. To do this effectively, they must have knowledge of how learning takes place. The successful teacher is one who applies this knowledge in an effective manner. He employs the various learning devices and methods in the areas where they can bring the best results.

PROFESSIONAL ATTITUDES

Teamwork is essential in order to provide a good cosmetology education. Teachers must, therefore, be serious and professional in their relationships with other members of the school staff. However, every teacher must be careful not to sacrifice individual initiative, imagination and inventiveness. Teamwork must recognize and emphasize the strengths of each teacher in the sharing and pooling of ideas.

The teacher's professional attitude can be evaluated in terms of the respect and admiration demonstrated for other members of the teaching profession. Special emphasis must be placed on the consideration of other teaching personnel at the school. In addition, there must be a direct relationship between the teacher's professional growth and deveolpment and his interest and participation in educational meetings, seminars and organizations.

COMMON TEACHING WEAKNESSES

A study of classroom teaching has identified a number of weaknesses in general teaching techniques. The attention of professional cosmetology teachers is directed to eight of the more common flaws in teaching practices. It might be wise for teachers to measure themselves in these areas to determine their own weaknesses.

Areas of Weaknesses:
1. Teachers do most of the talking, thus discouraging students from participating in the discussion.
2. Teachers do not make assignments definite, really interesting and worthwhile. They have the tendency to rush through or "slide over" this important educational area.
3. Teachers embarrass students by the use of sarcastic remarks. Every professional teacher knows that the use of sarcasm may have disastrous educational effects. However, too many teachers still resort to this discredited tactic.
4. Teachers still use examinations, not as educational tools, but in the most disagreeable and most unproductive manner. Students should be taught to accept examinations as a normal phase of the educational program. Test papers should be rated and returned to students while the subject is still fresh in their minds.
5. Teachers still fail to carefully plan their programs of instruction. Teaching is handicapped by poor planning of individual lessons and by the improper weighting of the material and poor allocation of time.
6. Teachers make statements of facts without any attempt to interpret them or to correlate them with the balance of the training program.
7. Teachers may direct all of their teaching efforts toward the "average" student. They make no attempt to offer a learning challenge to the exceptionally bright or gifted student. On the other hand, they also fail to help the student who is a slow learner and requires more attention.
8. Teachers who completely disregard student judgment and fail to include them in planning classroom programs and activities.

THE LEARNING PROCESS

Effective learning does not arise from memorizing isolated facts or developing a mastery over bits of operations separated from the entire technique. It develops from the understanding of the essential components and their relationship to the completed task. **Students learn in patterns and not in bits and pieces.** An essential part of learning is to understand the relationship of the parts, which results in the ability to generalize and develop complete concepts.

Students learn through the basic senses. These are the senses of sight, hearing, smell, touch and taste. **Most learning develops from the sense of sight.** However, all of the senses are important in some phase of the learning process.

All learning takes place as a result of stimulating one or more of the senses from which mental impressions are formed. A stimulus is anything, such as light or sound, which excites the sensory nerve endings.

It is the teacher's job to make certain that the proper stimulus is directed to the proper sense in order to create the desired learning pattern. Teaching is the process of helping students to learn.

SENSORY APPEAL

As previously stated, all information students obtain comes to them through the senses, with the sense of sight being by far the most important. It has been estimated that about 85 per cent of all learning is absorbed through the eyes. Some learning impressions are created through the sense of hearing and the sense of touch. In cosmetology, the senses of taste and smell are less important although there are certain situations where these also become essential.

The wise teacher employs those methods and devices which appeal strongest to the sense where learning most effectively takes place. For example, appeal to the sense of sight by the use of demonstrations, models, pictures, slides, illustrations, other graphic devices, and reading, particularly, but not exclusively, in connection with technical information.

The kinesthetic or muscular sense (touch) is also a very important sense in learning any manipulative skill. It results in the fine coordination which is characteristic of the artist or craftsman. For example: How tight to wind the hair makes use of the kinesthetic sense.

When more than one of the sense channels are employed, more learning will be likely to take place. Try to employ as many different kinds of senses in teaching as possible. For example: The teacher shows slides or a motion picture on how to perform a certain task (sight) and then requires that the student practice performing it (touch). The use of both of these senses will result in far more effective learning than if only student practice were employed.

Sight. The word "beauty" calls to mind a mental image, which is the result of seeing. One can learn to tell at a glance what is beautiful by seeing it many times.

Sound (Hearing). One may hear a door slam and recognize the sound immediately because of having heard it many times.

Smell. One may sniff some cosmetic product and classify it, depending upon the smelling sense, or the odor may not be familiar because it has not been experienced often enough to be properly classified.

Touch. The cosmetologist judges quality of the hair by feeling to determine its distinct properties.

Taste. If blindfolded and given a glass of orange juice, you would identify it as such by tasting, provided you had previously tasted orange juice frequently enough to establish its taste in your mind.

LEARNING PRINCIPLES

Each new learning area is a difficult experience. Each student requires patient guidance. Students must be carefully guided until they feel firmly grounded in the new learning.

First learnings are accompanied with resistance and frustration. But, as the student begins to understand the meaning of the subject, and begins to feel the joy of accomplishment, he seeks more learning and more accomplishment.

Learning is like a landslide. It requires a great deal of force to start the learning process. However, once it begins, it gathers strength and momentum. The development of a solution to each problem simplifies the learning and understanding of succeeding problems. As learning becomes easier it becomes more pleasant.

LAWS OF LEARNING

Learning is reacting; there is no learning without response and participation by the student. The teacher does not pour knowledge into a passive receptacle (the student) and then have it poured back to him by an examination. To remember, the student must actively participate in or experience what he is expected to learn. He must respond in a manner which will create new patterns in his mind or in his physical being which will result in new behavior patterns. It is only in the realization and use of the new knowledge and abilities that the learning process is complete.

The laws of learning apply equally to all students and serve as a basis for all activity and planning by the cosmetology teacher. Because learning is a very complex experience, it cannot be summarized or explained by a few brief statements or rules. However, some of the principles that apply to the learning process are fairly easily presented, understood and applied. We must realize however, that these are but a few of the factors involved in the process of learning and even if we know these principles we still do not have the answers to all of our teaching problems

Law of Readiness

Learning cannot be forced. It takes place only when the student is ready physically, mentally and emotionally. The student must therefore be prepared to learn before satisfactory results are obtainable. The "Law of Readiness" requires that the willingness, desire and interest to learn be present on the part of the student. These, in turn lead to effort being exerted by the student. Effort that does not spring from desire and interest becomes mere drudgery. If the teacher can arouse real interest then effort will flow and learning will take place.

Law of Primacy

It is a basic concept to say that the greater the attention at the time of teaching, the more effective will be the absorption and learning. First impressions are significant and most important because attention at that moment is intense. Thus, learning the right way the first time is easiest for the student.

In planning and presenting the lesson, the teacher must be exceedingly careful to be correct and accurate. If the presentation is not clear or essential factors are left out, great difficulties will be created in the learning pattern. Being taught incorrect information and then being required to unlearn what he had learned and to relearn new material may present a real hazard to progress in cosmetology education.

Law of Effect

Interest cannot be aroused unless we justify, to our students, the experience or material we are about to present to them. This justification, in cosmetology training, can be achieved either by leading them to understanding the practical value of what is to be learned or by so presenting the new concept that it appeals to a basic desire for additional information. If interest is an active attitude toward experience that arises from an understanding of its worth or importance, then we must reveal to the students the need for this experience or knowledge so that he may know definitely why his whole attention to the lesson is required.

Praise and encouragement will help the student achieve technical success.

Learning is easy when it is satisfying. To be required to relearn a lesson that has been erroneously taught, is certainly not satisfying. **Instructors must plan their work so that students begin to see success early in the training period.** If active interest is aroused by visible proof of successful accomplishment, effort for further learning becomes assured.

Law of Intensity

There is an old maxim in education to the effect that teaching is most successful when it is applied through as many senses as possible. It seems reasonable to state that as each sense is called into the learning process, new patterns are formed; that it is easier to restimulate one of three sense patterns than one of two. Thus, as we increase the number of senses to which we appeal, our areas of learning become enriched.

Learning comes best from vivid experience. When the instructor plans his presentation to many senses, the teaching program becomes more vivid, more stimulating and more effective.

Law of Exercise (Self-activity)

Much that has been presented previously emphasizes that learning takes place in direct proportion to the effort exerted by the student. Teaching, at best, is a process of arousing and directing the self-activity of the student toward a definite goal. Effective teaching provides a variety of ways in which students may apply their knowledge. In the final analysis, the students' reactions and ability to perform effectively, rather than the teachers' presentation, will determine their understanding and retention.

Other things being equal, the more frequently a new technique or theory is exercised the more effective its learning results. Such abilities and techniques as are established for any cosmetology skill are naturally strengthened by repetitions. Long disuse can result in forgetting.

The old adage "Practice makes perfect," is correct within certain limits. It is more important that the repetitions be well distributed than numerous. Practice should be regular and frequent — a little every day or every other day rather than innumerable times one day followed by a respite of two weeks. Technical skills tend to become dimmed unless reenacted; the more recent the practice the better do we know it. The most effective learning takes place when initial learning is followed immediately by application. Repetitions, with progressively increasing intervals, is far more productive than the same number of repetitions at regular intervals.

When students are given an opportunity to demonstrate their ability, the Laws of Readiness, Primacy, Intensity, Effect and Exercise start to operate.

THE PROFESSIONAL CLASSROOM ATMOSPHERE

Good teaching is dependent upon numerous factors in the classroom and in the teacher's technique and ability. The general atmosphere in the classroom often reveals a picture of the effectiveness of the teaching-learning situation.

1. **Classroom Activity.** The good, active cosmetology classroom does not exist in a vacuum. There is constant activity of serious students performing constructive work. The modern school of cosmetology keeps students involved in a host of constructive training activities.

2. **Individualized Training.** The good cosmetology teacher pays special attention to the student's individual training needs. The teacher and student must plan to work in accordance with the student's needs, capacities and interest. The training program must not be locked into a rigid, unflexible format that leaves many students hopelessly behind the set goals. Mass training and the educational "lock step" must be cast aside for individual learning.

3. **Flexibility of Teaching Methods.** There is no single, best way to teach in the modern cosmetology classroom. Teachers must use a variety of methods to be most effective. Every known teaching method should be employed during the teaching program. For best results every teaching device should be brought into play as needed.

4. **Realistic Approach.** The professional cosmetology teacher employs the realism of salon practice whenever possible. The good classroom does not function on a series of bogus projects or useless and unrealistic "busywork" programs.

5. **Objectives.** Both the students and the teachers know what they are doing at all times. They also are aware of the purpose served by their activities in helping to achieve either the short-term or long-term objectives of the teaching program.

6. **Problem Solving.** Both students and teachers take pride in finding solutions to cosmetology problems. They employ all of the resources available to them to arrive at their own solutions to various trade and technical problems. They refuse to accept "ready-made" unchallenged solutions to class problems.

7. **Teacher-Student Relations.** Teachers and students establish a good rapport among themselves. They approach the school programs in a professional and unified manner. Students and teachers approach the task of cosmetology training as a unified and coordinated team, each one eager and concerned with contributing to the overall success of the program.

8. **Classroom Cooperation.** In the good cosmetology classroom, students learn the techniques of living and working in cooperation with each other. They develop the abilities to reach group decisions, to plan together and to work together.

CLASSROOM TECHNIQUES

Teacher control of the classroom activities is of vital importance to successful learning. The following suggestions are offered to help professional teachers avoid some of the pitfalls commonly found in the classroom.

1. **Lesson Plans.** Every professional instructor is guided by carefully prepared lesson plans. While the lesson plans guide the program of teaching they should never be permitted to become "straight jackets." They should never be permitted to restrict teaching flexibility. Qualified teachers seek new ways to expand and develop the lesson and the learning opportunities of students.

2. **Textbook Control.** The most common weakness found in the cosmetology classroom is the teacher with a "textbook fixation." These are teachers who follow the textbook with absolute rigidity. The textbook is a very important and essential aid to good cosmetology education. However, the teacher should not be tied or glued to the textbook with absolute rigidity. The professional teacher introduces supplementary information, new references, audio-visuals, group discussions and other techniques to broaden the scope of learning.

3. **Directing (Guiding) Learning.** Each student learns in his own way, at his own pace. It is detrimental to educational or learning efficiency to demand that each student react in the same way. A teacher cannot succeed as a "dictator of learning," but the teacher's energies should be devoted to serving as a "director of learning." The teacher should "guide" students along the path to learning, but the students must learn for themselves. Teachers must never lock themselves, or their students, into a regimented, rigid routine of "dictated" learning in which each lesson is taught and learned by rote.

4. **Project Control.** Classroom projects are excellent teaching and learning techniques. However, careful control must be exercised over the number of projects being introduced. The planning or starting of too many unrelated projects drains the energies of both the students and the teacher. When projects become too numerous they begin to dilute or weaken their educational value and become disruptive influences. It is vital therefore, that the number of projects be carefully controlled.

5. **Interest in Learning.** Teacher enthusiasm and encouragement can do a great deal to involve students. However, learning takes place only when student interest is created in, and sustained by, the subject matter being taught. The challenge presented by the subject matter, together with the enthusiastic atmosphere created by the teacher, can maintain interest at a high level. This classroom condition helps to make the hard work of learning a pleasant experience.

6. **Verbal Control.** A very common fault in cosmetology education, and indeed in all education, is the exclusive or excessive use of verbal teaching. While it is true that "words are the chief medium of education," they should not be the exclusive means of education. Cosmetology classroom teaching lends itself readily to an appeal to all of the senses. Teaching should be diversified to utilize the eyes, the ears and the hands of the students. The amount and type of verbal instruction should be carefully controlled in the classroom.

7. **Teaching Aids.** Teaching aids of all types are important in the modern classroom. However, even this very valuable educational area can be overworked. Too many aids may soon detract from the teaching-learning atmosphere. Too many aids soon begin to clutter and litter the classroom until it resembles an untidy storage room. A professional teacher must not become overburdened with teaching aids. The aids should be used to illustrate or demonstrate a thought or even an entire lesson. However, control must be maintained over them and they must never be permitted to interfere with teaching flexibility.

ASSOCIATION OF IDEAS

An important aspect of learning is that people must understand the relationship of various elements before they can absorb entire concepts. This understanding expands into complete comprehension and the ability to generalize and develop knowledge. This association of ideas and concepts is the foundation upon which real learning is built.

Material to be learned must be "meaningful" to the student. The new material presented must become part of the whole within the mind of the student. It is important that new material, ideas and experiences be introduced in relation to familiar concepts and ideas.

Put YOURSELF in the student's place.

The wise teacher learns something of the background of students, their interests and their abilities, and uses this knowledge carefully in his classroom presentation.

If the material being taught is useful and beneficial, students will retain the knowledge better and are more likely to desire to learn more.

Learning something new is easier if it can be built upon something that is already known. It is best to start with simple steps that are related to material which is already known and then proceed to new and more difficult knowledge or techniques.

Learning takes place step by step. Every new thing we learn must be associated in as many ways as possible with things we already know. This can only be accomplished if the learning proceeds in an orderly step-by-step manner.

Learning experiences must be associated logically because of their similarity or their differences. It is a process of association of ideas, the new with the old, the unknown with the known. Students with considerable experience or knowledge find it easier to associate new ideas and concepts with knowledge already familiar to them. However, if suitable background experience is lacking, the cosmetology teacher must supply and develop the necessary information.

Students change from day to day, as their knowledge and skill increase and develop. Therefore, the instructor must constantly present new and up-to-date material to maintain this change and keep student development moving toward a goal. If the material is properly presented, the student's mind, acting in the manner of a blotter, absorbs the information a little at a time.

The student's mind absorbs information
like a blotter.

The transfer of knowledge from one area to another is directly in proportion to the degree that the student recognizes the similarity of situations. For example: Knowledge required to reason out a certain problem will not be transferred to a problem of the beauty salon unless the student recognizes a similarity in the two problems. If students understand this, then their reasoning ability can be used to great advantage in the transference of knowledge. Learning is affected by everything that influences the student. Included are home environment, school environment, nervous system, attitudes, and other factors.

Teachers may not assume that if a certain method of presentation is employed it will automatically get a certain response. Unless teachers take into consideration the many other factors which influence their students, they cannot be certain whether or not the method being employed will be the correct one for maximum response. Teaching is quite likely to be successful only in direct proportion to the teacher's own understanding and consideration of all factors affecting his students.

1. **In teaching logic, when do we judge that a new experience or technique is learned?**
   When that experience or technique has begun to function as a habit.

2. **In what two ways does a student do his own learning?**
   1. Through his own experience.
   2. Through his interpretation of the experiences of others.

3. **What is the basic function of the cosmetology teacher?**
   To provide effective guidance to his students.

4. **What is the cosmetology teacher's prime responsibility?**
   To make certain that the students acquire all the basic skills and techniques for services rendered in the beauty salon.

5. **Regardless of the teacher's efforts, in the final analysis, what is the only way in which the acquisition of knowledge can be accomplished?**
   Various learning devices and methods must be employed in the areas where they can bring the best results.

6. **Why is the professional attitude of the teacher essential to good cosmetology education?**
   A professional attitude permits and encourages a teamwork approach to the development of good cosmetology training.

7. **Why is it important that the teacher have some knowledge of the student's home and environment?**
   In order to properly understand the student and strengthen the ties between the teacher and the student.

8. **List eight weaknesses found in general teaching techniques.**
   1. Teachers do most of the talking.
   2. Teachers do not make assignments definite, interesting and worthwhile.
   3. Teachers embarrass students with sarcastic remarks.
   4. Teachers misuse examinations.
   5. Teachers fail to plan their program of instruction.
   6. Teachers make statements of facts without relating them to the training program.
   7. Teachers direct all efforts toward "average" students and neglect bright and slow students.
   8. Teachers disregard student judgment in planning programs and activities.

9. **How does effective learning develop?**
   It develops from an understanding of the essential components and their relationship to the completed task so as to form a pattern.

10. **Students learn through the basic senses. Name them and tell the most important sense for learning.**
    The five senses are sight, hearing, smell, touch and taste. Most learning develops through the sense of sight.

11. **Since learning develops as a result of stimulating one or more of the senses, define a suitable stimulus.**

A stimulus is anything, such as light or sound, which excites the sensory nerve endings.

12. **In regard to stimulus, what is the teacher's job?**

It is the teacher's job to make certain that the proper stimulus is directed at the proper sense to create the desired learning pattern.

13. **What percentage of all learning is absorbed through the eyes?**

Eighty-five percent.

14. **How would a wise teacher appeal to the sense of sight?**

By the use of demonstrations, models, pictures, slides, illustrations, other graphic devices, and reading.

15. **In what type of skill is the kinesthetic or muscular sense of touch important?**

Manipulative skill requires strong muscular sense.

16. **How does the good teacher make use of senses in his work?**

The good teacher combines as many of them as possible in teaching, such as appealing to sight by a motion picture; appealing to touch by having student practice; appealing to hearing by classroom instruction.

17. **What causes students to seek more learning and more accomplishment?**

When students begin to understand the meaning of a subject, success in learning encourages the desire for more learning.

18. **How do students react to first learnings?**

In general first learnings are accompanied by resistance and frustration.

19. **What are the five laws of learning? Define them.**
    1. Law of Readiness — the will to learn must be present in the student.
    2. Law of Primacy — learning the right way the first time is easier.
    3. Law of Effect — student must be convinced of the practical value of the teaching material.
    4. Law of Intensity — appeal to as many of the senses as possible in the teaching process.
    5. Law of Exercise (self-activity) — learning takes place in direct ratio to the effort exerted by the student.

20. **Students learn by practice. What is the more productive type of repetition?**

Repetition at progressively increasing intervals is more productive than the same number of repetitions at regular intervals.

21. **List the eight techniques employed by teachers to create a classroom atmosphere which is conducive to good learning.**
    1. Constant classroom activity.
    2. Individualized training.
    3. Flexibility of teaching methods.
    4. Realistic approach to teaching and learning.
    5. Full knowledge of objectives by teacher and students.
    6. Students involved in problem solving.
    7. Good rapport between teacher and students.
    8. Complete atmosphere of cooperation.

22. **List the seven controls exercised by professional teachers over classroom activities to promote good education.**
    1. Proper preparation and use of lesson plans.
    2. Control of the use of the textbook.
    3. Direct (Guide) Learning — not dictate.
    4. Careful control of classroom projects.
    5. Teacher enthusiasm to arouse student interest.
    6. Careful control of verbal teaching.
    7. Judicious use of teaching aids.

23. **In learning, why is the association of ideas important?**

    When the relationship of various elements is understood, then the student can absorb the entire concept.

24. **In learning new material, will a student with a broad background and knowledge find it easier than the student with a limited background?**

    The student with a broad background finds it easier to learn.

25. **In transferring knowledge from one area to another, what is important for the student to recognize?**

    It is important for the student to recognize any similarity of situations.

26. **What factors influence a difference in learning response?**

    Everything that influences the student affects his ability to learn. Included are home environment, school environment, nervous systems, attitudes, general health, and many other personal factors.

CHAPTER 6

STUDENT
LEARNING PRINCIPLES

STUDENT SUCCESS FACTORS

The first essential of successful student learning is a feeling of security. A feeling of fear or uncertainty serves to destroy the student's desire and ability to learn. On the other hand, a comfortable sense of security promotes the student's will to learn. The feeling of success gives a student confidence and improves his ability and desire to tackle new problems and new subject matter.

A classroom which is free from tensions and pressures is a far better place for learning than a classroom controlled by stresses and anxieties. Praise and recognition of progress serve to bolster the students' need for self respect and confidence. Positive, encouraging activities create a classroom atmosphere which is conducive to learning and achievement.

It is essential that teachers understand they must never disregard the total learning situation into which students are being directed. If students are pushed into impossible learning situations, it is inevitable that they will develop failure complexes. However, if students are guided into successful and satisfying learning experiences, they will take pride in the feeling of success and accomplishment, and seek additional learning experiences.

The belief that students are strengthened by threats and failures has been proven to be unsound and erroneous. The classroom should be a place for positive, constructive people, things and activities. If students make mistakes they should be corrected quietly and without embarrassment. When students have success they should be praised and encouraged to further accomplishment.

REASONS FOR STUDENT FAILURE

Every type of learning is difficult. Students who function in a state of continuous anxiety, apprehension and uncertainty cannot be expected to be successful learners.

There are a number of basic reasons for student failures. Professional teachers should be aware of the common reasons for student failures and be prepared to deal with them as they arise. Following are five of the most prevalent reasons for student failure.

1. **Students Do Not Know How To Study.**

   Teachers should guide students to the establishment of good study habits. They must be directed in:
   a) how to get prepared for study.
   b) how to set up proper study conditions.
   c) how to prevent interruptions.
   d) how to get the major ideas from a lesson.

2. **Students Are Afraid.**

   They fear the teacher, they are afraid of failure and they fear the subject matter. All these fears result in poor work and the failure to learn. Students with anxious minds cannot learn efficiently. Every student has a right to freedom from fear.

   Teachers must become aware of student anxieties and fears and exert every effort to overcome them. Freedom from fear will enable students to grasp and retain subject matter.

3. **Poor Reading Ability.**

   Many students are unable to understand the subject matter because they are poor readers. They do not have the ability to understand, remember and apply what they read.

   The teacher should take more time to help slower or poor readers; perhaps give more verbal instruction.

4. **Lack of Motivation for Learning.**

   Many students feel that they have no reason for studying and learning. They feel that the entire learning process is not worth the effort.

   The teacher must help these students to set goals which are important to them. They must be helped to understand that school study and application will assist them to attain desired goals.

5. **Students Study and Learn Only Those Things Which They Like Best.**

   They are inclined to push aside those areas of learning or techniques which they do not enjoy.

   The teacher must condition and guide students to get satisfaction from working in areas which they may not like. Teachers must encourage students to derive pleasure from performing difficult, even distasteful, tasks.

MOTIVATION

Motivate, using illustration.

To be successful, learning must be motivated. It takes place only when the desire or interest to learn is present. Further, a definite goal or objective must also be present. Teachers must stimulate and awaken the interest of their students and provide them with a clearly indicated goal, if learning is to be properly motivated.

In stimulating students, teachers must remember that the best motivation is both long-term and immediate. Students must know what part the material presented plays in their long-range goal. It is also important that the immediate significance of information be readily evident.

Motivation is probably the most basic factor in student learning. It is that element which influences a student to want to know, to understand, to believe, to act, to develop a new skill or gain new knowledge. The successful teacher recognizes the great importance of motivation and devises ways and means to introduce motivating factors into the learning process.

Long-Range Motivation

Some factors which contribute to the long-range motivation of cosmetology students are the:

1. Desire for financial security.
2. Seeking of new experiences.
3. Need for self-esteem.
4. Desire for artistic self-expression.
5. Desire to make others look nice.
6. Need for creativity.

Student Motivation for Learning

Some circumstances that motivate the student to learning are:

1. Student knows and understands requirements for a career in cosmetology.
2. Student enjoys cosmetology practice.
3. Student finds the school pleasant.
4. Student finds the subjects taught self-satisfying.
5. Student has acceptable or agreeable school hours.
6. Students are kept informed of proposed changes in schedules and study subjects.
7. Transportation to school is adequate.
8. Good recreational facilities are available.
9. School staff understands students' problems.
10. School and staff participates in community activities.
11. School has adequate and efficient management staff.
12. School creates a truly professional image.
13. Student's individual efforts are recognized.
14. Student has a feeling of accomplishment.
15. Student clearly recognizes long-term and short-term goals.

Teacher Motivation of Students

Ways in which the teacher can motivate students:

1. Help students to associate past experiences with learning situations.
2. Show students how the subject matter contributes to immediate needs.
3. Indicate how the subject matter contributes to future needs.
4. Give students opportunity to apply what they already know.
5. Awaken student curiosity as to new subject matter.
6. Direct students to the recognition and solution of problems.
7. Make certain that teaching-learning situation satisfies students' needs for action and movement.
8. Show students how facts and skills learned in school will be used in the beauty salon.
9. Show enthusiasm for subject and students will respond to that enthusiasm.
10. Make certain that students acquire feeling of success and accomplishment.
11. Bring new and fresh material to the classroom — keep student interest at a high pitch.
12. Gear classroom experiences to the individual needs of the students.

We must not conclude that motivation is the panacea for all teaching ills. It can do much to place teaching on a higher plane, but situations in which it impossible to motivate are not uncommon. Motivation at best, is justifying an experience, or information, in terms of present and obvious needs. In all teaching, occasions arise in which the **students must accept the teacher's judgment** that a particular set of facts or skills is necessary.

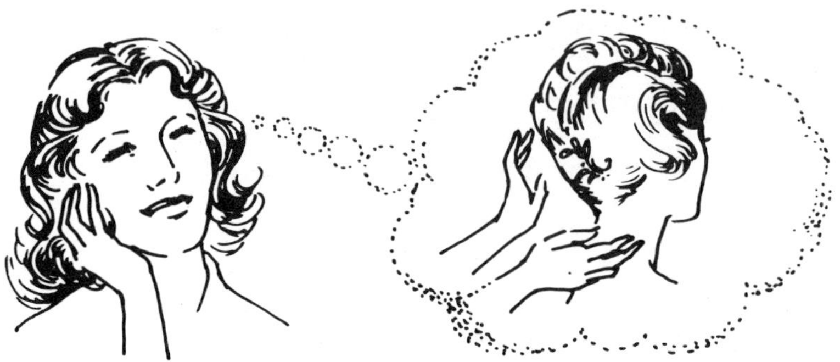

Every individual has the desire to create.

Make a good and proper introduction to each lesson, in line with the students' interests. Avoid any cosmetology practice exercises that fail to arouse and maintain their interest.

Interest is the basis of learning. Students learn that which is interesting and resist learning that which is uninteresting. A fundamental principle of teaching is that interest must be aroused before instruction can be effective. Creating a desire to learn, a readiness to learn, depends upon a number of factors, such as:

1. **Curiosity.** Cosmetology offers many opportunities for arousing curiosity and suspense as an interest-building device.

2. **Creativity.** All individuals desire to create something with their hands or minds; something better, or an easier way of performing a job. New developments, to be successful, must be based on fundamental principles. Successful cosmetology instructors teach these principles and their application to their students.

3. **Activity.** Students are bored when faced with inactivity for a period of time. They enjoy activity, which may be either physical or mental. Competent teachers always have enough planned activities on hand to make their students hustle a bit. Slight pressure on the job is a strong incentive to better workmanship. Creative thinking is a challenge to the student. However, the goal must not be too far ahead or seemingly out of reach or some will get discouraged and give up.

4. **Group Instinct** is present in most students; they love to work together. The instructor can, and must, foster the cooperative spirit. Some students work better in small groups; others can work successfully in larger groups; while a few are at their best when working alone. Wherever possible, use the group instinct as an interest-building device.

The group instinct
is a predominant
factor.

5. **Competition** has plus and minus values. It should not be entirely eliminated. Neither should it be overdone. In assigning group activities to students, members of the group should be as evenly balanced as possible. This promotes a competitive spirit since each wants to contribute as much as the others. If the group is badly out of balance the weaker student will let the others "do it" because they "want to," while the superior student will do most of the work because "the others can't." A word of caution is necessary. Do not carry competition to the point where it is more important than the learning involved. Use good judgment in determining the extent to which you can safely use competition as an interest builder.

6. **Pride of Accomplishment.** "Nothing succeeds like success." Students must feel that they are making progress toward some goal: accomplishing something worthwhile at all times. "Every job worth doing is worth doing well." Beauty salons are interested only in people who do well the tasks assigned to them. "Only your best is good enough for any job." Instructors must impress upon their students that these thoughts are more than mere slogans. They are the foundation of success in the beauty school and on the job. Students must be taught to take pride in doing a job and doing it well. Successful learning stimulates more learning. Failure to learn or to understand discourages further learning. The teacher must plan his instruction so that successful learning takes place each step in the program.

7. **Job Importance.** Every job and assignment should play its part in the development of students as a whole. When they can see their goal or objective, and can see the importance of the immediate job in attaining that goal, their interest will be stimulated. Teachers must avoid assignments which are independent learning units without regard to their place in the entire training program. Assignments "just to keep the students busy" have no place in a cosmetology training program.

8. **Knowledge and Skill.** Teachers encounter problems in cases where more preparatory knowledge and skill are needed. Recognition of this lack of knowledge and skill is essential. Recognizing the deficiencies, and the awakening of the desire to eliminate them, definitely establishes an interest basis for learning.

9. **Enthusiasm.** Enthusiasm is infectious. If instructors are genuinely enthusiastic about their subject, much of this enthusiasm will overflow to their students. If they are only "lukewarm," pupils will also have a "lukewarm" interest. Instructors who cannot become enthusiastic about their subject are a definite handicap to the program.

STUDENT PARTICIPATION

To really learn, students must actively participate in or experience the subject matter they are expected to absorb. They must take positive action to develop new patterns in their minds or muscles, which should result in new behavior patterns. The learning process is thorough and successful only when new information or new skills are actually put to use.

Learning is responding or reacting to outside stimuli. No learning occurs unless there is some definite reaction or response from the student. The teacher cannot pour information or knowledge into a passive receptacle and expect to have it poured back at a given signal. Learning requires an active joining of efforts by both teacher and student.

Learning by doing requires that the student constantly use the new material taught. If the ideas are abstract, then discussion and answering questions may be the best form of presentation. If they are scientific or mathematical, working out problems may give the best results. If the material is manipulative, actual practice of the operation will be necessary before it can be learned.

INDIVIDUAL DIFFERENCES

"Individual differences" is a term which could be applied to personal differences of a physical, emotional, moral or mental nature.

However, as a cosmetology instructor you are concerned mainly with the differences in individuals which affect their rate of learning, namely:

Differences in Emotional Reaction. Competent instructors adapt their approach to a teaching problem to the emotional makeup of their students. For example, a sensitive person requires the instructor to be consistently gentle. On the other hand, a constant complainer or a bully requires the instructor to be firm.

Difference in emotional reaction.

Differences in Ability. The ability of individuals varies greatly. When arousing a student's interest in a subject, you are faced with a challenging opportunity to develop that ability. For example, an abundance of related instructional material must be provided for a **fast learner.** On the other hand the **slow learner** requires more patience and understanding. Provide for many variations when presenting the same lesson in order to avoid monotony and loss of interest on the student's part.

Give each student his
share of your time.

Difference in Interest. The variety of student interests is one of the first things instructors will discover about their class. Sometimes in class it is impossible to cater to each individual's interest. When this is the case, choose an interest which is characteristic to almost all people, such as competition, general personal interest or some similar concept.

Planning for Individual Differences. Since teachers are faced with students of varying backgrounds, they must try to reach individuals according to their needs. Give as much instruction as possible on an individual basis.

Give individual help when needed.

In your introduction and presentation of material use as many different approaches as possible. If individual students do not understand one explanation, they will find something useful in another presentation.

While individual students all try equally hard, they may make very different progress. A good teacher appreciates both honest effort and high achievement and expends extra effort to bring along the slower students.

EMOTIONAL INFLUENCE ON LEARNING

Personal feelings and emotions play a critical role in the development of learning. Professional teachers are constantly seeking new ideas and programs to improve the emotional climate of the classroom and thus improve learning.

Teachers, as a result of their leadership role, have a very powerful influence upon the emotions of their students. The teacher's words, gestures or glances can make a student feel inadequate, inferior and a "natural loser." On the other hand, the teacher can also make the student feel confident, important, capable and worthwhile.

Techniques Which "Tear Down" Students

Unfortunately, some teachers take pleasure in degrading a student's ego and self-respect. Without realizing the extent of the damage they are doing, these teachers must gratify their own egos by making students feel inferior. Some of the tactics employed by these teachers are:

1. **Use of Superior Language.** Deliberately using words which the students do not understand. This tactic is designed to embarrass students, who will not reveal that they do not understand a question or a problem and are, therefore, unable to answer properly.

2. **Concentration on Fast Learners.** The most effective way to discourage and destroy a slow student is for the teacher to direct all teaching efforts toward high achievers. Those students unable to meet the very high standards set, soon feel completely left out of the learning situation. It does not take long to completely discourage the slow learner and have him ready to "drop out."

3. **Excessive Praise.** The use of excessive or immoderate praise for some trivial or minor task is actually detrimental. Students quickly recognize this extravagant praise as strictly "phony" and actually insulting. The instructor, in reality, is indicating that the student is incapable of any other task and is therefore being praised for this meaningless achievement. Even the slowest learners recognize this insincere approach.

4. **Arousing Student Guilt.** This is the superficial technique of making the student feel that he is "letting the teacher down." The teacher promotes the feeling that the student is failing the teacher personally. The teacher creates a guilty feeling in the student by developing the impression that he (the teacher) had worked so hard to help the student, who had deliberately failed to respond or make an effort to appreciate the teacher's great sacrifice. The foregoing tactics are demonstrated by rather sadistic teachers, who delight in "putting down" their students. The cause of professionalism in cosmetology education would be greatly advanced if these teachers were "weeded out" of the educational system.

TECHNIQUES WHICH "BUILD UP" STUDENTS

It is indeed fortunate for teaching in general and for cosmetology teaching in particular, that most teachers are concerned with "building up" their students rather than "tearing them down." The truly professional teacher devotes his energies to the development of student self-esteem, confidence and self-respect.

Professional teachers realize that successful teaching can take place only with the willingness and cooperation of students. No educational progress can be made in an antagonistic area which houses a perpetual war between teachers and students. Real learning and true education requires a cooperative and harmonious atmosphere of mutual respect and consideration.

Some of the practices followed by professional teachers to advance and improve learning are:

1. Students are given the opportunity to express their personal feelings. Respectful attention should be given to an honest expression of the students' attitudes, ideas, concerns and doubts.

   Students must feel that they may honestly express themselves without any fear of criticism or embarrassment. Under no circumstances should a student be subjected to ridicule, regardless of how unrealistic or unacceptable his statements may be.

2. Students are encouraged to believe that it is good and educationally worth-while to be individualistic and to think independently. It is assuring to students to be encouraged to explore their own minds and to be free to express their own thoughts. Students are made to feel that even if their ideas are "outlandish" and impractical they will not be humiliated in any way.

3. Competition in the classroom often serves to stimulate high achievers but discourages less able students. Therefore, it is advisable to avoid a competitive atmosphere in the classroom. Each student should be permitted to set his own learning pace. If any competition exists it should be with himself, rather than with others in the class.

Students must be encouraged to respect themselves as individuals and as students. They should be encouraged to expend every effort to learn and to grow as a student and as a human being.

REVIEW

1. **What is the first essential of successful student learning?**
   A feeling of security.

2. **How can the teacher create a classroom atmosphere which is conducive to learning?**
   By positive, encouraging activities.

3. **If students are pushed into impossible learning situations, what results are inevitable?**
   The development of failure complexes.

4. **List five basic reasons for student failure.**
   1. Students do not know how to study.
   2. Students are afraid.
   3. Poor reading ability.
   4. Lack of motivation for learning.
   5. Pushing aside areas of learning they do not like.

5. **What is the most basic factor in student learning?**
   Motivation.

6. **List twelve ways teachers can help motivate students.**
   1. Associate past experience with new learning.
   2. Point out how subject matter contributes to immediate needs.
   3. Indicate how subject matter contributes to future needs.
   4. Give opportunity for application of learning.
   5. Awaken curiosity in new subjects.
   6. Direct students in problem solving.
   7. Satisfy students' needs for action and movement.
   8. Associate new skills with beauty salon practice.
   9. Show enthusiasm.
   10. Direct student success and accomplishment.
   11. Maintain interest with new material.
   12. Meet student's individual needs.

7. **List nine ways to arouse interest and maintain student attention.**
    1. Curiosity.
    2. Creativity.
    3. Activity
    4. Group instinct.
    5. Competition.
    6. Pride of accomplishment
    7. Job importance.
    8. Knowledge and skill.
    9. Enthusiasm.

8. **How important is student participation?**
    To really learn, students must experience the subject matter they are expected to absorb.

9. **What are the individual differences in students which affect their rate of learning?**
    Differences in emotional reaction, differences in ability, and differences in interest.

10. **How does a teacher plan for individual differences?**
    By giving as much instruction as possible on an individual basis and using as many different approaches in the presentation of material as possible.

11. **List four of the tactics employed by teachers that tear down a student's confidence or desire to learn:**
    1. Use of superior language which students do not understand.
    2. Concentration on fast learners, which makes all other students feel completely left out and discouraged.
    3. Excessive praise for trivial things makes student feel that this is the limit of his capabilities.
    4. Arousing student guilt — makes student feel that he is letting the teacher down after great personal sacrifice.

12. **List three techniques employed by professional teachers to build up students.**
    1. Pay respectful attention to students' honest expressions of attitudes and ideas.
    2. Encourage students to be educationally individualistic and independent.
    3. Avoid competitive atmosphere in classroom; each student proceeds at his own pace.

CHAPTER 7

LESSON PLANNING

INTRODUCTION

Teaching without planning is like trying to navigate the ocean without a compass.

A great deal has been written in educational bulletins and other teacher references, on the subject of planning in its various aspects and especially on lesson planning. There is, however, a definite need for providing teachers with specific help and guidance in the preparation of lesson plans.

Planning begins the moment the teacher starts to think about any activity in the classroom. The aim of the teacher is to direct the teaching and learning activities of the class to achieve those objectives set up by the school. This can be achieved only if the teacher sets up a series of organized and sequential learning experiences that provide a smooth flow of related knowledge.

Continuity in cosmetology training is maintained and sequential development provided for, when the activities engaged in by students lead them to new, but related, learning experiences. The relationship of the sequence of instruction, the time allotments and the desired outcomes or aims of the teaching activities must be designed and directed to meet the objectives of the cosmetology training programs.

In order to develop the cosmetology educational program, the teacher should plan specifically, for each day, the aims, the content to be covered, the techniques and activities to be developed and the materials to be used. These daily lesson plans must be fairly flexible in nature, and may be informal in construction.

After the course has been carefully organized, the teacher is faced with the major responsibility of making sure that the day-by-day classroom activities relate directly to the general program. Planning the daily lesson centers around the device known as the **Lesson Plan.** This has been defined as follows: "Lesson Plan is the title given to a statement of the achievements to be realized and the specific means by which these are to be attained as a result of the activities engaged in during the period the class spends with the teacher."

VALUE OF DAILY LESSON PLAN

A large measure of an instructor's success depends upon his ability to effectively plan and present his subject. The importance of planning each lesson cannot be over-emphasized. No teacher can go to class unprepared and adequately present his subject. He must know exactly what he is going to teach and how he will teach it.

A teacher without a lesson plan is like a lawyer presenting a case in court without a brief or outline of the procedure he is to follow in conducting his case. The lawyer's client is not being properly represented and neither is a student being properly taught unless the teacher has an organized, definite plan of presentation.

The lesson plan charts the teaching-learning situation. It contains important guidelines and details which should not be trusted to memory. It directs all activities toward the achievement of specific objectives. It suggests new ideas, new approaches and an orderly sequence for the presentation of instructional material.

"Those who plan best, teach best."

BENEFITS FROM LESSON PLANNING

1. Lesson planning insures a definite objective (goal) for the lesson.
2. It insures a proper connection of new material with previous learning.
3. It insures organized selection of subject matter, material and activities.
4. It helps to advance the most desirable teaching procedure.
5. It provides for adequate summaries of the lesson.
6. It provides for efficient evaluation of the results of teaching.
7. It provides the teacher with key questions.
8. It provides for unity in lesson development.
9. It assures definite student assignments.
10. It provides for adequate flexibility to allow for individual differences in students.
11. It provides for the availability of teaching materials and teaching aids.
12. It gives a teacher confidence and provides for freedom in teaching, yet assures an orderly, organized presentation.

IMPORTANCE OF LESSON PLANNING IN TEACHING

Lesson planning is equal or greater in importance than planning the contents of the curriculum or the preparation of the course of study. A lesson plan enables the instructor to evaluate the results of the lesson in terms of the students, and allows the students to be in the foreground and the instructor in the background as a director of the learning activities of the class.

Lesson plans are outlines, blueprints, or guides, set up in a step-by-step fashion to cover the subject matter to be taught. A good lesson plan should include eleven basic steps, namely:

1. Specific objectives.
2. Teacher preparation.
3. Student preparation.
4. Presentation.
5. Safety precautions.
6. Demonstrations
7. Special problems.
8. Oral quiz to check students' understanding.
9. Application. (Students' participation.)
10. Summary.
11. Assignments.

A lesson plan should be flexible in order that it be functional. A well-outlined lesson plan assures the teacher that every phase of the subject will be covered. No point, however minute, will be overlooked. Lesson plans force instructors to carefully consider the selection of the subject matter, procedures and the preparation of tests to check the students' progress. Some kind of lesson planning must be carried out by all teachers regardless of their experience. An instructor who teaches without a lesson plan cannot be expected to be an effective teacher since his program becomes somewhat disorganized and lacks continuity.

Preparation of the lesson plan is a continuous and current educational program. A good instructor will not be satisfied with last year's outdated lesson plans, but will continually work to give his students the best in cosmetology education. His lesson plans will reflect his efforts to keep pace with the progress of his students and with new and modern cosmetology knowledge and understanding. Lesson plans not only reflect the teacher's desire to properly convey knowledge to students, but are an indication of the teacher's own effectiveness as an educator.

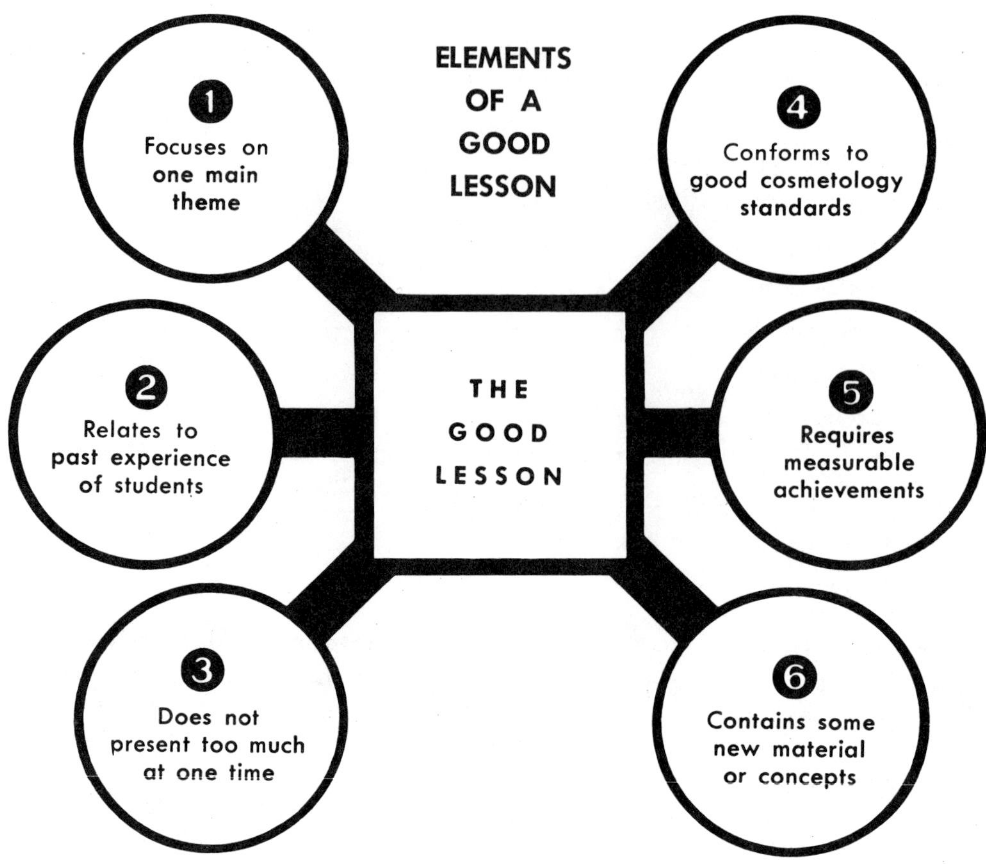

OUTLINE OF A LESSON PLAN

Of course, lesson plans will vary in content and form, according to conditions and circumstances. There is no hard, fast rule that commits you to a particular form; however, it may be helpful to consider the elements included in lesson plans of a comprehensive type.

1. **Aim (Objective).** The lesson plan should revolve around a concise statement of the immediate aims or aims of the lesson.

2. **Allocation of time.**

3. **Visual Aids and Materials.** Preparation should be made to assure availability of all aids and materials required for the lesson—both teacher's and students' needs must be met.

4. **Reference Material.** Where possible, lesson plans should contain specific textbook and workbook page references that will supplement classroom discussion.

5. **Presentation.** Methods and procedures for presenting the lesson material should be outlined. Indicate the order of presentation.

6. **Provide a number of key questions.**

7. **Summary.** It is appropriate to plan for summary statements which bring into focus the major points covered.

8. **Assignments.** Good lesson planning calls for assignments that:
   a) Are clear and comprehensible.
   b) Are meaningful and therefore, interesting to students.

Lesson Plan No. 12

SHAMPOOING

TOPIC: Introduction to Shampooing

OBJECTIVES: As a result of this lesson the student will:
1. Gain a sound background for shampooing.
2. Become familiar with the introductory material.

INSTRUCTOR'S PREPARATION

Facility to be used: Lecture room

Time: One hour

Materials and equipment
Model
Different kinds of shampoos
Neck strip
Towels
Shampoo cape
Comb and brush
Hair rinse

Printed material
Standard Textbook of Cosmetology or Van Dean Manual
Answers to Practical Workbook

Visual and Audio Aids
None

Preparatory assignment for students
Standard Textbook — Topic: Shampooing, Chapter 6 or
Van Dean Manual, Chapter 7
Practical Workbook — Unit #1

STUDENTS' PREPARATION — Bring to class:
Standard Textbook of Cosmetology or Van Dean Manual
Practical Workbook
Ball pen and paper

PRESENTATION

1. Greet the class.

2. Motivate students.
   Discuss with the students their experiences of poor shampoos and rough treatment, if any, employed on them.

3. State the purpose and importance of shampoos.

4. Explain water variances in different areas and importance of water knowledge.

5. Discuss the selection of the proper shampoo for different types of hair.

6. Discuss materials required for a shampoo.

7. Explain the importance of brushing techniques prior to a shampoo and, using model, show proper mantling technique.

8. Using model, discuss and demonstrate brushing technique.

9. **Questioning period — Leading questions**
   a) What is the purpose of a shampoo?
   b) What should a good shampoo accomplish?
   c) What kind of water do you have in your area?
   d) What determines proper shampoo selection?
   e) What are some exceptions to brushing before a shampoo?
   f) Why is it advisable to use only brushes with natural bristles?

10. **Practice session** — Under supervision
    Have students practice brushing technique on each other.

11. **Summary Statement**
    Re-emphasize the importance of a good shampoo and its effects on the patron.

12. **Make new assignment**
    Standard Textbook: Topic — Plain Shampoo, Chapter 6 or
    Van Dean Manual, Chapter 7
    Practical Workbook — Unit 1

This Lesson Plan is taken from . . .

"COSMETOLOGY LESSON PLANS

AND

LESSON PLANNING"

By JOSEPH S. JUNELL and GERALD J. AHERN

ITEMS TO CONSIDER IN LESSON CONSTRUCTION

There is a definite limit to the time an instructor can maintain interest in a lesson. This amount of time is about one-half hour of teacher lecture, unless there is a great deal of student participation in the lesson.

Organize lessons to fit the required time schedule.

Always consider the time factor when actually presenting the lesson. Plan the lesson in its complete form. Changes due to a lack of time can be made while the lesson is being presented. If possible, teachers should plan their teaching in order to allow enough time to complete a lesson.

Select the lesson according to the following factors:

1. What are the objectives of the lesson?

   If there are more than four or five closely related objectives in the lesson, divide it into several lessons.

2. Does the lesson meet the needs of the student?

   Make all instruction student-centered. What is taught is only of value as it contributes to the development of the student.

3. Does the lesson deal with only one major topic or job?

   Do not confuse the student with too many ideas or topics at one time.

Don't confuse the students with too many ideas.

4. Does the lesson contain new ideas or procedures?

   If there are no new elements in the lesson, treat it as a review lesson.

   If there are more than six or seven new elements to be learned, divide them into several lessons.

5. Is the lesson based on previous information?

   Unless the lesson starts a new unit of work, it should relate to the previous lesson.

6. Does the lesson lead into more advanced work?

Unless the lesson is the last one in a unit of work, plan it to be followed by additional information.

7. Is the lesson too short?

If the lesson lacks enough material to give a test on the information presented, it may not be a lesson, but merely a bit of information. If possible, combine several small lessons into a large unit of instruction.

8. Is the lesson too long?

A lesson should not take longer than 30 minutes to present, if possible. If there is too much material, divide it into several lessons.

GUIDING PRINCIPLES FOR PREPARING LESSON PLANS

The following suggestions or guiding principles are designed to help cosmetology teachers develop their lesson plans. These principles are intended to help teachers make their lesson plans become more effective working instruments in the daily teaching program.

1. Prepare the lesson plan so it can be easily followed.

    The plan can be followed easily if:
    a) The writing is clear and legible.
    b) Ample writing space is used.
    c) Plans are organized in a clear and definite pattern.
    d) Space is reserved for comments, notes and reminders.

2. Use all available sources of subject matter, teaching aids, and all school resources. Make use of all resources available.
    a) Course of study, teaching guides, manuals and handbooks
    b) Sets of slides, filmstrips, tapes, films
    c) Reference books
    d) Periodicals, catalogues

3. Check to be sure that all course areas are included and provision is made for including all facets of each cosmetology skill area.

4. Keep in mind the sequence and the continuity of the subject matter and the steps in each cosmetology skill area.

    The sequence and the continuity in cosmetology training have a bearing on the degree of growth in knowledge and skills. They are based upon careful analysis of student cosmetology growth and development. The course of study indicates the sequence for development in cosmetology training.

5. Integrate the training areas in order to achieve a unified approach to the cosmetology subject matter.

    Integrated training draws upon several curriculum areas. This integration is best achieved in the development of cosmetology techniques.

    However, almost every lesson should contain some quality of integration as the professional cosmetology teacher cuts across subject and curriculum areas to develop cosmetology skill techniques.

6. The plan should approach the work area with consideration of the time allotment for each specific training area.

In a well-integrated cosmetology program, it is difficult to allot time exactly to each cosmetology skill or to the subject matter. While most cosmetology programs indicate specific time allotments for the various skill areas, proper education permits some flexibility in the training program.

7. Indicate specific concepts, subject matter or cosmetology skill to be taught.

8. Indicate the skills and the activities within the specific cosmetology technique, as well as those skills and activities associated with it.

9. The plan should indicate the activities for the class as a whole and for students with individual differences.

   a) The teacher plans to work with the entire class when:
      1. Teaching a new subject or a new skill.
      2. The class requires additional training in a specific technique.
      3. A class discussion is desirable.
      4. Evaluating training progress.

   b) The teacher plans to work with individual students in order to:
      1. Help students overcome specific weaknesses.
      2. Encourage students with special abilities and talents.

10. List specific teaching aids to be used, such as audio-visual aids, text, reference books and cosmetology materials.

11. Provide for a maximum amount of student participation in carrying out the cosmetology training activities.

12. Include plans for continuous evaluation of student progress; also plan for student follow-up, based on the indicated needs of the class or individual students.

   Teachers use various methods to determine student needs, such as:
   a) Tests — various types
   b) Observation of students' activities
   c) Comparison of students' work (periodically)

1. **Define the term "lesson plan."**

   Lesson plan is the title given to a statement of the achievements to be realized and the specific means by which these are to be attained as a result of the activities engaged in during the period the class spends with the teacher.

2. **What is the value of a daily lesson plan?**

   For effective teaching, the instructor must know exactly what he is going to teach and how he will teach it.

3. **What are the benefits of lesson planning? Name twelve.**
   1. Insures a goal for the lesson.
   2. Insures connection of new with previous material.
   3. Insures organized selection of subject matter.
   4. Advances most desirable teaching procedure.
   5. Provides summaries of lesson.
   6. Provides efficient evaluation of teaching results.
   7. Provides key questions.
   8. Provides unity in lesson development.
   9. Assures definite student assignments.
   10. Provides flexibility for individual differences in students.
   11. Provides the availability of teaching materials and aids.
   12. Gives teacher confidence.

4. **What are the eleven basic steps in lesson planning?**
   1. Specific objectives.
   2. Teacher preparation.
   3. Student preparation.
   4. Presentation.
   5. Safety precautions.
   6. Demonstration.
   7. Special problems.
   8. Oral quiz
   9. Application.
   10. Summary
   11. Assignments.

5. **What are the elements of a good lesson? Name six.**
   1. Focuses on one main theme.
   2. Relates to past experience of students.
   3. Does not present too much at one time.
   4. Conforms to good cosmetology standards.
   5. Requires measurable achievements.
   6. Contains some new material or concepts.

6. **How should you start your lesson plan?**

   With a statement of the aim of the lesson.

7. **What type of materials should be ready before the lesson starts?**

   All visual aids and and materials for teacher and students plus reference material.

8. **What presentation details should be defined for better teaching guidance?**
Methods and procedures should be outlined, a list of key questions prepared, and time allocated to each topic.

9. **What two ways can you check a good assignment?**
   1. It is clear and comprehensible.
   2. The student realizes that it is meaningful.

10. **What is the amount of time that an instructor can usually maintain interest in a lecture?**
About one-half hour of teacher lecture, unless there is a great deal of student participation in the lesson.

11. **How will you select lesson material to meet the time factor?**
Consider the lesson objectives. Be certain there are not too many for one lesson.

12. **How should a lesson meet the need of the student?**
The lesson should be built around the topic which will contribute to the development of the student.

13. **What should be considered concerning the development of the lesson?**
It should be based on a previous lesson and lead into future classes of advanced information.

14. **How can you evaluate if the lesson is too short?**
If there is not enough material to give a test, it may not add up to a lesson and should be combined with other material.

15. **List the twelve basic principles for preparing a lesson plan.**
   1. Prepare the plan so it is easy to follow.
   2. Use all available sources of subject matter.
   3. Check to be certain that all areas are included.
   4. Watch sequence and continuity of subject matter.
   5. Integrate training areas to achieve a unified approach.
   6. Consider time allotted to each area.
   7. Indicate specific concepts, subject matter or skills to be taught.
   8. Indicate skill and techniques in specific and associated areas.
   9. Plan activities for class—provide for individual differences.
   10. List teaching aids to be used
   11. Provide for maximum student participation.
   12. Include plan for student progress evaluation.

CHAPTER 8

THE FOUR-STEP TEACHING PLAN

INTRODUCTION

Cosmetology teachers cannot hope to succeed unless they clearly understand the general purpose and function of cosmetology education. While it is true that the most immediate aim is to prepare the student to practice in the beauty salon, there should be a broader and more far-reaching objective to be achieved. It might be more educationally sound to say that the purpose and function of cosmetology education is "to develop in each student the knowledge, interests, ideals, habits and skills whereby he can function competently in the beauty salon and, in addition, to continue to shape both himself and the practice of cosmetology into an ever-nobler professional status." This broader concept demands that the teacher apply a wide and comprehensive knowledge, in order to achieve the proper fulfillment of his objective.

Teaching and learning are equal partners in a cooperative enterprise. The teacher must understand the students and how they will respond to various teaching situations and techniques, if learning is to take place. Effective teaching is based on the correct application of planned and organized educational procedures. How students react to the teacher's efforts will determine the effectiveness of the teaching program.

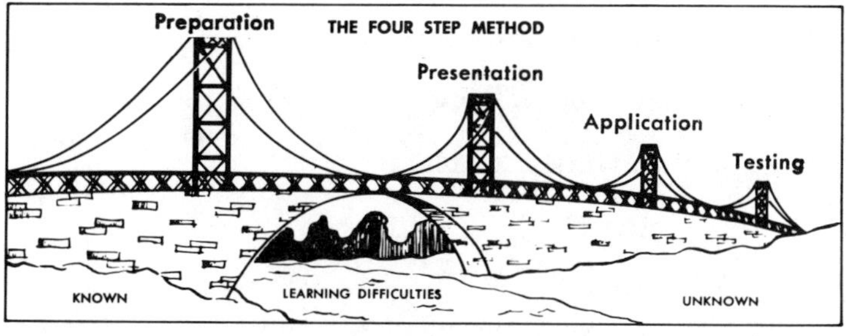

FOUR-STEP METHOD

The natural procedure applicable to cosmetology training is the Four-Step Method of Teaching. It is basically logical to proceed in accordance with this orderly and effective plan in educational development. It is a system or plan of teaching that is based on the application of logic and good common sense. The first step is to arouse the attention and interest of students. Only when this is accomplished can the teacher present the information, subject matter or technique to be learned. The next step would naturally be to give students the opportunity to practice the new material or techniques presented. The final step in the procedure is to determine that the students have actually learned. Thus the four-step teaching plan or method is revealed as a simple, orderly and basically sound program of instruction.

The four steps are:

Step I: Preparation.

Step II: Presentation.

Step III: Application.

Step IV: Testing.

The real problems in using the four-step method of instruction grow out of the failure of the instructor to interpret them properly when confronted with specific teaching situations.

Every step is important in the overall learning pattern. However, great care must be exercised by the teacher to use judgment, understanding and common sense in their application.

STEP I: PREPARATION

This step includes preparation of:

1. The teacher.

2. The classroom.

3. Teaching aids.

4. The student.

Teacher

Know the subject thoroughly.

Keep in mind the objective of the lesson.

Break down material into small, easy-to-master steps.

Plan your work, then work your plan.

Prepare the lesson plan.

1. Don't memorize it.

2. Be familiar enough with the plan to conduct your class by referring to it only occasionally.

3. Know the objective of the lesson.

4. Know the motivation to be employed.

5. Know what teaching method or methods to use in order to be most effective.

6. Prepare teaching supplies, equipment, and teaching aids.
   a) Charts.
   b) Chalk-board.
   c) Hand-out material.
   d) Others.

7. Arrive in class early so that final preparations can be made prior to the arrival of students.

Arrive early! Prepare yourself, the room, teaching aids before students arrive.

Classroom

The teacher is responsible for the condition of the classroom: the environment should stimulate learning. Some things to be considered are:

1. Sanitary conditions.
2. Proper lighting.
3. Heat and ventilation.
4. Seating arrangements.
5. Equipment properly placed for maximum teaching efficiency.
6. General classroom atmosphere.

Use adequate lighting.

Provide proper ventilation

Teaching Aids

It is the responsibility of the teacher to make certain that all necessary teaching aids are available before starting the lesson. Teaching aids should be:

1. Placed where they are easily seen by all students.
2. Available for use without delay.
3. In proper working order.
4. Placed for maximum lighting and acoustical effectiveness.

Students

Students must be properly seated in order that they may see and hear without straining.

1. Get attention of class.
2. Develop interest in lesson.
3. Stimulate the desire for learning.
4. Student must be convinced of need to learn.

Students will not learn unless they are ready for learning. They must have the desire and the willingness to learn.

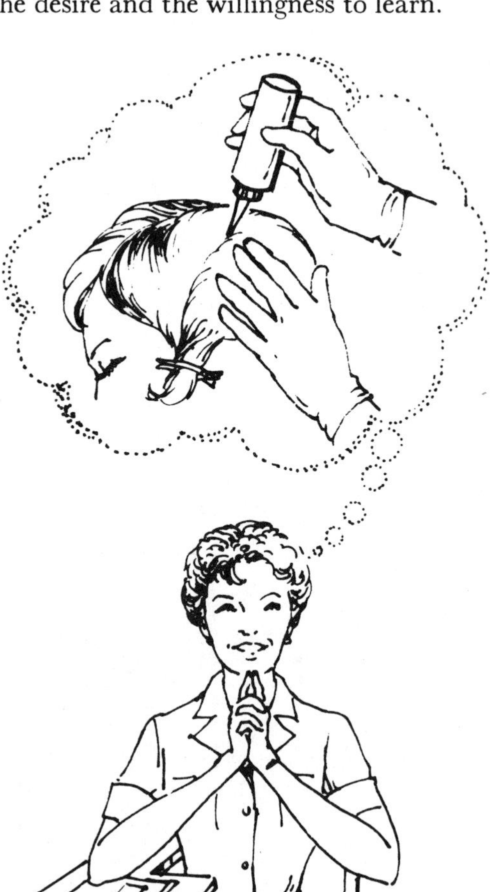

Get the students thinking about the lesson.

It is the teacher's responsibility to create this willingness and desire for learning.

1. Get students thinking about the lesson.
2. Tell them what to expect.
3. State objective of the lesson.
4. Develop in students a sense of security and confidence in their ability to master the subject.
5. Make certain that students understand reasons for learning the subject matter.
6. Give brief outline of class procedure to be followed.
7. Ask thought-provoking questions.

If student interest and desire for learning are aroused, the teacher may proceed with confidence to a presentation of the lesson.

SUMMARY

Preparation of students.

1. Put them at ease.
2. Tell them what is to be taught.
3. Arouse their interest.
4. Create enthusiasm.

STEP II: PRESENTATION

The objective of this step in the teaching process is to impart new knowledge or skills to the students. This step must be related to known ideas and experiences. It is the instructor's responsibility to arrange the teaching material in an effective and interesting manner, placing emphasis on the most essential areas.

The lesson plan is the teacher's blueprint of the program to be followed and the objectives to be accomplished. It is wise for the instructor to refer to the lesson plan to be certain that he is accurate and complete in his presentation.

The learning process is not instantaneous. Students must be treated with patience, understanding and consideration.

It is important that the instructor be able to see all students and observe their reactions during the presentation. It is equally important that the students be able to see and hear the teacher clearly and observe his actions and reactions. Both of these can be better accomplished if the teacher will remember to remain standing during the entire presentation.

A teacher should always talk directly to the class — not off into space or to a chalkboard. He should be careful to speak clearly and distinctly so that he will be easily heard and understood by the entire class.

The instructor demonstrates and explains

The instructor demonstrates and asks questions to check the students' understanding.

It is difficult to ascertain from the facial expressions of students whether or not they understand. A number of specific questions directed at individual students will help to test their understanding. Instructors must make certain that the class understands each point before going on.

Students should be required to take notes of the important points of a lesson as an aid in organizing knowledge, providing study material to be reviewed for tests or for future reference. However, note-taking would be a complete waste of time if the material could be duplicated for student use. **Workbooks** should be employed to assist students in organizing knowledge and providing review material.

Summary

Presentation of lesson.

1. Step-by-step presentation.
2. Explain how technique is to be performed.
3. Demonstrate performance of technique.
4. Stress key points.
5. Explain safety measures involved.
6. Present no more than can be absorbed or mastered in a single lesson.

STEP III: APPLICATION

This step in the learning process gives students the opportunity to put into use the information previously prepared and presented. It should reveal the student's grasp of the new material and his readiness to progress.

In this phase of the learning process students are asked to perform the skills taught and these are checked along two lines:

1. Do they know and understand the subject matter?
2. Are they able to perform properly?

It is the usual practice to teach a theory lesson before presenting the manual skills or techniques with which it is associated. The theory lays the foundation for certain ideas or abilities involved in the practice lesson which follows. Occasions may arise where the theory lesson may follow the practice lesson; this occurs when the application of certain skills and techniques uncover a need for specific information. This need provides the motivation for the theory lesson which follows.

The separation of manual skills and techniques from theoretical information in organizing and teaching cosmetology may seem to be a rather artificial arrangement, since the two must be woven and coordinated together when applied in the salon. We must consider, however, that when students are attempting to learn techniques they are attempting to acquire manipulative skills and habits. If we require them, at the same time, to carry through the thought processes connected with the learning of related information, the result may be to impair one or both types of learning. Educators have found that the learning of both types of material is made easier by teaching them separately and then weaving them together.

This does not mean that a few important points of information are never presented or discussed during a practice lesson. When there is a considerable amount of new material to be introduced however, it is important to organize and present it as a separate lesson. The instructor, at every opportunity, should show the relationships of what is being taught to the practical work in the salon. This will make the instruction more meaningful, create greater interest, and encourage students to apply the knowledge or information to the problems connected with the application of manual techniques.

The student displays her ability to perform the skills and explains the movements.

The instructor employs the application step both to give the student training in required skills and to find weak points in the student's knowledge or understanding of the lesson. At the conclusion of this step, the teacher should feel certain that the student has thoroughly mastered the lesson which was taught. The teacher must use care and judgment to determine just when to assist learners and just how to assist them. **In no case should instructors do the work for the student.** Of course, the teacher should be prepared to show them some particular step in the process which they did not understand. Each student should be required to go through the entire procedure a sufficient number of times to master all points.

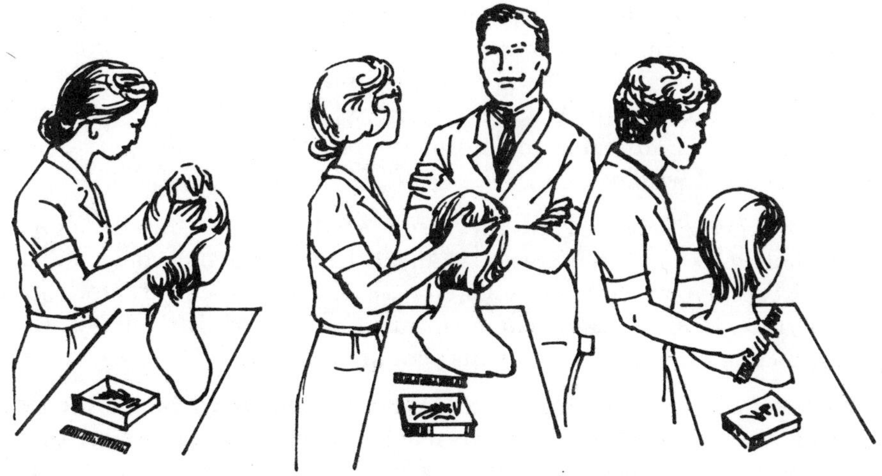

All students perform techniques under supervision

Have students practice, hold discussions, ask questions and get answers in applying the points presented. Help them to assimilate this knowledge by providing for demonstrations and student projects.

Summary

Application. Student performance under supervision.
1. Have students explain technique.
2. Students demonstrate performance.
3. Correct student errors. Explain.
4. Encourage students to find their own errors.
5. Compliment students on their good performance.

STEP IV: TESTING

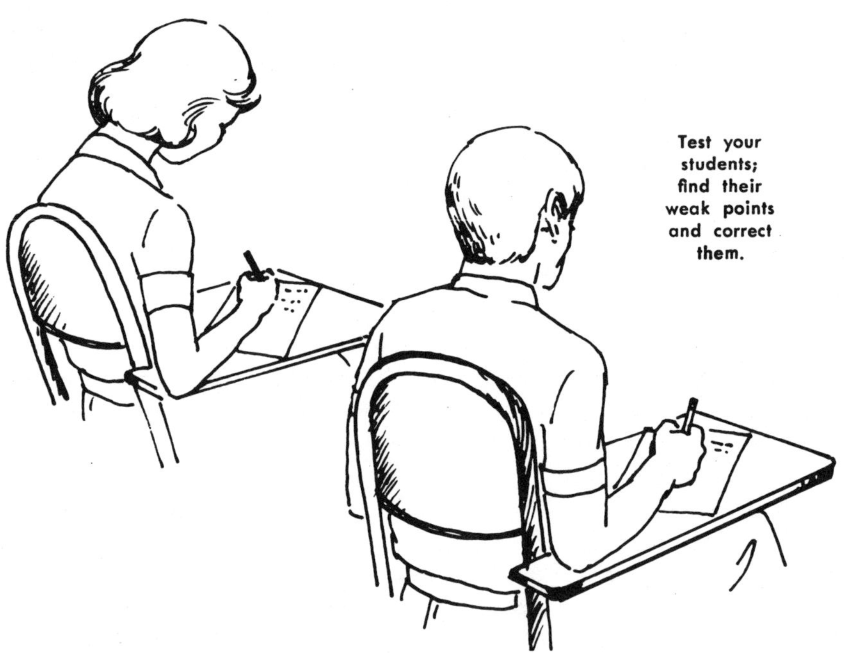

The testing step in the teaching process may be regarded as the final evaluation of the student's accomplishments. The instructor is concerned with determining the present skills of students and their readiness to move on to a new area of instruction. Whether such tests be oral, written or performance examinations, it is advisable to inform the students of their success or failure and their areas of weakness.

The teacher should regard the result of the test as unsatisfactory if the student fails to perform without assistance. If this occurs it would indicate that either the teaching process was not well carried out, or the instructor's judgment was incorrect. In either case, teaching must be repeated. If the lesson was properly planned and taught, all students should be successful on the examination.

Each step in the teaching process must be completed before the next step is started. In carrying out the three teaching steps, any failure on the part of the cosmetology teacher to carefully complete one step before the next step is undertaken, results in an accumulation of difficulties.

Without proper **preparation** there will be improper **presentation,** and as a result, the process of **application** will indicate areas of failure in the learning process. If the application has not been properly carried out, students will fail in the final step, the test. Instructors must therefore be positive that each step has been thoroughly and completely carried out before proceeding to the next one.

Summary

Testing students.

1. Question on performance of technique.
2. Check performance and speed.
3. Check quality of work and safety measures employed.
4. Correct mistakes—reteach points missed.
5. Be sure student can perform service without help.

CHECKLIST FOR FOUR STEPS OF STUDENT INSTRUCTION

1. **Preparation of Students.**
   a) Put them at ease.
   b) Tell them what is to be taught.
   c) Arouse their interest.
   d) Create enthusiasm

2. **Presentation of Lesson.**
   a) Step-by-step presentation.
   b) Explain how technique is to be performed.
   c) Demonstrate performance of technique.
   d) Stress key points.
   e) Explain safety measures involved.
   f) Present no more than can be absorbed or mastered in a single lesson.

3. **Application.** Student performance under supervision.
   a) Have students explain technique.
   b) Students demonstrate performance.
   c) Correct student errors. Explain.
   d) Encourage students to find their own errors.
   e) Compliment students on their good performance.

4. **Testing Students.**
   a) Question on performance of technique.
   b) Check performance and speed.
   c) Check quality of work and safety measures employed.
   d) Correct mistakes—reteach points missed.
   e) Be sure student can perform service without help.

REVIEW

1. **What is the broad concept of the beauty culture teacher's function?**
   To develop in each student the knowledge, interests, ideals, habits, and skills whereby he can function competently in the beauty salon and, in addition, continue to shape both himself and the practice of cosmetology into an ever-nobler professional status.

2. **What are the steps in the Four-Step Method of Instruction?**
   1. Preparation.   2. Presentation.   3. Application.   4. Testing.

3. **What is involved in the preparation step?**
   Preparation of the teacher, the classroom, the teaching aids and the student.

4. **What is the most important factor in teaching preparation?**
   Know your subject thoroughly and arrive early to prepare yourself, the room and teaching aids, before your students arrive.

5. **Why is it important to have all equipment, materials and supplies ready before the class begins?**
   To be sure that they are available and in working order so that a complete lesson may be conducted.

6. **What are the steps in the preparation of the students?**
   1. Put them at ease.   3. Arouse their interest.
   2. Tell them what is to be taught.   4. Create enthusiasm.

7. **Why is it important that the teacher stress safety precautions in his presentation?**
   For the proper protection of the patron and the cosmetologist.

8. **Indicate one way the teacher can check the effects of his presentation.**
   By observing the students' reactions closely.

9. **Why should safety measures be observed throughout student practical performances?**
   Students must be indoctrinated with the importance of practicing safety from their very start in the practice of cosmetology.

10. **Before the teacher moves to a new point in his presentation, what should be checked?**
    The instructor should be certain that the class understands each point before going on to the next one.

11. **In stressing application, what type of lesson is presented first?**
    The theory is taught first, followed by a demonstration of the manual skills or techniques with which it is associated.

12. **Why is it important to teach theory and manipulative skills separately?**
    Most students are unable to absorb manipulative skills and theory at the same time.

13. **What should oral, written or performance examinations reveal to the student?**
    They tell the student of his success or failure and the areas of weakness. Also, the instructor must analyze his teaching methods to be sure they convey the proper information.

CHAPTER 9

BASIC
TEACHING METHODS

INTRODUCTION

Learning is never a passive process of absorbing knowledge without expending any effort. Quite the contrary, learning takes place only during activity. It is a very active process of acting and reacting to some definite stimulus. **Student involvement in this teaching-learning action is the key to all cosmetology learning.**

When students are ready to have new knowledge or techniques introduced, the teacher must be ready to present them in a manner which will be interesting and effective.

A method is nothing more than a form of procedure. It is the manner in which the teacher uses the material at his disposal to produce or achieve a desired educational objective.

Learning, in cosmetology, is a never-ending process. There is always a better way , a newer or more effective method or a better and more productive technique. As a result, change, innovation and creativity are essential ingredients if cosmetology educational progress is to take place. If teaching or teaching methods become static, cosmetology learning hits a plateau and begins to go down hill. To make the learning process real and productive both the subject matter and the teaching method employed must be relevant and effective.

TEACHING METHODS

The method employed by the teacher may be judged either good or bad, depending on whether or not the instructional activity produces the desired results. If there is a poor method, there will be poor results; if there is a good method, there will be good results. Excellence of method exhibits itself in the selection of material and that form of presentation calculated to yield, in the most efficient manner, the highest quality of learning.

While stressing the importance of methods we must at the same time warn teachers that formal procedures in instruction, like procedures in any other field, may easily become a fetish; they may corrupt good teaching; they may confine activity rather than give it freedom. These are the abuses, not the uses of method.

> **Methods must be flexible; they must serve as general guides; they must not be worshiped as idols; they must be used as instruments.**

Following the selection and arrangement of the subject matter, the next step is the determination of the best method to be employed. Some methods are more effective than others, depending upon the type of lesson to be taught. A combination of methods is usually more desirable than the use of any particular one. It is advisable to vary the methods of presentation in order to involve the greatest possible use of the students' senses. For example:

1. Demonstrations and visual aids utilize the senses of sight and hearing.
2. Lectures, discussions and question-answer methods involve hearing.
3. The performance of manipulative techniques utilizes the sense of touch.
4. Methods involving the sense of smell can also be devised for successful cosmetology instruction. Products may be identified by smell.
5. The sense of taste is seldom used in cosmetology teaching.

Many effective methods may be successfully employed in the school of beauty culture. In many cosmetology areas a combination of methods is essential for effective instruction. The teaching method or methods that best fit the particular instructional situation must be the method or methods employed. Some of the factors which influence the choice of method are: type of subject matter, objective of lesson, size of class, need for individual instruction and physical conditions present.

There are a number of methods of instruction in general use in cosmetology schools, such as:

1. Lecture.
2. Workbook.
3. Instruction sheet.
4. Demonstration.
5. Discussion.
6. Conference.
7. Project.
8. Question and answer.
9. Field Trips.

LECTURE METHOD

The lecture method is essentially a detailed explanation of some major idea or concept. This method, while primarily a system of explaining something, makes extensive use of narration and description. It offers the opportunity to convey useful information and essential facts at a minimum expenditure of time. It is the most commonly used method and is usually at its best when employed in combination with some other method of instruction.

The most significant advantages of the lecture method are:

1. It is used to introduce a new topic.
2. It is employed to arouse interest.
3. It economizes on time.
4. It provides the opportunity to supplement textbook information.
5. It offers the opportunity to impart information.
6. It is used to supplement other methods.
7. It is useful to summarize essentials.
8. It is important in teaching allied or related sciences, such as anatomy and chemistry.

Planning is the first essential of a well-developed lecture. To make the lesson effective, objectives have to be clearly understood, the main points clearly defined and the supporting materials well organized.

The teacher can only communicate with students on their own language level. Therefore, the vocabulary used by the teacher could make the difference between success and failure.

Redundancy and repetition are often used in this type of presentation to clarify and reinforce major ideas, key words, principles and important concepts. This is a very powerful technique which can be employed to good advantage in focusing and highlighting important points.

To be most effective students should be encouraged to participate. If students do not understand points they should be encouraged to ask questions.

WORKBOOKS AS ADJUNCTS TO INSTRUCTIONAL MATERIAL

Theory and practical workbooks should be employed as very important adjuncts to many instructional methods.

These workbooks combine all the advantages of note books, review books and classroom study material. They also offer a ready source of important data for homework and classroom assignments.

Theory workbook

Practical workbook

The workbook, if properly employed, offers a very effective instrument for obtaining complete student participation in the classroom presentation.

Instructors will find workbooks to be very essential teaching aids for more successful and satisfying learning results.

Some of the advantages of workbooks are:

1. Offer detailed coverage of each subject.
2. Encourage student participation.
3. Help motivate learning.
4. Promote uniform learning habits.
5. Help in the development of student study habits.
6. Serve as complete review books.
7. Serve as classroom note books.
8. Supply supplemental material.
9. Offer opportunity for fast students to move ahead at their own pace.
10. Assist with individual instruction for slower learners.
11. Provide a continuity of learning material.
12. Help maintain student interest.
13. Help both students and instructor to place emphasis on the most important points of each lesson.

14. Help organize the subject matter into easily manageable units.
15. Assist teachers to remedy learning difficulties as they arise.
16. Help absent students to keep up with class.

INSTRUCTiON SHEETS

Instruction sheets are used primarily as a supplement to some other method of instruction. When properly used they are a very effective method of presenting information.

Instruction sheets should never be used as a substitute for personal instruction, but must be used in conjunction therewith. If improperly used they could lead to a waste of material, incorrect interpretations, improper use of tools or equipment and possible danger of accidents.

In cosmetology training well-prepared instruction sheets can be especially useful as guides during the students' application of a particular technique. The instruction sheet should present a clear step-by-step outline of the procedure to be followed in order to obtain proper results.

The advantages of the use of instruction sheets as a method of teaching are:
1. Assure complete coverage of subject matter.
2. Assure more uniform instruction.
3. Provide practice in following written instructions.
4. Allow students to progress at their own rate.
5. Assist in the handling of large groups efficiently.
6. Help students to develop habits of self-reliance.
7. Permit students to make individual reviews of material.
8. Used to affirm a principle.
9. Provide a continuity of learning.
10. Maintain a variety of activities.

DEMONSTRATION METHOD

The demonstration method is employed to assist the student, in an economical and effective manner, to understand and master some new procedure. Demonstration has the great merit of being effective, of permitting the teacher to exhibit a technique and to call attention (while the process or technique is unfolding before the student) to its important aspects.

This method of instruction should be followed immediately by student practice, with the students performing the same or a similar activity.

If a demonstration is to be interesting and educationally effective it must be performed smoothly and like a well-oiled machine. To accomplish this the teacher must prepare everything required before the demonstration is to begin. It is advisable that the teacher run through the operation beforehand, in order to be certain that it will be performed perfectly and accomplish its objective.

The demonstration must always be performed with exactly the same materials as the students will use. The teacher should make certain that students will have available the same materials for the same performance.

Students should not be made to feel that they cannot perform adequately because they were given different materials to work with than those used in the demonstration.

Demonstrations should be short, frequent and well planned. They should always be accompanied by a brief explanation of what the students are to observe and special techniques to look for.

> **Before starting the demonstration the teacher should check carefully to be certain that the necessary implements, equipment, materials and teaching aids are available and close at hand.**

The technique being demonstrated must be performed carefully and each step clearly explained. The techniques employed will depend upon the subject matter and the previous experience of the students. The professional cosmetology teacher goes through the demonstration step by step, taking as much time as is required. The work may be stopped at various spots to point out important details or to be certain that nothing escapes the attention of the students. In teaching cosmetology techniques it is **essential to point out health and safety factors** and to explain why they are important. At all times the instructor must emphasize how to perform the technique safely and efficiently.

The demonstration should be followed by a discussion, a summary of key points, and perhaps a question and answer period covering the same material.

During and following the demonstration, oral questions can be used to excellent advantage. These questions may serve several purposes. By bringing in the element of repetition, they tend to fix in the minds of the students the techniques demonstrated. They assist students to discover how well they have understood the demonstration, particularly the reasons for performing the work in the manner followed by the teacher. If the questioning is well done, the student may readily identify those areas which he does not understand. Doubtful areas of knowledge may also be clarified by answers given by other students. They may ask questions of the instructor which help to clarify the subject matter.

Oral questioning helps to stimulate thinking and tends to keep students alert. The teacher may use a few carefully selected questions, as the demonstration proceeds, to roughly check the manner in which his performance and explanations are being received and understood by the entire class and by individual students.

The demonstration method is most helpful to:

1. Illustrate a manipulative procedure.
2. Clarify a principle.
3. Illustrate use of equipment or implements.
4. Demonstrate correct procedure.

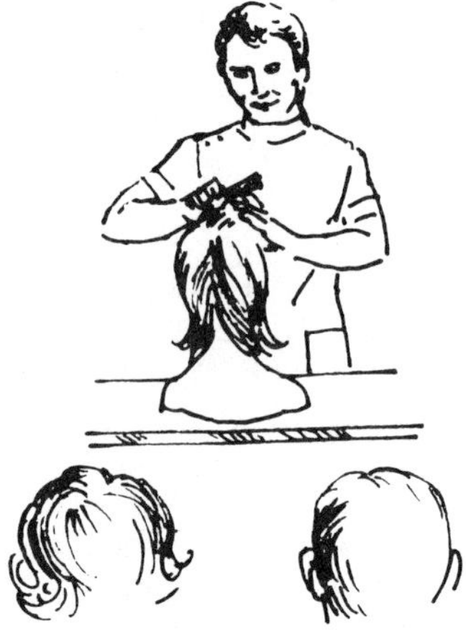

Demonstration

The demonstration may easily fail to accomplish its objectives unless certain precautions are observed.

1. Review the lesson objectives to be certain that the demonstration will meet them.
2. Do not carry the demonstration beyond the limits of the present lesson.
3. Prepare and follow a lesson plan.
4. Be certain that every student can see and hear clearly.
5. Avoid distractions.
6. Explain new terms to students.
7. Perform the demonstration slowly and deliberately, making sure that students do not miss key points.
8. Associate new techniques with familiar material.
9. Use clear and simple language.
10. Be absolutely certain that all material, supplies and equipment required are at hand and in good working order.

DISCUSSION METHOD

The discussion method presents opportunities to avoid many of the weaknesses of the lecture method of teaching. In a lesson conducted by a competent teacher the student shares in, and in fact becomes, the active center of the entire procedure. The student cannot assume a passive attitude; he is responsible for more than absorbing in sponge-like fashion; he is called upon to exercise his ability to think and to reason clearly by helping in the solution of the problems being discussed.

The teacher and the student are in close contact: the stimulation of the group alerts the mind of each student present. Every opportunity is given to observe the extent to which the problem is being understood and the solution developed. The student is encouraged to ask for further explanations at the points of special difficulty, and consequently the rate of instruction is synchronized with the speed of learning.

This method permits student interest to be maintained by the give and take of discussion and by the eventual understanding of the participants. The student is in a position to challenge the interpretations of the instructor and is able to free himself from arbitrary presentation and decisions.

The danger exists in this method of instruction that if the teacher is not skilled and well trained, discussions may be diverted into irrelevant and unimportant channels. The teacher must therefore be alert to prevent the intrusion of idle and tedious comments which contribute nothing to the subject matter under discussion.

For best results, the discussion method should be used together with other methods of instruction. It should be concluded with a summary of the important points covered and the conclusions reached.

The discussion method is of special value to:

1. Warm up or review.

2. Promote understanding.

3. Stimulate student participation.

4. Encourage student desire for learning.

Suggestions for Using the Discussion Method

> The discussion method is one which requires careful preparation before it is introduced. It also requires proper control by the teacher when it is being used.

If this method is to be successfully employed the following suggestions should be followed:

1. Prepare in advance a number of written questions, to be asked to encourage discussion. These questions should be asked at intervals to guide and stimulate the discussion.

2. Make it clear to your students that **everyone** is expected to take part in the discussion.

3. Diplomatically discourage comments or questions which lead the discussion off at tangents.

4. Maintain discipline and have pupils answer questions or make comments in an orderly fashion, and signal for recognition when they wish to speak.

5. Try to have every student participate in the discussion. The teacher should make a special effort to call upon students who are less inclined to participate.

6. It is quite helpful to list key points on the chalkboard as they are developed in the course of the discussion. This policy will assist the class to follow the progress of the discussion and to relate different ideas.

7. Prevent the discussion from turning into a debate or argument. Do not permit time-consuming cross discussion between students.

8. The discussion should not be allowed to continue for too long a period of time. Make certain that the discussion progresses properly, that all elements of the subject are covered and that the discussion period ends with definite information developed by the students.

9. Be certain to summarize, briefly, at the end of the discussion. The ideas developed should be listed on the chalkboard and final comments made on each.

CONFERENCE METHOD

The conference method of instruction is very similar to the discussion method in its application.

This method is favored by many educators because it serves to develop ideas and expressions from members of the class. Here again, every student is a contributor to the discussion and should be working to the limit of his capacity.

The skilled instructor directs the attention and interest of the group into the desired channels, using the "How, When and Why" approach.

This method offers great opportunities for student self-expression and should be a part of every educational plan. It is best used when students have some knowledge of the subject which is to be further developed.

The Conference Method

The conference method can best be used to:

1. Encourage group thinking.
2. Expand on previous learning.
3. Get new opinions and ideas.
4. Modify or correct erroneous thinking.
5. Develop understanding.
6. Insure participation by all students.

PROJECT METHOD

The project method is employed to afford students the opportunity to demonstrate an effective manual performance or show adequate understanding of some previously taught technique.

The planning and execution of a good training project is excellent experience in the development of cosmetology students. However, great care must be exercised to be certain that the task is sufficiently interesting and challenging to stimulate and maintain student interest. The danger exists that it might become strictly routine and dull, in which case its value as a teaching device is greatly diminished.

If the project method is to be employed for maximum learning benefits, the teacher must be sure that the student gains confidence in his own power by carrying out a plan to a successful conclusion.

The project method is used to impart knowledge, skills, attitudes and technical appreciation. Its basic value is in training the students to organize instructional material for the attainment of planned results.

The project method can be used to:

1. Furnish an opportunity to develop and practice skills.
2. Provide fundamental principles of instruction.
3. Practice development of principles from the simple to the complex.
4. Arouse and maintain students' interest.
5. Practice the realization of objectives.
6. Encourage creative thinking by students.

QUESTION AND ANSWER METHOD

The question and answer method is frequently used in all cosmetology schools. The instructor's ability to use this method effectively is one of the prerequisites of good teaching.

Questions are, or should be, part of all methods of presentation in order to force student participation.

The question and answer technique can be used to great advantage to:

1. Discover interests, knowledge and abilities of students.

2. Arouse interest and direct the attention of students.

3. Stimulate discussion.

4. Assist in analyzing students' problems and planning their work.

5. Test the students' knowledge and evaluate the effectiveness of teaching.

6. Review and summarize areas of knowledge.

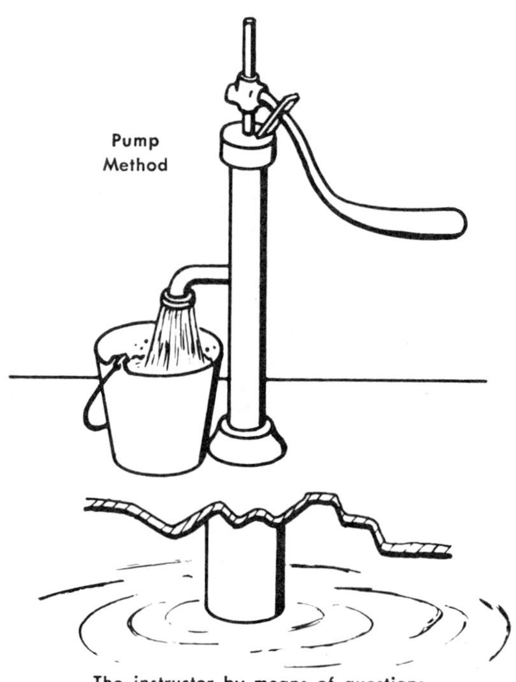

The instructor by means of questions, can pump out information.

The procedure to be followed in asking questions:

1. State the question to the entire group, requiring all students to think of the answer.
2. Pause for a moment to permit students to formulate answers.
3. Call on a student, by name, to answer the question.
4. Evaluate the answer and perhaps expound and comment on it.

Good cosmetology teachers should be exceedingly careful in their manner of questioning.

Basic rules for asking questions:
1. Speak clearly and distinctly.
2. Permit only one student to answer at a time.
3. Call on students in all parts of the room.
4. Avoid calling on certain bright students only.
5. Avoid a two-way discussion on a question, with one student.
6. Call on inattentive or unruly students.
7. Avoid asking questions and calling on students in any sort of rotation or in alphabetical order.

Good questions, which accomplish their purpose, are not easy to create. Even after they have been properly formed their value and effectiveness may be destroyed if they are not properly used.

The value of the question as an aid to successful teaching cannot be over-estimated. It not only helps students to think constructively, but also helps the teacher to discover the effectiveness of his instruction.

It is important to keep the following points in mind when the question and answer method is employed:
1. Think out your questions carefully and state them clearly.
2. Make your questions short and to the point.
3. Avoid all ambiguities.
4. Require that answers be expressed in complete, clear sentences.
5. Do not ask questions which can be answered "yes" or "no."
6. Do not repeat answers given by students; do not amplify their answers.
7. Do not permit group or chorus answers.
8. Do not use a fixed order for calling on students; make certain that every student is given an opportunity to answer.
9. Do not embarrass a student by commenting unfavorably on his inability to answer a question. (Keep in mind that questions are being asked to instruct, not to cross examine.)
10. Take into consideration the individual abilities of your students, Select, very carefully, the student to answer your question.
11. Ask the question. Give students time to formulate their answers, then call on those you wish to answer.
12. Ask questions in logical sequence which lead students to find conclusions, thus developing learning.
13. Do not reveal answers by facial expressions, tone of voice or mannerisms.
14. Avoid using the same questions in two or three different ways; this destroys interest.

The teacher must know the purpose of each question being asked and frame it properly to achieve the desired purpose. Questions may be of any of the following types:
1. **Memory or Recall Questions.** Such questions require the student to recall an idea or a fact. The recall question is used for the purpose of review, repetition or emphasis. Example: What determines the choice of rods in cold waving?

2. **Questions to Test Understanding.** After a demonstration is concluded, it is important that students understand why the skill was performed in the particular manner demonstrated and why certain key points of the operation are important. For this purpose the teacher uses questions which will reveal how well each student understands these points. Example: Which type of hair treatment is given prior to a pastel color or toner application?

3. **Thought Questions** require the student to apply his knowledge and arrive at some decision as to the best procedures or methods. These are the judgment-forming kind of questions. Example: What procedure should be followed when preparing the hair for a pastel color toner application?

FIELD TRIPS

A very important method of instruction, widely used in schools of beauty culture is the field trip. These excursions are organized and conducted by the school as part of the training program. Field trips vary widely in purpose from observation and demonstration meetings to practice and performance trips in hospitals, old age homes and retirement homes.

While field trips may possibly be questionable as an actual method of instruction, they can be used to very good advantage in the overall teaching-learning program.

Field trips are important, in cosmetology education, for a number of reasons:

1. They strengthen vital images. Important impressions and techniques involved in the teaching process become stronger.
2. They give wider experience than is available in the clinic or classroom.
3. They add variety to student activities. They help to add interest and eliminate the monotony of the classroom.
4. They reinforce learning. Techniques learned in school are reinforced by observing their actual performance in a professional environment.
5. They help to build interest in various important areas of cosmetology practice.
6. They help to develop a more intensive understanding of the entire practice of cosmetology.
7. They assist the slower students in learning.
8. They are an aid to other methods of instruction.
9. They help to show the relationships of different areas of cosmetology training.
10. They serve to broaden the understanding of cosmetology as a complete profession.

Types of Trips

Among the various kinds of field trips the following are typical:

1. **Visits to beauty salons.** These are valuable in order to observe the actual practice of cosmetology techniques and skills by licensed professionals. They are also important to absorb the atmosphere of an actual salon in operation.
2. **Trips to trade shows or seminars.** These are important in order to learn the latest techniques and newest business methods employed by practicing cosmetologists.

3. **Visits to Cosmetic Manufacturers.** These are important in order to observe the actual preparation of beauty salon products and their methods of application.

4. **Trips to Color Training Centers.** These are important in order to learn the latest methods and techniques in hair tinting.

5. **Trips to Permanent Wave Manufacturers.** These are important in order to observe and to learn the newest techniques in permanent waving.

6. **Trips to hospitals, old age homes or retirement homes.** Students receive invaluable experience in performing free services for the patients and residents of these establishments. At the same time they hlp to raise the spirits and morale of the individuals receiving these services. Trips to these institutions are also very valuable for raising the professional image of the school. Of equal importance is the fact that the performance of services on the elderly, disabled or ill individuals is a tremendous morale booster for the students themselves.

REVIEW

1. **What is the definition of "Teaching Method?"**
   It is the manner in which teachers use the material at their disposal to produce or achieve a desired educational objective.

2. **How do you evaluate a good teaching method?**
   To the extent it produces the desired results.

3. **Name a factor which influences the choice of teaching method.**
   The choice depends on the type of lesson to be taught.

4. **Name four elements which affect the type of lesson.**
   1. Objective of the lesson.
   2. Size of class.
   3. Need for individual instruction.
   4. Physical conditions present.

5. **Name nine methods of instruction in general use in cosmetology schools.**
   1. Lecture.
   2. Workbook.
   3. Instruction sheet.
   4. Demonstration.
   5. Discussion.
   6. Conference.
   7. Project.
   8. Question and answer.
   9. Field trips.

6. **What is an imprtant advantage of the lecture method?**
   It offers the opportunity to convey useful information and essential facts with a minimum expenditure of time.

7. **Why are workbooks one of the most useful methods of instruction?**
   Workbooks combine all the advantages of note books, review books and study material, as well as providing a ready reference source.

8. **In what way will workbooks help (a) slow learners? (b) fast learners?**
   a) Slow learners can keep up with the class by studying at their own pace.
   b) It offers the fast student the opportunity to move ahead at his own pace.

9. **How will workbooks help the absent students?**
   It will give the absent students the opportunity to catch up with the class.

10. **How are instruction sheets used?**
    Primarily, instruction sheets are used as a supplement to other methods of instruction.

11. **How is the demonstration method used?**

The demonstration method is used to exhibit a new procedure and to call attention to its important aspects as the process is unfolding before the student.

12. **What is the advantage of the discussion method of teaching?**

In the discussion method of teaching, the student cannot maintain a passive attitude and must become involved in the problem under discussion.

13. **How does the conference method of teaching differ from the discussion method?**

They are very similar, but the conference method is best used when the students have some knowledge of the subject which should be further developed.

14. **What care must be taken when utilizing the project method in teaching?**

The training project must be sufficiently interesting and challenging in order to maintain student interest.

15. **What two important educational benefits are derived from the question and answer method?**

The question and answer technique is an excellent one for reviewing and summarizing knowledge.

16. **Name three types of questions utilized in the Question and Answer Method.**
    1. Memory or recall questions.
    2. Questions to test understanding.
    3. Thought questions.

17. **List 10 important reasons for field trips.**
    1. They strengthen vital images.
    2. They give wider experience.
    3. They add variety to student activities.
    4. They reinforce learning.
    5. They help to build interest.
    6. They assist slower students.
    7. They are aids to other methods.
    8. They help to show relationships of different areas of cosmetology training.
    9. They help develop a more intensive understanding.
    10. They broaden the understanding of cosmetology as a complete profession.

18. **List the six most typical kinds of field trips taken by beauty culture students.**
    1. Visits to beauty salons.
    2. Trips to trade shows and seminars.
    3. Visits to cosmetic manufacturers.
    4. Trips to color training centers.
    5. Trips to permanent wave manufacturers.
    6. Trips to hospitals, old-age homes and retirement homes.

CHAPTER 10

TEACHING
AIDS

THE IMPORTANCE OF TEACHING AIDS

Creative and innovative methods of teaching must be introduced if a cosmetology educational program is to be successful. This is one of the important reasons for using audio-visual aids whenever possible. These aids give the cosmetology teacher the opportunity to vary the instructional techniques employed. It is this variety of approach which permits the teacher to keep interest high among cosmetology students, who otherwise might become bored and restless by traditional teaching methods.

Most educators agree that the use of audio-visual techniques provide an interesting change of pace and help to clarify important information. Further, when students see an educational presentation, as well as hear it, they learn faster and remember longer.

The cosmetology instructor has at his disposal a large variety of excellent teaching aids to help in the development and presentation of the subject matter. As stated earlier, all people learn through their senses. Most teaching aids appeal directly to these senses and make a sharp impact on learning. Among the most commonly used teaching aids are: films, filmstrips, transparencies, flip charts, pictures, chalkboards, pegboards, models and cutaway models, books, workbooks, slides and tests. Actual field trips can also be classified as teaching aids.

The selection of the teaching aid for any particular subject requires careful thought and consideration. Teachers must be certain that the device they are to employ is the most effective learning accessory available for the particular subject. They must be certain that it is clear, understandable by students and illustrates the desired subject matter. Teaching aids must be selected in advance, checked to be sure that they are in good working order, and be available when required.

CLASSIFICATION OF TEACHING AIDS

1. Projection Aids (Enlarged on screen):
   a) Slides
   b) Filmstrips
   c) Films (Motion Pictures)
   d) Transparencies (Overhead projection)

2. Display Aids:
   a) Chalkboard
   b) Charts, Pictures, Posters
   c) Flip Charts
   d) Pegboards

3. Duplicated and Printed Aids:
   a) Mimeograph Sheets
   b) Project Sheets
   c) Program Sheets
   d) Instruction Sheets
   e) Textbooks
   f) Workbooks

4. Three-Dimensional Aids:
   a) Mannequins
   b) Mock-ups
   c) Models
   d) Cutaway Forms

CHARACTERISTICS OF GOOD VISUAL AIDS

A visual aid is a film, filmstrip, set of slides, transparencies, model or device which will assist learning through the sense of sight. When selecting or preparing a visual aid the following points must be considered:

1. It should explain an idea, show a relationship or present a procedure in the best possible manner.

2. It must be clearly visible to all members of the class. An aid is of no teaching value if it cannot be seen.

3. Printed matter must be large enough and clear enough to avoid eye-strain from any point in the room.

4. The meaning of the words must clear and understandable to all students. Terms employed must be acceptable and in common usage throughout the industry.

5. Bright colors should be used whenever possible to aid effectiveness.

6. Models should be made to scale. To avoid confusion all parts should be in proper proportion.

7. The aid should be constructed of good materials.

8. A proper visual aid should be constructed with good workmanship.

9. It should be portable to permit re-use in other locations.

10. It should be covered with a good protective material to prolong its life.

SELECTION AND USE OF GOOD VISUAL AIDS

It is unfortunate that sometimes important audio-visual demonstrations fail to develop the expected learning. If learning does not take place, the probability exists that the teacher failed to carefully prepare for the visual presentation. Audio-visual presentations are ineffective if the teacher fails to:

1. Preview visual aids.
   a) Be sure it does what teacher intends.
   b) Avoid misleading titles.
2. Properly prepare students.
   a) Tell them what to watch for.
   b) Tell them what to expect to learn.
   c) Give proper explanations.
3. Follow up the presentation.
   a) Explain difficult or misunderstood points.
   b) Have students ask questions.
   c) Encourage group discussion.
   d) Check on what has been learned.
4. Explain vocabulary.
   a) Define and explain new words.

FILMS, FILMSTRIPS, SLIDES AND TRANSPARENCIES

Most learning takes place through the sense of sight. Films, filmstrips, slides and transparencies make a direct appeal to this sense.

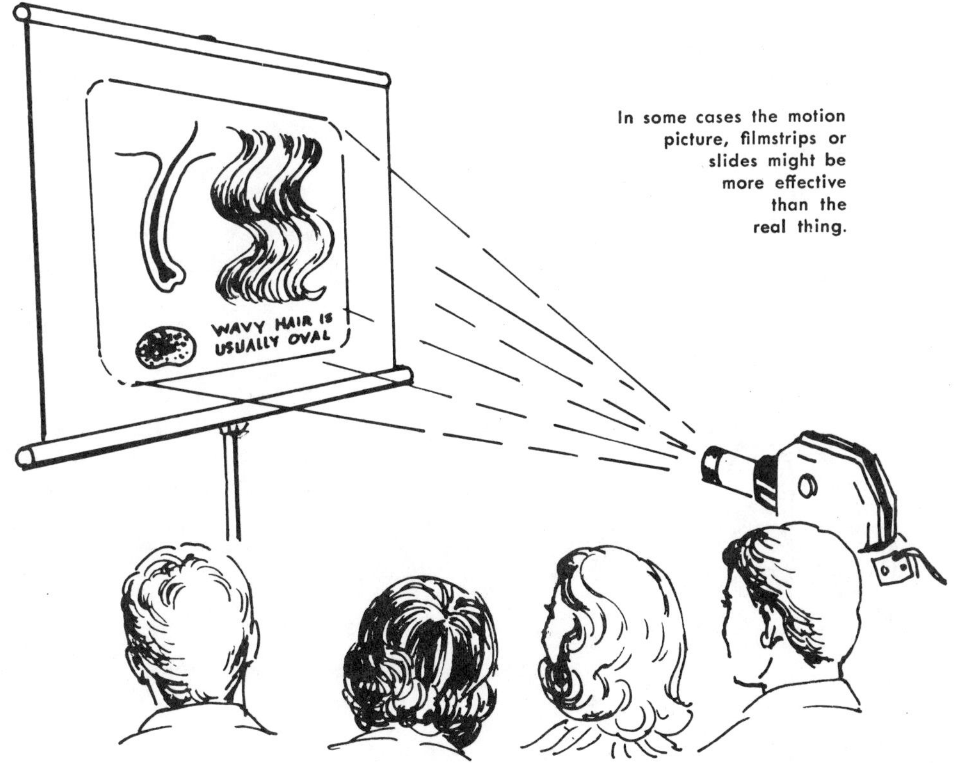

In some cases the motion picture, filmstrips or slides might be more effective than the real thing.

Since most students learn more easily and quickly through the sense of sight, films, filmstrips, slides and transparencies would seem to be ideal teaching aids. Through these devices students are presented with ready-made "mental images." They are saved the problem of trying to build these images from word pictures created by the teacher. The picture is presented faster and is more clearly understood than the spoken word.

A picture is second best to the real thing. **In some cases the films, filmstrips, slides or transparencies might be more effective teaching aids than the "real thing" itself.**

However, before selecting films as teaching aids, keep in mind the following:
1. Use films as an aid, not a substitute for the teacher.
2. Do not use a film if a more effective aid is available.
3. Instructional films are **not to be used** as entertainment features.
4. Schedule films at proper time.

Selection and Use of Films

To be most effective, select the film which best fits the subject matter to be taught:
1. Preview the film before showing it in class.
   a) Does it meet the objectives of the lesson?
   b) Make notes on areas to be clarified verbally.
2. Prepare the room. Place seats and projector so that all students can see and hear clearly.
3. Introduce the film.
   a) Advise class of what to expect.
   b) Advise of special areas to look for.
4. Show film.
   a) Do not leave the room.
   b) Show a definite interest in the film.
5. Discussion of film—stress key points.
6. Rescreen film within a short period.
   a) Most films contain too much information to grasp in a single viewing.
7. Test. If desired, the teacher should examine students on what they have learned from the film.

FILMSTRIPS

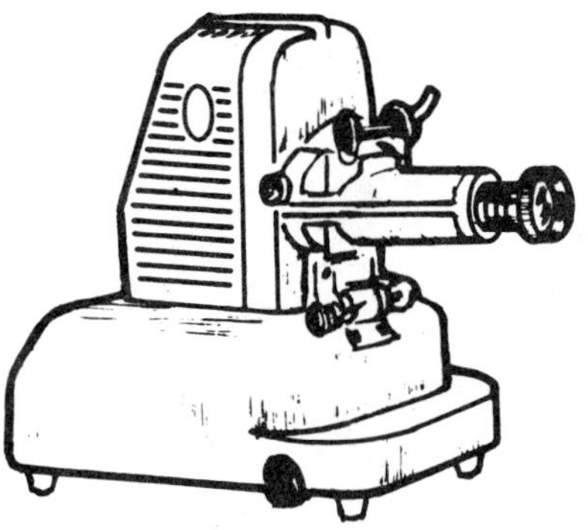

Filmstrip projector

The filmstrip is only one of many visual aids. However, this instructional aid has proven to be tremendously effective in cosmetology education, while they have remained relatively inexpensive.

The filmstrips are carefully selected and used when they will help to present subject matter in the most effective manner.

Filmstrips are employed where they will help to shorten the teacher's presentation and/or will increase its effectiveness.

Filmstrips are employed when they will adequately illustrate or demonstrate the various steps in a cosmetology service.

Filmstrips can very effectively present the step by step performance of various cosmetology techniques.

Advantages of Filmstrips

1. Relatively inexpensive as compared to other visual aids.

2. Can be prepared to parallel the units of the textbook.

3. Step by step procedures can be slowly and effectively shown while they are explained by the teacher.

4. An individual frame (picture) can be kept on the screen while it is being discussed and until it is understood by the students.

5. The teacher's comments can be tailored to meet the need of the class.

6. The entire mechanism is fairly simple to operate.

7. The teacher may be very selective in emphasizing those frames deemed most essential.

8. The teacher may prepare questions to ask the class with reference to individual frames and thus help to maintain student alertness and involvement.

9. As the various frames are projected the teacher may point out those areas deemed most essential.

Reminders and Precautions

In order to obtain the maximum teaching benefits from the filmstrips certain precautions must be taken:

1. The teacher should review the filmstrip before presentation to the class to check for accuracy.

2. Teacher questions and remarks must be directed to the students and not to the screen.

3. Captions and printed material should be read very slowly for student comprehension.

4. A filmstrip with errors or one that is technically outmoded or inaccurate should never be shown.

5. The material presented by the filmstrip should be summarized and discussed as part of the presentation.

SLIDES

An outstanding development in modern education is the increasing use of slides as an important aid to instruction.

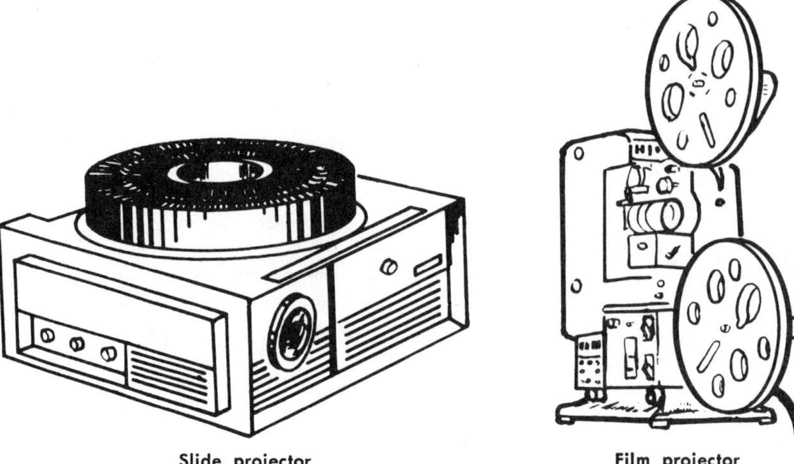

Slides are among the best of the audio-visual teaching aids. They offer one of the most effective means of aiding students to absorb and retain the subject matter being taught. Slides are among the most potent student motivators and attention-holders in the learning spectrum. They help to create a desire for learning on the part of the student, which aids tremendously in making teaching more effective. They serve to add interest and vitality to any training situation and as a result help students to learn faster, remember longer, gain more accurate information, and receive and understand concepts and meanings more clearly.

Plan carefully when using slides, in order to receive maximum teaching benefits:

1. Determine exact point in teaching program where you believe the slides will prove to be most beneficial.

2. Arrange slides in proper order.

3. Set up projector and screen.

4. Check students' seating so that all have unobstructed vision.

5. Check lighting of room

6. Make sure projector is in proper working condition.

7. Introduce slides with brief description and objective of viewing.

8. Present slides with complete and accurate commentary.

9. Stop at important slides, to point out pertinent information.

10. Sometimes a single slide may warrant an entire teaching session.

11. Complete discussion after viewing.

12. Students must have opportunity to practice information if it lends itself to physical practice.

13. Review.

Transparencies are used for the same teaching reasons as are slides. They are also used in almost the same manner as slides.

Transparencies are drawings or photographs on transparent material through which light is passed for projection on a screen. If the teacher will use good common sense and imagination transparencies can be used to give great flexibility in the presentation of the visual aids. By using color, new interest and attractiveness are added. Multiple overlays (additional transparencies placed over another transparency) may be used to add additional information to the basic drawing. Masks may also be used and removed at appropriate times to reveal additional content and information.

Transparencies are convenient to use and are usually cheaper and easier to produce than other training aids. They add great flexibility to the entire teaching program because they can be made easily and inexpensively, to keep up with changing conditions.

DISPLAY AIDS

Characteristics of good cosmetology display aids:

1. The purpose for which the material is to be used is clearly identified.
2. The subject matter materials are acceptable for the class interest level.
3. The materials offer a challenge to learning progress.
4. The language is professional in tone.
5. The sentences are written in acceptable, familiar language.
6. The materials encourage reasoning and contain evaluating devices to help determine learning progress.
7. The directions are simple and clear and can be followed with little difficulty.
8. The material is designed to encourage maximum progress, according to the individual student's ability.
9. The materials depict realistic cosmetology situations.
10. The material is presented in such form that each lesson teaches a single concept or thoroughly covers a small number of concepts.
11. The skills and concepts to be taught are presented in sequential, logical order.

CHALKBOARD

When using a blackboard (chalkboard), flip charts, wall charts or other visual aid, the teacher should always face the class. At no time does he turn his back to the class.

If it becomes necessary to take a few steps either toward or away from the visual aid, the teacher does it in a manner permitting a view of the class at all times. In this way, the teacher never loses contact with the class.

The chalkboard is a most flexible and practical teaching aid. Its use is limited only by the teacher's imagination and drawing ability. Some of its uses are to illustrate, diagram, emphasize key points and to develop a solution to a problem during conference procedure.

When using the chalkboard:

1. Write or print clearly
2. Use a pointer.
3. Stand to one side.
4. Face and talk to the class.

The following suggestions for the use of the chalkboard could definitely increase its effectiveness as a visual aid:

1. Don't crowd the chalkboard. A few important points could be most effective.

2. The subject matter should be fairly simple. Short concise statements are most productive.

3. Plan the use of the chalkboard in advance.

4. Gather in advance all supplies to be used with the chalkboard: chalk, ruler, eraser, etc.

5. Check lighting; avoid chalkboard glare.

6. Use color whenever possible.

7. Print all captions and drawings on a large scale. The material must be clearly visible to each student.

8. Erase all unrelated material—avoid material that distracts.

9. Keep chalkboard clean.

10. Prepare complicated chalkboard set-up before the class meets.

11. Keep chalkboard covered until ready to reveal the material.

CHARTS, PICTURES AND POSTERS

Charts and pictures are adaptable to almost any classroom teaching situation. They present graphic illustrations of subject matter already taught or to be presented to the class. **Care should be exercised in their use, as follows:**

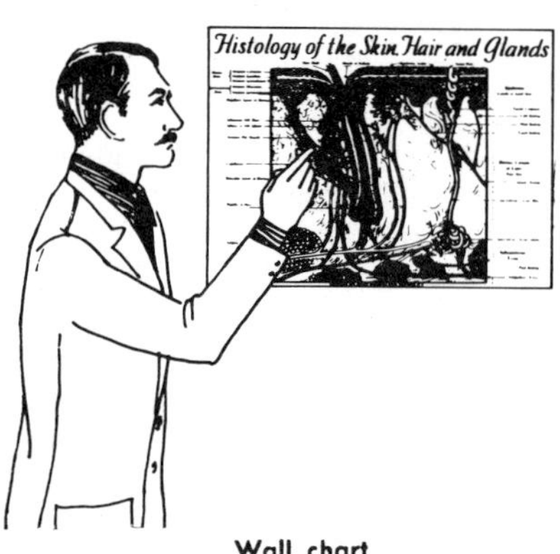

Wall chart

1. Select or prepare aids that will help emphasize or illustrate points in the lesson.

2. Mount posters where they are usable. Cover them so they cannot be seen until needed.

3. Plan how and when the aid will be used.

4. Use the aid. Always stand to one side of the chart, use a pointer and face and talk to the class.

5. Develop and stress important points.

FLIP CHARTS

Flip charts are important assets to an instructor when he is presenting a progression of steps in the development of an area of knowledge or a technical skill. They are especially important because they permit the instructor to pace his display with the progress of the class. They also give him the opportunity to stop at any single chart and thoroughly discuss it for as long as necessary. **Flip charts help the instructor to:**

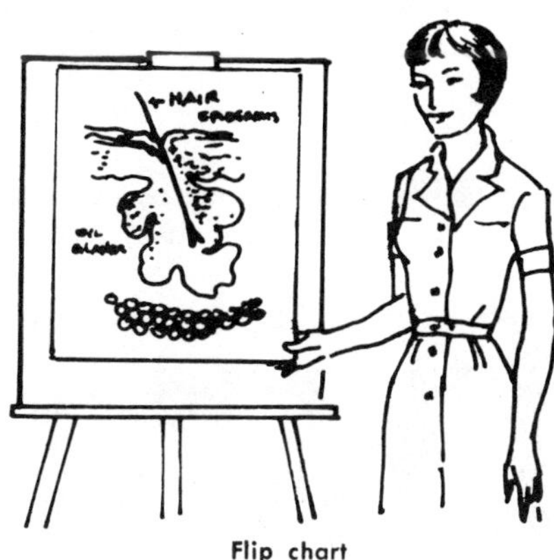
Flip chart

1. Show what an object looks like.
2. Show how different elements work together.
3. Teach relationships between different components.
4. Show useful data to the entire class at one time.
5. Show comparisons needed for making decisions.
6. Show progress of the class.
7. Motivate classroom learning.

PEGBOARD

Pegboards are teaching aids which enable the instructor to set up permanent and semi-permanent displays for student guidance. They permit the instructor to readily change such pictorial or written data exhibits without too much expenditure of time or money. Pegboards furnish the instructor with a method to exhibit complicated or detailed drawings which are too difficult or time consuming to be placed on the chalkboard.

Peg-Board (cork-board).

MANNEQUINS AND CUTAWAY FORMS

Using mannequins in classroom presentations has several distinct advantages as follows:

1. No darkened room is needed.
2. They may be seen, handled and examined by students.
3. Exact relationship of parts and areas are shown in realistic manner.
4. They are extremely valuable for close examination and adjustment.

Mannequins offer students a fairly realistic model upon which to practice various techniques.

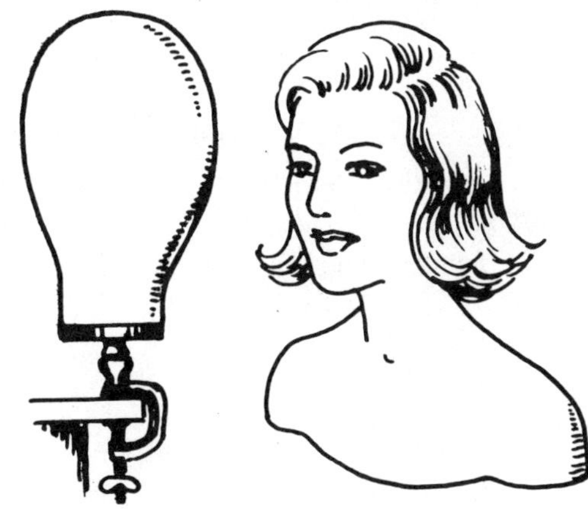
Canvas block.   Mannequin

When using mannequins, be sure to:

1. Select the proper mannequin to fit the subject matter.
2. Mount mannequin so that all students have a clear view.
3. Place it for convenient use.
4. Introduce it into the lesson.
5. Avoid passing it around while talking.
6. Develop and stress its importance as an aid to learning.

Cutaway forms in the beauty culture field are used primarily to show parts of the skin, scalp and hair, with the same advantages as mannequins.

TEXTBOOKS

The textbook is probably the most widely accepted teaching aid in general use by all schools. It serves as a source of subject matter, ideas and information in the planning and presentation of lessons in the classroom.

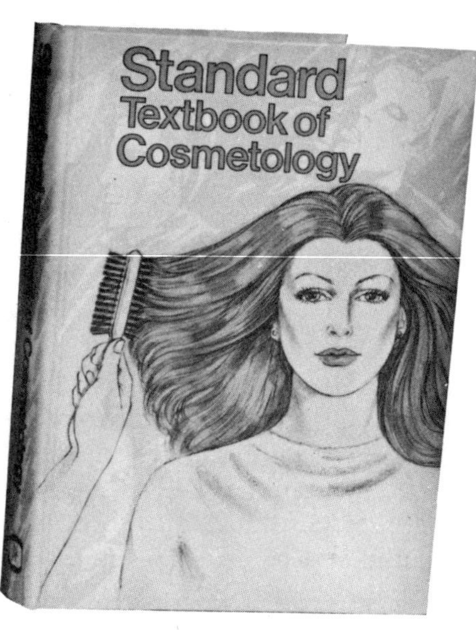

The Textbooks that create a Professional Image to the industry

All or only part of some books may be suitable for class use. It is the teacher's responsibility to review the book and to determine which areas can best be employed in the learning pattern.

It is of utmost importance that the teacher does not expect the textbook to do the teaching. The text is a teaching aid—an important and valuable teaching aid—but the actual instruction must be given by the teacher.

In making an assignment from a textbook, make it definite by using the following ideas:

1. Identify the book clearly.
2. Know the source and location of the book.
3. Specify the exact areas to be covered.
4. Define the purpose of the assignment.
5. Explain clearly what to do. Tell students whether they are only to study, or to write notes or a review, or to make an outline of the material for class presentation.
6. Give students the opportunity to ask questions in order to clarify the assignment.

The workbook has a place in modern education because of the unique contribution it makes to teaching and learning activities.

As a study and learning guide, the workbook encourages students to help themselves under the supervision of the teacher. In the workbook will be found a variety of exercises, problems, work sheets, visual aids and other instructional materials, together with directions for use, space for recording answers and means for grading the finished work. At its best, the workbook is an essential aid to study, planning and the application of important facts and skills.

A good workbook should have the following features:
1. Follows well-established objectives of the curriculum.
2. Motivates students to do better work.
3. Provides for a series of drills, reviews and tests.
4. Promotes the maximum growth and development of the student's mental capacity.
5. Coincides with the textbook being used.

The workbook method appeals to beauty culture teachers because of the following benefits:
1. **Effective teaching.** Following an organized system of teaching helps to emphasize and review essential facts and skills.
2. **Reduces failures.** Students take a greater interest and pride in their work, and tend to develop good study and learning habits.
3. **Saves teacher's time.** Relieves teachers of such arduous tasks as keeping detailed notes, dictating and writing exercises on the chalkboard.
4. **Saves student's time.** Relieves students of the need to copy exercises, notes and assignments.
5. **Absentee students make up lost time.** Without interfering with the rest of the class, students have a chance to catch up with the work that has been missed.
6. **Fast learners** are permitted to move ahead at an accelerated pace by advance exercises in the workbook.
7. **Slow learners** are provided with a means of keeping pace with the class. Workbook exercises and practice lessons can be studied and performed at home, thus giving these slower students the additional time they require.

REFERENCE LIBRARY

In addition to the textbooks and workbooks, the teacher must plan to make efficient use of reference books. Use the following suggestions:

1. Have a definite place for storing the books when not in use.
2. Have a plan for distributing the books for use in class and for checking them in at the end of the session.
3. If a reference book becomes obsolete or unavailable, substitute another book to serve the need of the course.
4. If students have difficulty in making efficient use of reference books, they should be given assistance in how to use them to best advantage.

DUPLICATED AIDS

MIMEOGRAPH SHEETS

Mimeograph sheets, prepared by the teacher, are important aids in connection with his classroom presentation.

1. They help the teacher to emphasize and to present to the students the most important facts discussed in the classroom.
2. The mimeographed sheets help to clarify unclear areas in the subject matter presented.
3. They save the teacher considerable time by eliminating the necessity for writing out lengthy material on the chalkboard.
4. They save the student time in taking notes and permit closer attention and concentration on the teacher's presentation.
5. They permit students who may have been absent to catch-up with the class.
6. They also provide very important and exceptionally good review material.

PROJECT SHEETS

1. The project sheet is an important aid in the development of a new technique.
2. It provides a definite assignment to students.
3. It provides step by step instructions in how a project should be carried out.
4. It helps to develop student confidence because they are able to perform adequately if they follow the instructions provided.
5. It helps to give individual instruction to each student.

PROGRAM SHEETS

1. The program sheet is important in the fact that it keeps students informed, in advance, of what they can look forward to.
2. It helps to arouse student interest in the overall program.

3. It helps to motivate students to progress from one area to another.
4. It helps to show students the importance of each area in the overall program.
5. It helps to establish a continuity in the teaching-learning program.

INSTRUCTION SHEETS

1. Instruction sheets can very effectively be used, by the teacher, for presenting information to the class.
2. If properly prepared, they assure complete coverage of the subject matter.
3. They offer a method of presenting uniform instruction to all students.
4. They permit students to proceed at their own pace.
5. They save time of both the teacher and the students in writing long, tedious notes.
6. They prevent the misunderstanding of instructions.
7. They train students to follow written instructions.
8. They help students to develop self-confidence.

RECOMMENDATIONS FOR USING VISUAL AIDS

Teacher Preparation

1. Know what you expect to accomplish.
2. Carefully preview each film, filmstrip, slide, etc., before showing to class.
3. Rehearse the use of the teaching aid and plan appropriate and informative comments.
4. Have everything ready before the class meets.
   a) Check projection equipment.
   b) Have spare bulb.
   c) Arrange screen and seats for most effective viewing.
5. If chalkboard drawings are very detailed and require a long time to create, draw them before the class starts. You might have a very light pattern on the board which you can follow quickly.
6. Cover or hide displays until required, so they will not distract your students.

Classroom Presentation

1. Visual aids should not be a substitute for the teacher. They should be used to aid the teacher—not to replace him. The teacher must be present to make comments and ask questions.
2. Employ each aid at just the proper time in the teaching pattern. Choose and schedule the particular aid for use where it will most effectively make a specific and essential contribution to the subject matter being taught. Keep visual aid out of sight until ready to be used.
3. Face and speak to your class—not to the visual aid.
4. If any form of illustration or model is used as part of the classroom presentation, do not pass it around while the discussion is going on. This can be very distracting. The students can examine it later.
5. If motion pictures, filmstrips, or slides are to be used, your students should know what they are looking for. Avoid the danger of the students missing the important points, emphasizing unimportant data, or considering the whole thing as a form of entertainment.

6. If necessary, reshow any film or other teaching aid to emphasize a point which may have been missed.

7. Audio-visual aids should never be used without some follow-up activity which capitalizes on the presentation.

TESTING

This subject will receive detailed coverage in following chapter.

REVIEW

1. **What is the most important consideration in selecting a teaching aid?**
   The instructor must be aware that it is the most effective learning accessory available for the particular subject.

2. **Name ten characteristics of a good visual aid.**
   1. It should explain an idea.
   2. It must be clearly visible.
   3. Printed matter must be large enough.
   4. Wording must be simple.
   5. Bright colors should be used.
   6. Models should be made to scale.
   7. The aid should be constructed of good materials.
   8. The aid should be well made.
   9. It should be portable.
   10. It should be covered with a good protective material.

3. **Films, filmstrips and slides make a direct appeal to the most important sense in learning. What is it?**
   The sense of sight.

4. **Can the motion pictures sometimes be more effective than "the real thing"?**
   Yes.

5. **List the steps in the selection and use of films as a teaching aid.**
   1. Preview it for suitability.
   2. Prepare room.
   3. Introduce the film.
   4. Show film, remaining in room.
   5. Discuss film.
   6. Rescreen film within a short period.
   7. Test.

6. **Why should motion pictures and filmstrips be previewed before they are shown to the class?**
   The teacher must decide whether or not all of the material is to be shown to the class. The teacher must also determine what is to be emphasized and at what time the visual aid is to be shown.

7. **Why should the teacher tell students what they are to look for and what they should learn from the aid?**
   If these things are not called to the attention of students, they will miss important facts and may fail to learn.

8. **What two things should the teacher do to make the maximum use of the aid?**

Make informative comments and ask questions of students.

9. **Under what conditions would the teacher reshow a visual aid?**

If the students obviously have not learned from the first showing.

10. **Why are slides among the best of the audio-visual teaching aids?**

They aid the student in absorbing and retaining the subject matter being taught.

11. **How should slides be used to give maximum teaching benefits? List the 13 steps.**
    1. Determine most beneficial point to use them in teaching program.
    2. Arrange them in order.
    3. Set up projector and screen.
    4. Check students' seating for visibility.
    5. Check lighting.
    6. Check working order of projector.
    7. Introduce slides.
    8. Present slides with complete and accurate commentary.
    9. Stop at important slides.
    10. Remember sometimes a single slide could be the basis for a teaching session.
    11. Discuss after viewing.
    12. Let students practice information, if possible.
    13. Review.

12. **Why are charts, pictures and posters adaptable to almost any classroom teaching situation?**

They present graphic illustrations of subject matter.

13. **Why are flip charts important teaching assets?**

Flip charts permit the instructor to pace his display with the progress of the class.

14. **Why is the chalkboard one of the more flexible and practical teaching aids?**

The chalkboard is useful in illustrating, diagraming, emphasizing key points and developing a solution to a problem.

15. **What type of display does the pegboard facilitate?**

Pegboards enable the instructor to set up permanent and semi-permanent displays for student guidance.

16. **What is the value of mannequins and cutaway forms as teaching aids?**

The value of mannequins and cutaway forms is that they can be handled directly by the students and show parts in a realistic manner.

17. **How would you solidify the value of a field trip?**

Classroom discussion should always follow a field trip to solidify the educational value of the trip.

18. **How does the textbook rate as a teaching aid?**

The textbook is the most widely accepted teaching aid in general use.

19. **What point must the teacher consider in using a textbook?**

The teacher must always realize that actual instruction must be given by the teacher.

20. **Give six ideas which assist in making assignments from a textbook.**
    1. Identify the book clearly.
    2. Know the source and location of the book.
    3. Specify exact areas to be covered.
    4. Define purpose of the assignment.
    5. Explain clearly what is to be done.
    6. Give students opportunity to ask questions.

21. **Name five features of a good workbook.**
    1. Follow objectives of the curriculum.
    2. Motivate students.
    3. Has series of drills, reviews and tests.
    4. Promotes maximum growth of student's mental capacity.
    5. Coincides with textbook being used.

22. **List seven ways in which the workbook method appeals to beauty culture teachers.**
    1. Effective teaching in an organized system emphasizes essential facts and skills.
    2. Reduces failures.
    3. Saves teacher's time.
    4. Saves pupil's time.
    5. Absentee students can make up lost time.
    6. Fast learners can move ahead.
    7. Slow learners can keep pace with class, using workbook at home.

23. **How should the teacher make use of a reference library?**
    1. Have a definite place for storing the reference material.
    2. Have a plan for distribution in class and collecting the material after class.
    3. If a reference book is unavailable, substitute another to fill the need of the course.
    4. Assist students in the use of reference books.

24. **Give two general recommendations for the use of visual aids.**
    1. Know what you expect to accomplish.
    2. Prepare beforehand for its use.

25. **In what way should visual aids be used?**

Visual aids are exactly what they are called and should be used as aids to the teacher—not as a replacement for him. The teacher must be present to make comments, ask questions and direct the class activities.

CHAPTER 11

TESTING

INTRODUCTION

Until very recently examinations were used almost exclusively as a means of awarding final grades for educational performance. In fact, the present dislike and dread of examinations is probably a carry-over of teacher misuse of tests: using them as punishment, or over-emphasizing their importance in setting final school grades.

Modern educators have discovered that examinations serve a number of very important functions in the overall educational pattern. It has been found that properly prepared and administered examinations are excellent educational aids and teaching tools to advance the learning program. Examinations are used as instructional aids; instruments to evaluate training results, techniques and programs; and as essential tools in the educational structure. This chapter will discuss in detail the types of examinations, their uses and how they fit into the educational pattern.

Cosmetology teaching and training programs must have specific objectives and definite standards which should be met before the instruction can be considered successful. Therefore, it is essential that the cosmetology teacher make comprehensive periodic checks to determine whether or not satisfactory progress is being made. To decide whether each lesson, series of lessons or even a complete program is successful, the teacher must use tests and careful evaluations that compare actual results with desired objectives.

If a predetermined degree of capability is to be expected of students at the termination of a basic educational program, standards of competency must be established. No teacher can assume that he has taught well unless some concrete evidence of the students knowledge, skill and understanding is determined. Without some form of examining, the teacher can never be crtain that both the students and teacher have reached the learning objectives. Educationally, the best tool developed for discovering student ability and potential is appraisal by a carefully prepared examination.

Tests have been developed to measure or evaluate many different things such as:

1. Intelligence.
2. Abilities or aptitudes.
3. Areas of interest.
4. Individual personalities—strengths and weaknesses.
5. Student achievement.

Cosmetology teachers are primarily interested in student achievement tests of all types.

The cosmetology teacher must make decisions based on the results of adequate testing. If a sound approach is not taken, neither the teacher nor the school administration can ever be certain that the students will achieve the planned objectives in terms of skills and knowledge. Skill in the development of student tests is demonstrated by the creation of examinations which provide great accuracy in measuring achievement of cosmetology skills and the acquiring of subject-matter knowledge.

Some of the important uses of tests in cosmetology education are:
1. Measurement of general student ability.
2. Measurement of student achievement.
3. Diagnosis of student weaknesses.
4. Diagnosis of teaching effectiveness and weaknesses.
5. Direction of effective study habits.
6. Motivation for study.
7. Isolation of areas which require further instruction.

MEASUREMENT OF GENERAL STUDENT ABILITY

The measurement of general student ability enables the teacher to gauge the possible progress of the student under normal conditions. It enables the school to separate students into groups of comparable ability so that all may

work at full capacity. It also enables the instructor to formulate different standards of achievement to care for varied abilities when separation is not practical. This allows faster students to move ahead at an accelerated pace without penalizing the slower student.

MEASUREMENT OF STUDENT ACHIEVEMENT

This is the time-honored purpose for which examinations have been used in the field of education. This still remains a very important reason for testing, although not as much emphasis is being placed upon tests in this area as in former years.

DIAGNOSIS OF STUDENT WEAKNESSES

The use of tests to diagnose student weaknesses has become one of their most valuable purposes. Just as the doctor recognizes a correct diagnosis of the patient's illness as the first prerequisite to a possible cure, so teachers have come to consider a proper diagnosis of the students' weaknesses essential to any corrective procedure they may employ. Areas of weakness in the learning pattern are isolated by means of examinations. Tests also permit teachers to determine the rate of student comprehension and readiness to profit by more advanced information.

DIAGNOSIS OF TEACHING EFFECTIVENESS AND WEAKNESSES

Classroom examinations point out areas of learning which were ineffectively taught. It is not enough to diagnose student difficulties. Many so-called student weaknesses are the result of poor teaching procedures. The teacher should recognize that an examination, properly prepared, may function as a two-edged sword. It points out the weaknesses of the student, and also reveals shortcomings of the teacher. The examination which reveals a lack of true understanding of the material, not by one student but by an entire class, clearly indicates teacher failure and retraining becomes necessary.

DIRECTION OF EFFECTIVE STUDY HABITS

Educators have only recently become aware of the value of examinations as a means of guiding students into correct study habits. If the teacher calls the attention of students to the areas of learning to be examined, placing emphasis upon certain important elements, students will be directed to a careful study of these units. Possibly at no point in the learning experience of students can the desire to master the art of good study habits be so effectively motivated as in the desire to do well on examinations.

MOTIVATION FOR STUDY

Questionable as this purpose of the examination may be from the idealistic point of view, practically, it is a very important factor in teaching procedure.

Tests may imbue students with the desire to study. The knowledge that they will be examined on the subject matter will usually be an effective influence in forcing students to study. In preparing for examinations students review past work and solidify learning.

If the student has the opportunity to review his test, with the errors indicated, he is frequently motivated to study more and harder to improve the weak areas revealed.

The fact that students may perform satisfactorily under direct teacher supervision is no guarantee that they will continue to do so when acting without this supervision. Consequently, cosmetology instructors should follow up their presentation with a test or inspection of the work performance of students. If errors in execution or procedure are found, correction and retraining should be undertaken at once.

RULES TO BE FOLLOWED IN RETRAINING

1. Students should function "on their own."
   a) They must be permitted to perform by doing the job themselves.
2. Teacher should check frequently.
3. Teacher should suggest improvements in techniques.
4. Encourage students to look for key items as they progress.
5. Encourage students to seek improvement in weak areas.
6. Examine students' work frequently.
7. Teacher should take advantage of the opportunity to fill in important gaps in the students' knowledge and techniques.

EVALUATING INSTRUCTION

By giving an examination after teaching some new cosmetology technique or subject matter, the teacher can judge whether or not:

1. The sequence of instruction is effective.
2. The lesson plans provide for thorough and adequate coverage of the subject matter.
3. The teaching aids employed were adequate, or others should be used.
4. The proper method or methods were employed in presenting the subject matter.
5. The teaching techniques employed were effective.
6. The tests indicate that certain areas of the subject matter should be retaught.

EFFECTIVE TESTING

Types of Tests

Although there are many kinds of tests, the three basic types of examinations used in cosmetology schools are:

1. **Oral Quizzes.** Used in the classroom for review and in order to determine mastery of subject matter.
2. **Written Tests.** Used to measure how well students have learned cosmetology theory and techniques.
3. **Performance (Practical) Tests.** Used to measure the achievement of cosmetology skills.

Qualities of a Good Test

1. It measures accurately the student's knowledge, understanding or skill.
2. The directions and the questions are clear, concise and complete.
3. It is easy to give, easy to take, easy to correct and easy to score.
4. Questions are valued fairly and accurately.

Guidelines for Effective Testing

1. The test scores are only as valuable as the procedures employed to arrive at that score.

2. A test is only a sampling of achievement. To be of any value, the test must seek specific information. In the case of performance testing, it is essential that the test be appropriate and evaluate skills that had already been taught.

3. Performance tests, properly prepared and administered, can be very valid because they test identifiable techniques.

4. The teacher should make every effort to evaluate the method and technique employed in examining. The test itself should be judged for effectiveness, objectivity and accuracy.

5. The directions for the test must be clear and understandable by the students and should be carefully followed.

6. A test should never be an end in itself. It should only be an indicator, a teaching aid, a technique employed by the teacher to help develop and increase knowledge or improve skills.

Checklist for Evaluating a Test

1. Is the content on the achievement level attained by students?

2. Is the language of the test on the students' vocabulary level?

3. Are the directions clear, concise and easily understood by students? Do they result in a minimum of test-taking errors?

4. How valid is the test? Does it actually test that for which it is intended?

5. Is it easily, quickly and accurately scored?

6. Is it easy to give?

7. Is it easy to take?

8. How reliable is the test? Does it consistently give results that would indicate its reliability?

ORAL EXAMINATIONS (QUIZZES)

In the regular course of cosmetology teaching, frequent oral quizzes are often more revealing and helpful than long examinations given occasionally.

Any type of classroom teaching almost necessarily involves oral questions and answers. However, when using oral questions as an examination device, teachers must be extremely careful in the composition and employment of them. Unless careful precautions are taken, oral questions may be especially subjective and lack reliability.

In order that oral questions have any merit as evaluation instruments they must be thoroughly and carefully prepared. Not only should the questions be composed and listed in advance but the acceptable answers should also be listed.

Every student should have an equal opportunity to hear well-prepared questions and be permitted to give acceptable answers. Questions should be asked of all students in the same tone of voice. Any clues to the answers by tonal emphasis, tonal inflection or by facial expressions must be carefully avoided. Scoring should be done while the questioning is in progress.

PERFORMANCE TESTS

Since the practice of cosmetology requires complete training in the actual manual performance of the various techniques, the practical test is especially important. A good practical test should be able to predict actual performance ability and should cover the important skills and techniques which will be required for competent service in the beauty salon.

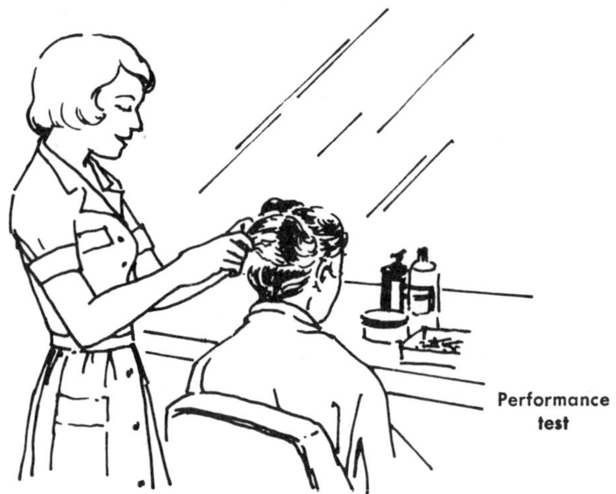

In preparing this type of test, teachers must consider the following:

1. What are the important skills, techniques and information required?

2. Which manual operations best represent the salon services?

3. The selection of test items which will best demonstrate manual dexterity and manipulative skills.

4. Observation Areas:
    a) Skill and accuracy in performance
    b) Speed.
    c) Combinations for better performance.
    d) The quality of the finished job.

5. Examination must be effective, consistent, efficient and economical.

6. Time to be allotted to different techniques.

7. Required equipment, implements and supplies.

8. Organization of equipment, implements and supplies.

9. Assistance and direction required in conducting examinations.

10. Score sheets, checklists and observation sheets required.

Rules for Performance Testing

1. Test must be given to all students in the same way.

2. Rating and evaluating must be the same for all students.

WRITTEN EXAMINATIONS

The written examination requires the same careful planning and preparation as the performance test. This careful preparatory work is revealed in the type of questions used, the area of knowledge selected, the emphasis being placed on critical areas, the choice of test items and the number of questions.

Types of Written Tests in General Use

1. Essay.
2. True or False.
3. Matching.
4. Completion.
5. Multiple Choice.
6. Identification.

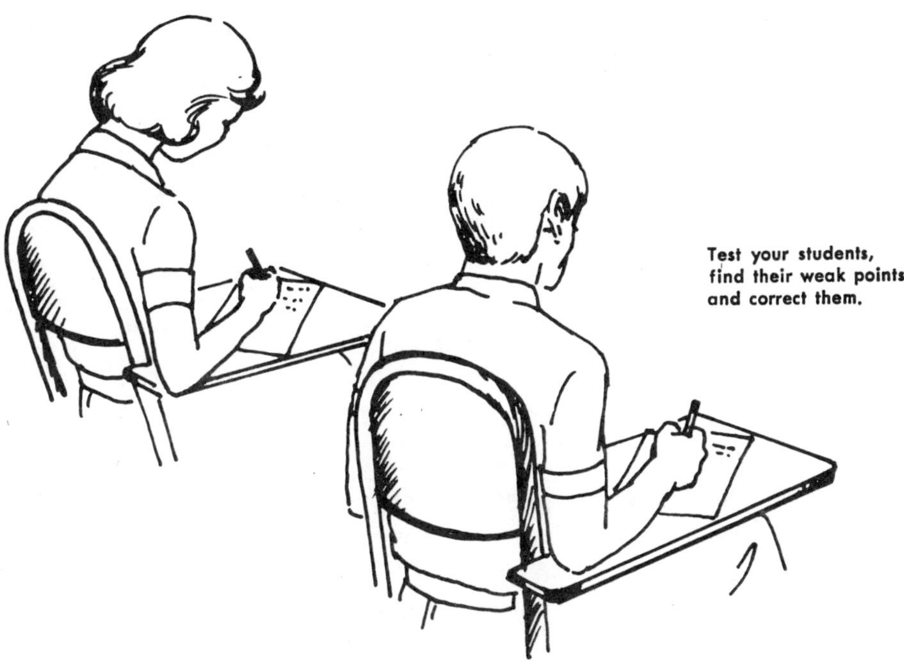

Rules for Written Test Preparation and Administration

1. **An examination is not an endurance contest.** The objective is to evaluate the knowledge and understanding of students. To include all of the items pertinent to the subject matter might make the test inefficiently long. The principle to be applied is that a sufficient number of test items be used to indicate the degree of knowledge possessed, without allowing the element of fatigue to influence the examination.

2. The best type of examination uses two or three of the various types of test items. It makes the examination more interesting and is more productive as a method of evaluating student knowledge.

3. It is also advisable to include both easy and difficult items on the examination.

4. Tests should be arranged from the easy items to the more difficult.

5. Directions should be in writing and be clear and precise.

6. Organize items so that scoring is simple, rapid and accurate.

7. Tests should be administered to all groups in the same way, under the best possible physical conditions.

8. Tests should be easy to give, easy to take and easy to rate.

The teacher must be aware of the different types of written tests, be able to prepare and administer them and recognize their strengths and weaknesses.

THE ESSAY EXAMINATION

The traditional essay question is firmly fixed in testing practice. It is the type of question with which all teachers are quite familiar. Essay questions are still being used for special purposes.

The nature of the essay examination makes it an ideal instrument for evaluating the student's ability to express himself in writing. It permits the testing of the ability to write in a correct, convincing and interesting manner. However, when a test is intended to measure factors other than writing ability, the essay examination has very little merit. A cosmetology classroom test should be designed to evaluate the students' knowledge of subject matter, not writing proficiency; therefore the essay has very limited use in cosmetology education.

Although essay questions have very little value in the school of beauty culture, the teacher should understand their merits and demerits.

Advantages

1. They are very easy to prepare.
2. They are very simple to give
3. They can be given under almost any conditions.
4. They require very little supervision.

Disadvantages

1. They lack objectivity.
2. Rating them is very subjective (subject to individual judgment, emotions and other irrelevant features).
3. They emphasize the ability to write well.
4. They permit only a limited range of questions. The number of questions is too limited to give an adequate sampling.
5. They create an atmosphere of unfairness.
6. They are very difficult to rate.
7. They do not lend themselves to the evaluation of cosmetology knowledge.

OBJECTIVE QUESTIONS

The tendency in all test development should be to simplify test questions. Simplification is necessary in order to reduce to a minimum the possibility of invalidating their results through improper usage. The more complex a test becomes in form or in administration, the less reliable the results are likely to be.

Each type of test question varies in its construction. As a means of avoiding the faults of the essay question, objective (or limited response) questions are now being used in the classroom. With the refinement of test construction, new or variations of familiar question forms are constantly being developed. The most common of the objective questions are the true-false, multiple choice, matching, completion and identification.

All objective type questions are far more difficult to prepare than the essay question. However, all are well worth the extra effort involved because they help do the best possible measuring job.

The objective type of question lends itself to purely objective rating: (It is) either right or wrong.

Writing is practically eliminated, since all answers are strictly limited. The unrelated factors of speed and quality of handwriting and ability in written composition are not involved.

The students can answer a large number of objective questions in a short time. Each test can cover a very wide range of material within a limited time.

Because the rating is highly objective, the results will be identical regardless of who rates the examination, or when they are rated.

TRUE-FALSE TEST

The true-false test consists of a series of statements, of which some are true and the rest are false. The true statements are in conformity with the facts or general principles the student is supposed to know. The false statements are not in accord with the accepted facts.

The test requires the student to apply the knowledge acquired in the classroom to determine which statements are accurate and which are not. The ability to discriminate between truth and falsity is one method of measuring the student's knowledge of the subject matter covered.

Sample Questions

1. Under normal conditions average healthy hair, when dry, can be stretched 20% of its own length .... T   F
2. Since hair consists mainly of keratin it is not flexible and cannot be stretched. .... T   F

The fact that true-false questions are widely used is no mere accident. This type of question is among the best known of all of the objective types.

Advantages

1. Simplest and most adaptable of all types of questions.
2. Relatively easy to prepare.
3. Very easy to score.
4. Lends itself very well to cosmetology.
5. Easy to understand
6. Easy to take.
7. Can cover a wide area in a short time.

Disadvantages

1. Less reliable than other objective questions.
2. Permits guessing at answers.
3. Care must be exercised to avoid ambiguities in preparing statements.

Rules for Preparing True-False Questions

1. A good true-false statement should allow the student to understand an important fact or generalization presented in the form of a statement.
2. A good true-false statement should be clear and definite. It must be free from any ambiguities which permit more than one interpretation of the statement.

3. A good true-false statement should be a short sentence which covers one definite idea.

4. A good true-false statement should not give the answer to other statements on the same test.

5. A good true-false statement must be absolutely "true" or absolutely "false."

6. A good true-false statement must be so accurate and so universal that it permits no qualification and no exceptions.

7. A good true-false statement should not be tricky in any way.

8. A good true-false test should make some provision in the scoring to adjust for guessing.

MATCHING QUESTIONS

The matching question is among the most popular of the objective types. While they are not easy to prepare, they offer an evaluation of the student's ability to associate and connect important items in cosmetology. They require a single, definite answer which leaves no room for subjective analysis.

The matching question provides two lists of words or phrases. Each item on the first list has a close relationship to a specific item on the second list. The student is required to mark the items on one list which are closely related to the items on the other.

In answering matching questions the student is required to write only a code letter or number identifying the related item. The two lists should have unequal numbers of items, but each item should have only one correct answer. It is important that the instructions given be clear and definite.

Sample Question

Find the item in Column I which is closely related to an item in Column II and place the number of that item in the appropriate bracket.

Column I	Column II
1 Coarse	( ) Cross bond
2 Croquignole	( ) Resilience
3 Sulphur	( ) Rotary
4 Density	( ) Texture
5 Elastic	( ) Skin test
6 Porosity	( ) Hair root
7 Allergy	( ) Mitosis
8 Tinting	( ) Winding
9 Follicle	( ) Thick hair
10 Neuron	( ) Absorption
	( ) Paraffin
	( ) Aniline derivative
	( ) Nervous system

COMPLETION QUESTIONS

Completion questions are those in which a statement is presented with a critical word or phrase missing. The student is expected to complete the statement by supplying the missing word or phrase which will give the statement correct and accurate meaning.

The completion question is the best of the objective questions to test for thoroughness of knowledge. It motivates the development of the ability to recall and apply accurately the subject matter learned. The brief answers make it possible to cover a large amount of subject matter in a relatively short period, thus the sampling of cosmetology knowledge is greater. The rate at which students can answer questions is slower than with the true-false or multiple choice questions, but the test is more difficult. The necessity for the student to supply his own answers makes a demand upon his own initiative and self-reliance.

The well-prepared completion test practically eliminates any chances for guessing the correct answers. In order to recall, from a vast amount of subject matter, the precise answers required, the student's knowledge must be thorough and accurate.

Completion questions are considered to be less confusing, fairer because of less guessing, less likely to give wrong impressions, more thorough, and require more thought and ability than any other type of objective question.

The preparation of good completion questions requires much thought, concentration and time. It is the most difficult type of question to make objective, since great care must be taken in the construction of each item to make sure that only one word or phrase will be correct. It is one of the slowest types of objective questions to score. However, item for item it is probably the most reliable of all the objective questions.

Items to be considered in the preparation of completion questions:
1. Avoid loose, ambiguous items which cannot be answered with one or two words.
2. Try to place the blank near or at the end of the statement.
3. Avoid extraneous clues to the correct answer.

Sample Question

Under normal conditions, average healthy hair, when dry, can be stretched ....

MULTIPLE CHOICE QUESTIONS

The multiple choice item consists of an introductory question or incomplete statement, called the stem, and a number of suggested answers or completions, called the responses. The number of suggested responses varies from three to seven or more; one is the correct or best response, and the others are incorrect. The test requires the student to rcognize the correct response. To reduce the possibility of guessing in the multiple choice question, increase the number of responses.

The multiple choice question makes a demand upon the judgment and upon the ability to select the best from among several possibilities. To be able to select the correct answer from among several erroneous ones is a good test of the student's knowledge of the cosmetology material taught.

The multiple choice question merits wide use. It is among the best of all objective questions. While it is more difficult to prepare than other types of questions, it is easy to give and to score. With an answer key or scoring template it can be scored with great ease and rapidity.

The multiple choice question is especially adaptable to testing in schools of cosmetology. It is easy to take, easy to give, definite, fair and thorough. The fact that there is less chance for guessing makes a special appeal. The guessing element is reduced in proportion to the number of answers suggested for each statement. If four possible choices are given, the chances of getting the correct answer by pure guessing is only one in four. If more responses are given the chances of guessing are further reduced.

The multiple choice question stimulates mental attitudes and activities of a practical nature. It requires knowledge of facts and the application of this information. It demands sound judgment and a careful appraisal of facts. The multiple choice question does not measure merely the possession of isolated facts; it also measures the ability to apply the subject matter knowledge.

A good multiple choice question requires great care in its preparation. It cannot be thrown together in a haphazard manner. The proper preparation of multiple choice questions requires a knowledge of the techniques of the construction of such items. Following are some of the rules to be considered in preparing multiple choice items:

1. Use at least four or five choices whenever possible, to minimize guessing.
2. Select responses that have some degree of plausibility. Each alternative must literally be a possible answer.
3. A question should not present an absurd situation or a ridiculous choice.
4. Avoid words which serve as clues.
5. Avoid the use of "a" or "an" as the final word of the stem; these words act as hints or clues.
6. A statement should be clear, straightforward and unambiguous.
7. An item should present a situation which is possible and likely.
8. An item should be stated positively, not negatively.
9. The items should be realistic and practical.

The properly prepared multiple choice question is especially satisfactory for use in schools of cosmetology. It is practical in its makeup and application, it is strictly objective in rating, it is easy to administer, it is fair and it is thorough, requiring definite knowledge to answer it correctly.

Sample Of Multiple Choice Question

Under normal circumstances, average healthy hair, when dry, can be stretched:

a) 10%	c) 30%
b) 20%	d) 40% --------------

IDENTIFICATION QUESTIONS

Identification tests are used in cosmetology primarily in the study of anatomy. This type of test is used when students are required to identify various components or parts of a human structure or some object.

The students are presented with a drawing or photo of some area of the human body or object with certain points or areas numbered. They are required to identify those areas numbered.

TEST CONSTRUCTION

The professional cosmetology teacher should be able to develop and construct an effective test as part of the educational program.

1. Consideration in selecting the type of test or questions:
   a) Materials to be examined.
   b) Review of the material to be covered.
   c) Time to be devoted to test.
   d) Facilities available.
   e) Student preparation.
   f) Type of questions to use to achieve objectives.
   g) Which areas of subject matter to emphasize.

2. Arrangement of material:
   a) Progress from simple to complex.
   b) Mix some easy and some difficult questions.
   c) Plan questions to facilitate test administration.
   d) Plan test construction to facilitate scoring.
   e) Decide on order of questions.

3. Construction of questions:
   a) Develop card file of questions.
   b) Review each question before using.
   c) Carefully construct questions in accordance with rules previously discussed.
   d) Check wording of questions for clarity.
   e) Arrange questions in the order they are to appear on examination.

4. Preparation of examination:
   a) Proper order, spacing, alignment.
   b) Preparation of scoring template or answer key.

REVIEW

1. **In addition to providing a means of awarding a final grade for work done, of what other use is a test?**

    Modern educators have found that tests are excellent teaching devices.

2. **Name seven important uses of tests in education.**
    1. Measurement of ability.
    2. Measurement of achievement.
    3. Diagnosis of weaknesses.
    4. Diagnosis of teaching strengths and weaknesses.
    5. Direction of study habits.
    6. Motivation for study.
    7. Isolating areas requiring further instruction.

3. **Why is it important for a teacher to measure general student ability?**

    So that she may formulate different standards of achievement for the varied abilities in her class.

4. **List six areas that may be indicated by a test which help to evaluate the effectiveness of teaching.**
    1. Proper sequence of instruction.
    2. Lesson plans provide for adequate coverage.
    3. Teaching aids were effective.
    4. Proper teaching method or methods were employed.
    5. Teaching techniques employed were effective.
    6. Certain areas must be retaught.

5. **What are the rules to be followed in retraining? Name seven.**
    1. Students should be permitted to perform on their own.
    2. Teacher should check frequently.
    3. Teacher should suggest improvements in techniques.
    4. Encourage students to look for key items as they progress.
    5. Encourage students to seek improvement in weak areas.
    6. Examine students' work frequently.
    7. Teacher should fill in gaps in students' knowledge.

6. **What are the three most frequently used types of tests?**

    Performance, written, and oral tests.

7. **What are the four basic qualities of a good test?**
    1. It measures accurately.
    2. Directions are clear, concise and complete.
    3. It is easy to give, easy to take, easy to mark.
    4. Questions are valued fairly and accurately.

8. **List the eight items to check in evaluating a test.**
    1. Is content based on students' achievement level?
    2. Is language on students' vocabulary level?
    3. Are directions clear, concise and easily understood?
    4. Does it actually test what it is intended to test? (Validity.)
    5. Is it easily, quickly and accurately scored?
    6. Is it easy to give?
    7. Is it easy to take?
    8. Does it consistently give results that would indicate reliability?

9. **In which area of the educational program are oral questions most effective?**
In classroom quizzes for evaluation of daily learning progress.

10. **In giving a performance test, what two rules are to be followed?**
    1. Test must be given to all students in the same way.
    2. Rating and evaluating must be the same for all students.

11. **List six different types of written tests in general use.**
    1. Essay.
    2. True or false.
    3. Matching.
    4. Completion
    5. Multiple choice.
    6. Identification.

12. **How can a teacher keep a written examination from becoming an endurance contest?**
The examination should be composed so that a sufficient number of test items are used to indicate the degree of knowledge possessed without allowing the element of fatigue to influence the examination.

13. **Why should you use two or three different types of test items in your examination?**
It makes the examination more interesting and is more productive as a method of evaluating students' knowledge.

14. **In what order should test items be arranged?**
Tests should be arranged from the easy items to the more difficult.

15. **What are the four advantages of the essay type examination?**
    1. Easy to prepare.
    2. Easy to give.
    3. Given under almost any conditions.
    4. Very little supervision.

16. **List the seven disadvantages of the essay type examination.**
    1. Lacks objectivity.
    2. Very subjective and unreliable rating.
    3. Emphasizes the ability to write well.
    4. Permits only a limited range of questions.
    5. Creates an atmosphere of unfairness.
    6. Very difficult to rate.
    7. Does not lend itself to the evaluation of cosmetology knowledge.

17. **Why are objective type examinations suitable for testing in cosmetology?**
They are purely objective, they evaluate knowledge of subject matter, they practically eliminate writing, they can cover a very wide area in a short time, they are easily and fairly scored.

18. **List the seven advantages of the true-false examination.**
    1. Simplest type of question.
    2. Easy to prepare.
    3. Very easy to score.
    4. Lends itself well to cosmetology.
    5. Easy to understand.
    6. Easy to take.
    7. Covers wide area in short time.

19. **List the three disadvantages of the true-false examination.**
    1. Lacks reliability.
    2. Permits guessing at answers.
    3. Susceptible to ambiguities in statements.

20. **Why are matching questions important in cosmetology teaching?**
    They offer an evaluation of the student's ability to associate and connect important items in cosmetology.

21. **Why are completion questions one of the best of the objective type questions?**
    They are less confusing, fairer because they permit less guessing, less likely to give wrong impressions, are more thorough, and require more thought and ability to answer.

22. **List the nine rules to be followed in the preparation of multiple choice questions.**
    1. Use at least four of five responses to minimize guessing.
    2. All responses (correct or incorrect) must have some degree of plausibility.
    3. A question should not present an absurd situation.
    4. Avoid words which serve as clues.
    5. Avoid "a" or "an" as the final word in the stem.
    6. Each statement should be clear, straightforward and unambiguous.
    7. Each item should present a situation which is possible and likely.
    8. Each item should be stated positively, not negatively.
    9. The items should be realistic and practical.

23. **When are identification tests used in cosmetology?**
    Primarily used in the study of anatomy. Students are required to identify various parts of the body from a drawing or photo on which numbers have been substituted for the anatomical terms.

24. **What are the four general areas to be considered in test construction?**
    1. Type of test or questions.
    2. Arrangement of material.
    3. Construction of questions.
    4. Preparation of examination.

CHAPTER 12

CLASSROOM MANAGEMENT

INTRODUCTION

Good classroom management by the cosmetology teacher is as important as sound teaching techniques. Efficient management in the classroom and in the clinic can make a major contribution to learning effectiveness. The teacher's management skill profoundly influences the entire teaching-learning pattern as follows:

1. It can make the teaching proceed far more smoothly, with a minimum of unpleasant incidents and accidents.
2. It can influence students' attitudes toward safety, neatness, performance standards, use of time, and cooperation with fellow students.

CLASSROOM ATMOSPHERE

It is often difficult to understand why some students are disinterested, noisy, inattentive and unruly with one teacher, but serious, well mannered and attentive with another.

Effective classroom management and control is the sole responsibility of the teacher. It is essential that the teacher control his own reactions in all classroom situations. Students tend to take their cues from the teacher's behavior, and act accordingly. If the teacher fails to approach the work seriously and with a professional attitude and purpose, the students will do likewise. The teacher's own attitudes, classroom habits and teaching conduct are usually clearly reflected in students' attitudes, habits and behavior.

Teachers must at all times maintain complete control of the class. However, the teacher must also establish the atmosphere of the classroom if effective classroom control is to take place. No teacher can control an unusual classroom situation if that teacher conducts himself like one of the students. The teacher's attitude toward day-to-day problems, as well as unusual occurrences, is an important element in classroom management. If the teacher is excitable or lacks maturity and self-control, it is very probable that the entire class will reflect that excitement and lack of control. The teacher's attitudes and actions are usually mirrored by students' reactions.

Other very important requisites for good classroom management are the teacher's skill, knowledge of the subject and a feeling of complete security. The teacher's own confidence, personal ability and feeling encourages the development of a classroom atmosphere conducive to good learning and permits good teacher-student relations to flourish.

There are certain times during the teaching period when it is particularly important for the teacher to be in control of the entire class and to have the attention of all students. The beginning of the period is one of these times.

The manner in which the class is received and in which the work is begun is vitally important on the first day the teacher meets the class and for the first few days thereafter. This also is of considerable importance throughout the course.

First impressions are lasting and the whole attitude of the class toward the teacher and toward the work may be determined by the way in which the class period is started.

It may be advisable for the teacher to give a brief talk in which he introduces himself and writes his name on the chalkboard, so that students may address him properly. He should also outline briefly the aims to be achieved and discuss quickly some of the rules of the school and salon activities.

However, it is a good plan for the teacher to get started on the first lesson of the course as soon as possible on the first day. The first class period should not, however, be a talking period; therefore the instructor should swing into the work as soon as possible.

Each time a class period begins, the teacher should secure the attention of the entire class, to complete as quickly as possible the routine matters of roll call, special announcements and other matters. Then as soon as possible after the beginning routine has been completed the class should be busily engaged in the program of the day.

RECORDS AND REPORTS

Competent instructors should be able to satisfactorily handle all phases of the job. This includes the preparation of all classroom records and reports.

Use special forms to report sickness, requisition and inventory.

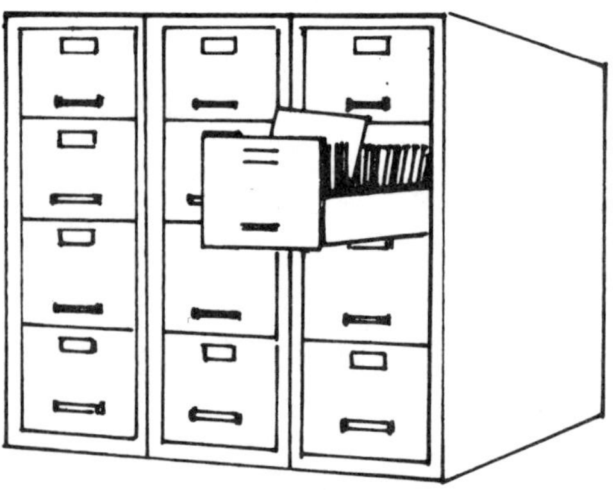

Have a good filing system —keep accurate records.

Cosmetology instructors must keep records for different kinds of reports, such as attendance, excuses for absence and tardiness. Where instructional supplies and materials are involved, requisition and inventory forms are used. Cosmetology instructors must learn early that incomplete and inaccurate records and reports are of no value to anyone and may become costly and wasteful.

Successful cosmetology training requires that instruction be put on an individual basis. This means that students must know what is expected of them throughout the course, that they will progress at their own rate, and that a record will be kept which will clearly show individual achievement. Such records are commonly called "progress charts."

Record in the proper area the total number of hours of training and a rating or grade for each completed unit. Obviously no student should be permitted to advance to a new unit until he has attained a satisfactory achievement standard in previous units. Since the purpose of cosmetology training is to prepare for satisfactory employment, it is essential that employment standards in a beauty salon become training standards in the school.

SAFETY MEASURES

Safety in cosmetology training is not an isolated subject. Safety measures are part of every cosmetology operation and every manual technique taught. At each step in the training program the teacher should stress the applicable safety factors. This helps to develop safety as an attitude and a habit, which will be of vital importance throughout the student's professional career.

To help stress the importance of general safety practices, the teacher should display posters, show films and employ other teaching aids designed to emphasize safety factors.

Human Factors Causing Accidents

1. Ignorance.
2. Carelessness.
3. Fatigue—caused by:
   a) Overwork.
   b) Poor lighting.
   c) Poor ventilation.
   d) Monotony.
4. Wrong attitude toward safety measures.
   a) Teacher's or student's attitudes of careless complacency.

HOUSEKEEPING

Materials, Supplies and Implements

One of the first requirements of good teaching is good housekeeping. Floors cluttered with materials and supplies or hair are not only unsightly but dangerous. Provide storage space for all implements when not in use. At the end of each class period, all implements should be sanitized thoroughly and placed in a dry sanitizer. Stock rooms should have all materials stored safely on shelves or racks. Keep dust and dirt out of corners and hard-to-clean places. Bookshelves and reading tables, displays, bulletin boards, etc., should be arranged neatly. The teacher's desk should set a reasonable example of good housekeeping. When visiting a class, the "housekeeping" catches the eye first.

A place for everything and everything in its place.

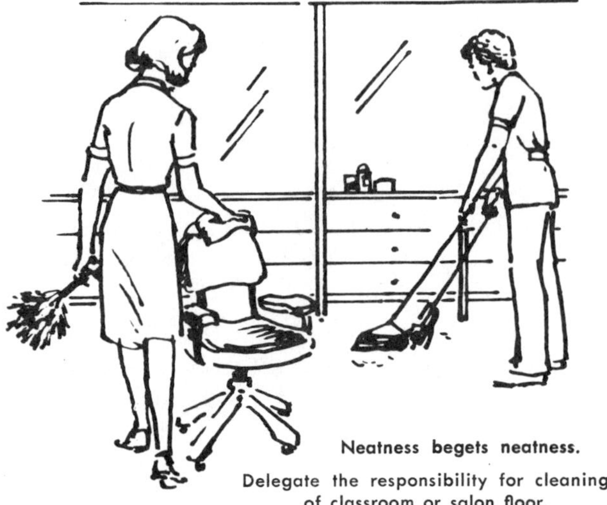

Neatness begets neatness.
Delegate the responsibility for cleaning of classroom or salon floor.

One indication of the instructor's management ability is the amount of waste material and supplies which accumulate. By careful planning, this waste may be kept to a minimum. Beauty salons watch waste carefully and this watchfulness must be drilled into the students as part of their training. The successful cosmetology instructor will plan ahead so that necessary materials and supplies will be available when needed.

Avoid wasting material

Skilled cosmetologists keep their implements in first-class condition. Successful instructors plan their work so that time is allowed for students to keep implements in good operating order. Frequent inspection and repair will catch the little things before they result in greater damage.

Classroom Conditions

The cosmetology instructor is responsible for the physical condition of the classroom.

Check the classroom's temperature and ventilation. High temperatures and stuffy classroooms or work areas are conducive to sleep and a sleeping student gathers little wisdom.

Check the lighting. Both direction and intensity are important in lighting. Keep lights above and behind students. Do not make them face a bright light while they are trying to watch the instructor or writing on the chalkboard.

Aim for undivided attention. You lose every time you try to compete with interruptions.

See that projectors and
slide trays are not
spilled or abused.

Be safety-conscious and avoid accidents.

Check the seating in the classroom. Seating arrangements should be such that all the students can see and hear without straining. Arrange the proper number of chairs in the proper manner. Watch the spacing. Students are more comfortable when they are not crowded too close together. Do not allow the students to lounge or sprawl.

Try to anticipate all problems so that nothing will interfere with the smooth operation of the class.

Check for the comfort and safety of your students in the classroom. Safety rules have resulted in a tremendous reduction of accidents and injuries. The cosmetology instructor must plan to make his classroom and equipment as safe as it is humanly possible. When accidents do occur, they are usually the result of carelessness, either on the part of the instructor, the student or both.

TEACHER'S CHECKLIST FOR CLASSROOM AND CLINIC

Physical Setup

1. Sufficient space for program activities.
2. Adequate lighting.
3. Adequate ventilation.
4. Adequate heat or cooling.
5. Elimination of unnecessary hazards.

Student Work Areas

1. Clear visibility for all students.
2. Cleanliness of student areas.
3. Orderliness of furniture and equipment.
4. Clinic work stations properly set up.
5. Clear aisles.

Storage Areas

1. Efficiently organized — supplies easily accessible.
2. Perpetual and visual inventory.
3. Sufficient shelves, bins, racks to minimize danger of breakage.
4. Systems for controlling flow — avoid "stale" products and spoilage.
5. Maintain protection against theft.

MAINTENANCE OF EQUIPMENT

The maintenance of implements and equipment is of vital importance to the school and in developing a desirable attitude by students.

1. Establish responsibility for certain implements and equipment.
2. Repair and replace broken equipment.
2. Keep equipment clean and polished.
4. Keep equipment in top operating condition.

CLASS SUPERVISION

As a "manager," cosmetology instructors must plan their work, what they will teach, what materials they will use, how to care for their room and equipment, and many other things. The remaining problem is to get the job done in order to carry out the plans which should have been made.

Cosmetology instructors must create an atmosphere which is conducive to serious, thoughtful work and the development of good work attitudes and habits. **There is no shortcut to success.** The sooner students understand this, the sooner they will start to develop proper work attitudes and habits.

Cosmetology instructors should plan their time and distribute it fairly among the students. Some require more help than others. Too often, the better students are neglected. All students should be brought up to an established standard, with some progressing far beyond. Students should be expected to do their best. Successful cosmetology instructors will plan their time to render the maximum help possible to all students.

"A job for everyone and everyone at his job" is a goal which all cosmetology instructors should strive to attain. It can be realized through good class management and supervision. However, it is not good education to create jobs just to keep students busy. Assigned tasks should be constructive, meaningful and contribute definitely to the learning pattern.

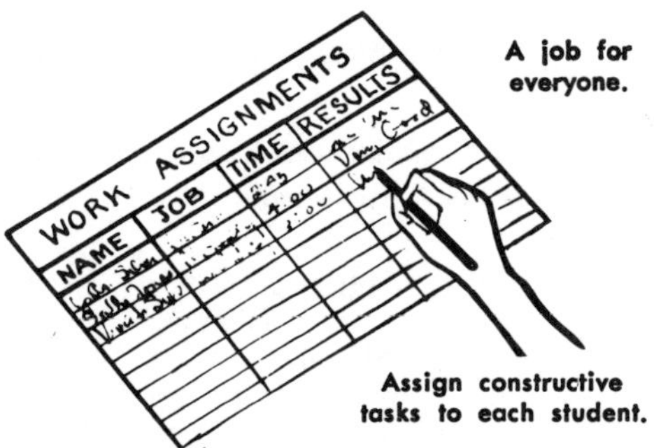

The instructor should circulate among students and be on hand when help is needed. Successful cosmetology instructors get to each student as quickly as possible when help is required. Instructors cannot successfully conduct a class while sitting at a desk in the office. Planning their time properly will enable them to take care of everything, even though it may require hours beyond the regular school day. Successful teaching is hard work, and to remain in the teaching profession calls for much effort.

Discipline. Be firm—but fair—and speak kindly.

CLASSROOM CONTROL

Student Discipline

In cosmetology classes, maintain interest at so high a pitch that discipline is not a problem. Sometimes the class can become so informal that it gets out of control. Every class has at least one individual who lives for the sole purpose of creating disturbance. Students who cannot become interested in the subject or who do not desire to prepare themselves as cosmetologists should be dropped. However, such cases are not common. When found, they should be studied carefully by instructors to be certain that they themselves have not fallen down in their contacts with the students.

Avoid Confusion

Confusion can be avoided by using a simplified step-by-step procedure of presentation of the subject matter. Presenting too much material at any one time will overwhelm the student and only serve to confuse.

STEPS OF LEARNING

Start with the simple and work toward the complex.

It is difficult enough for a student to learn without the instructor complicating the learning process. Give the student a chance to learn. Don't try to cram everything into one lesson. Start with a simple presentation. When the student has a basic understanding of the subject, gradually build learning upon learning until the difficult has been mastered.

Humor

Training is no longer a grim business. Use a joke, a play on words, or a pun when it is effective in directing attention or emphasizing a point.

However, avoid being a comedian. This is not your function.

REVIEW

1. **How does proper teacher management of the classroom influence the teacher-learning pattern?**

   It can make teaching proceed smoothly with a minimum of unpleasant incidents. It can influence students' attitudes.

2. **List five areas where students' attitudes may be affected by proper classroom management.**

   Attitudes toward: (1) safety, (2) neatness, (3) performance standards, (4) use of time and (5) cooperation with fellow students.

3. **Where does the responsibility lie for effective classroom management and control?**

   Solely with the teacher.

4. **How does the teacher's attitude create an atmosphere in the classroom which is conducive to good learning?**

   The teacher's own confidence, personal ability and feeling of security will be reflected in the students' attitudes.

5. **What school task must never be delegates to students?**

   Teachers must be careful not to delegate the job of teaching to the students.

6. **What time during the teaching period is a particularly important one for the teacher to be in control of the entire class, and why?**

   The beginning of the period is an important time for the teacher to make a good first impression on the class.

7. **Why should the teacher get started on the first lesson of the course on the first day?**

   The instructor should swing into the course work as soon as possible.

8. **What type of records must a cosmetology instructor keep?**

   Reports, such as attentance, excuses for absence and tardiness, requisition and inventory forms for instructional supplies and materials.

9. **List the four major human factors which cause accidents.**
   1. Ignorance.
   2. Carelessness.
   3. Fatigue.
   4. Wrong attitude toward safety measures.

10. **What are some of the rules for good housekeeping?**
    1. Floors are kept clean and clear of material.
    2. Storage space is provided for all implements when not in use.
    3. After class, all implements sanitized.
    4. Bookshelves and displays, etc. are arranged neatly.
    5. The teacher's desk sets the example of good housekeeping.

11. **Give one indication of the instructor's management ability.**
    Waste materials are kept to a minimum.

12. **How can wear and tear on equipment be minimized?**
    A skilled cosmetologist keeps equipment in first-class condition. Frequent inspection and repair will be helpful.

13. **How does a good cosmetology instructor take care of the physical condition of the classroom.**
    1. Check on temperature, ventilation and lighting.
    2. Aim for undivided attention.
    3. Check seating arrangements.
    4. Try to anticipate all problems.
    5. Check for safety in the classroom.

14. **List the five factors which must be checked for all classrooms.**
    1. Space.
    2. Lighting.
    3. Ventilation.
    4. Heating and cooling.
    5. Elimination of hazards.

15. **List five factors which must be considered for student work areas.**
    1. Clear visibility.
    2. Cleanliness.
    3. Orderliness.
    4. Proper work stations.
    5. Clear aisles.

16. **List five factors to consider in setting up a storage area.**
    1. Efficiently organized.
    2. Perpetual and visual inventory.
    3. Sufficient shelves, bins, racks.
    4. Control of flow to avoid spoilage.
    5. Protection against theft.

17. **Why is the proper maintenance of implements and equipment of vital importance?**
    It protects the property in the teacher's care and develops a desirable attitude by students.

18. **What type of atmosphere must the instructor create in the classroom?**
    It must be conducive to serious, thoughtful work and the development of good work attitudes and habits.

19. **How should cosmetology instructors plan their time with the students?**
    The time should be scheduled so that all students are brought up to an established standard, with some progressing far beyond.

20. **What is the best method to avoid a discipline problem?**
    Keep interest at such a high pitch that there is no time for behavior problems.

21. **How can the teacher avoid confusion?**
    By concentrating on a step-by-step procedure of presenting the subject matter, from the simple to the complicated.

22. **Is a "light touch" advisable?**
    The instructor with a well-developed sense of humor is a popular one, but comedians cannot function as teachers.

CHAPTER 13

TEACHING ADULTS

INTRODUCTION

For many years, the practice of cosmetology has been one of the most consistent income producing areas open to wage earners. Over an extended period of time, the entire field of cosmetology, with all of its many branches, has been among the top ten industries in the modern economy. It is one vocation which continuously employs several millions of people in its many, diversified segments. Because it is a consistent vocation, because it creates no obstacles for different age brackets and because it is available to all individuals, it offers special inducements to mature people to join its ranks.

The professional practice of cosmetology offers special encouragement to those individuals seeking a means of earning a livelihood and supporting a family. It invites not only the teenager seeking a career, but adults who are looking for a means of earning a continuous income.

The practice of cosmetology also presents special advantages because it is an area where individuals can be trained to serve adequately within a comparatively short period of time. Thus, adults seeking some measure of income security, and who cannot afford to spend years in training, are especially attracted to the practice of cosmetology.

Due to the fact that cosmetology is so appealing, so inviting and so encouraging to adults, it confronts cosmetology education, and educators, with a rather difficult situation. Schools of Beauty Culture are faced with the problem of not only teaching teenagers or teaching adults, but teaching teenagers and adults in the same class, at the same time and under similar conditions.

FORTY AND OVER

Those individuals that are 40 and over may desire to take a Cosmetology Course for the following reasons:

Those women whose children have grown up and/or married, may need a vocation to keep them busy or give them added income.

Those women or men who may not be satisfied with their present vocation, and want to improve their financial position.

Retired women or men who find themselves bored and need a vocation to re-inspire them as useful individuals.

Many men turn to cosmetology when their jobs have phased out.

Barbers who want to learn **Hairstyling.**

Objectives

This chapter is designed to help cosmetology teachers of adult students to gain a better understanding of these students, of their goals, their weaknesses and their problems.

The value of the material depends, to a great degree, upon the teacher's understanding of its purposes and of its limitations.

It is not intended to be a neatly packaged program to be used without careful consideration of a particular situation or of the special needs of any classroom. There is no way of supplying teachers with a magic "pill" or "injection" which will immediately substitute for careful planning and development of a well coordinated educational program.

This information is offered as a guide, which, when used with other teaching guides and materials supplied in the **Cosmetotlogy Teacher-Training Manual,** will be of some assistance in handling and training **adult cosmetology students.**

TEACHING ADULTS IS DIFFERENT

For years, cosmetology teachers have been finding out for themselves, that teaching adults is quite different from teaching teenagers. While, basically, rules, theories and methods of training are the same, other essential factors make teaching adults a different experience.

Ther are a number of reasons why adult students are found to be different. To list just a few differences, teachers find that with adult students:

1. The motivation for learning is different.
2. The teacher lacks authoritarian powers over the adults.
3. Many students are older than the teacher.
4. Adult students have more worldly experience than the teacher.
5. Adult students demand faster and more visual results.
6. Adult students require more careful handling.
7. Adult students require more individualized instruction.
8. Adult students have more outside problems which interfere with training.
9. Adult students may not learn as rapidly.
10. Vision and hearing may not be as good.
11. Adult training is only a part-time activity.

Professional teachers understand that the rules of learning and the methods and techniques of teaching are basically the same for all students. The major differences that exist between teenage and adult students are to be found in the students themselves. While differences do not exist in the methods and techniques of teaching and learning, they do and must exist in the application of those methods and techniques. The greatest success in cosmetology teaching is achieved by those teachers who understand this difference and apply themselves to the special handling required by adult students.

OBSTACLES TO LEARNING

Most adult cosmetology students are self-motivated. They enroll in a school of beauty culture and attend classes because they want to, not because they are forced to. Yet, because of previous experiences, self-created fears, anxieties and doubts, they must be constantly re-motivated.

Many adult students turn to cosmetology after personal failures in other vocations or in other educational efforts. If they had been successful in a previous field of endeavor or had been successful in previous schooling they would not have turned to cosmetology. However, earlier failures have forced them to try beauty culture as a means of earning a livelihood or supporting a family.

As a result of earlier failures many adult students have developed certain feelings of resentment, they have built-in fears of yet another failure. They fear ridicule or exposure to other defeats and as a result, they need constant reassurance. These feelings, emotions and attitudes, in adult students, have created unnatural obstacles to learning. Some of these self-created obstacles are inside the students, and cannot be controlled or affected by the teacher. However, a number of "Obstacles to Learning" may be controlled and their effects minimized by teacher planning, attitudes and professional techniques. Some of the learning obstacles which may be minimized by the instructor are:

1. **Irritation** — Annoying teacher mannerisms, poor teacher/student relations, unreasonable and unnecessary interruptions and delays, can create this type of obstacle.

2. **Confusion** — The teacher may create confusion by making contradictory statements or fail to associate new material with previous learning. The teacher may further create bewilderment by presenting too many ideas at one time, or introducing overly complex material without the proper groundwork.

3. **Fear** — A very common "obstacle in learning", found among adult students, is "fear"; fear of failure, fear of ridicule or fear of being hurt. The teacher can minimize this emotional fear by making sure that the student achieves some success each day.

4. **Boredom** — Adult students easily become bored if they find the work too easy or too hard. The tasks presented should offer a challenge, but must not be beyond the capabilities of the student. The teacher must motivate the student and must constantly develop and maintain student attention and interest.

LEARNING AREAS WHERE ADULTS MAY DIFFER

The professional cosmetology teacher realizes that most individuals, especially adults, differ in their mental capacities as well as in their physical makeup. The good teacher makes provisions for adapting training techniques to best fit the learning capacities of each student.

Following are some of the factors which greatly influence the adult student's ability to learn and which the teacher must recognize and make provision for, in any program of "individualized" instruction.

1. **Concentration** — It is often difficult for an adult, beset with outside problems, to fix his attention on one idea for very long. In order to learn, the student must be encouraged to exercise his "power of concentration" and refocus his attention quickly when the mind wanders.

2. **Intelligence** — Intelligence is the ability to respond quickly and successfully to new situations and subject matter. The intelligence of the student enables him to associate new ideas or material with past experiences and knowledge. While "native" intelligence changes very little throughout a person's lifetime, teachers must recognize its scope and limitations and adapt the teaching program to it.

3. **Interest** — Without student interest, cosmetology teaching is more or less futile. An adult learns well those things and that material in which he has a vital, sustained interest. Teachers find that adults rebel and refuse to learn when they become bored or fail to see the importance of the material in the over-all learning program. It is the teacher's responsibility to arouse and maintain interest at a high level. All material taught must be associated with the course objective and the benefits to the adult students indicated.

4. **Well-Being** — The student's power of concentration and ability to learn is closely associated with his well-being. Mental and physical comfort increases the student's power of concentration. Mental processes are greatly hindered by pain, discomfort, emotional upset such as grief, irritation, anger and worry. The good cosmetology teacher extends every effort to put adult students at ease and tries to maintain a cheerful frame of mind.

5. **Past Experiences** — The adult student usually has a wide range of background experience. The professional teacher recognizes this wide experience and tries to use this experience as a basis for imparting additional knowledge.

6. **Memory** — Any person's ability to remember is extremely important to learning. Some of the factors which influence memory are vividness, uniqueness, frequency and relative importance. Contrary to the belief of some individuals, adults are able to remember, as well as young people. It may take adults a little longer to commit material to memory. However, when they learn the material they retain it longer.

7. **Imagination** — Imagination is the power and ability to form mental images or pictures of things which are not actually present. A good imagination is of vital importance to success as a hairstylist. It is important that the cosmetologist have the ability to visualize the appearance of the style before beginning to execute or create the style. The effective cosmetology teacher stimulates and encourages the use of imagination by all students (especially adults) of cosmetology.

8. **Self Confidence** — A major problem presented by adult students is a lack of self confidence. This lack of confidence had probably been created and developed by failures prior to their enrollment in school. Learning is enhanced and developed and becomes successful when the student believes that he can learn and be successful. The good cosmetology teacher encourages and develops the self confidence of adult students. Teachers should

never, purposely, assign a task which is beyond the ability of the student to perform. Every assignment, every task must be designed to build and develop confidence.

TEACHER-STUDENT RELATIONS

Adult emotions and frustrations are demonstrated in various ways, and it is important that the teacher recognize them for what they are, and be prepared to deal with them. A few emotional signs recognized by teachers are:

1. **Rationalization** — The student finds explanations for actions, which may sound reasonable, but which do not get to the real facts or heart of the matter.

2. **Flight** — The student is always trying to escape from any frustrating situation. Finds excuses for being absent or leaving school.

3. **Resignation** — The student is ready to give up, drop out of school or show little or no interest in the class proceedings.

4. **Projection of Blame** — Always finding someone else or something else to blame for a lack of understanding or any weakness (usually blames the teacher).

5. **Aggressiveness** — The student displays anger, discourtesy, contempt and is loud in accusations; all to cover up some personal weakness or frustration.

The truly professional teacher quickly recognizes emotional reactions in students and is prepared to deal with them. However, educational growth and teaching maturity is demonstrated by the teacher who plans to prevent and eliminate these obstacles to learning. Good teacher-student relationships will usually create a classroom atmosphere which is conducive to good learning and will help minimize or eliminate student emotional displays. There are four basic teacher-student practices which should be followed for good cosmetology education.

1. **The teacher should help students to set reasonable, attainable goals for themselves.** Students are frequently frustrated and completely demoralized when they are unable to attain certain goals, which were completely out of reach before they started. The teacher should add to student satisfaction and confidence by pointing out areas of work where the student does excel. Under all circumstances, goals must be attainable by students.

2. **Guide students to help themselves.** Students may flounder, become frustrated and seek help from the teacher. The teacher must be understanding, and show the student that he is willing and anxious to help, guide and encourage the student to a correct solution of the problem. The teacher must not work out the problem, but guide the student to his own solution. This appeals to the student ego, builds up self-confidence and develops a feeling of accomplishment.

3. **Keep students informed.** Students, especially adults, should be advised of the overall objectives of the entire educational program. They should be familiar with the complete course and understand the relationship of daily work with the long range objectives. They will better understand and participate in all teaching-learning activities if they understand their purpose and importance.

4. **Encourage students to evaluate the teaching programs,** the most effective teaching methods employed and the teacher as a guide and director of learning. Encourage students to make suggestions for the improvement of teaching and learning efficiency.

Above all, and at all times, under every condition, treat each student as an adult and not as a child.

CLASSROOM CONDITIONS

Classroom conditions for a good teaching situation do not just happen. They must be carefully developed, built upon and motivated by the teacher. There are four basic classroom conditions for effective learning. There may be many more, but the four conditions discussed here are essential to all learning.

1. The atmosphere in the classroom must be warm, friendly and free from pressures or threats. Adult students are filled with anxieties, to start with. They are doubtful of their ability to get along with others; they are anxious and uneasy about their ability to learn and to maintain a level of performance. These anxieties become of major concern if they sense a feeling of rejection by the teacher or by the students, or their efforts are accepted coldly and without enthusiasm. If this reaction takes place there is little desire, enthusiasm or effort left for dealing with the problems of learning.

2. Student imagination and experimentation should be encouraged. The warm and friendly atmosphere of the classroom should not become an over-protective blanket which limits and neutralizes the students freedom of thought and expression. Students should be encouraged to experiment with new ideas, new techniques and new methods. It is very important that students be protected against ridicule when mistakes are made during experimentation.

3. Students must be encouraged to gradually become independent of the teacher's learning supports. Students must not become so overly dependent upon the teacher that they are helpless without the teacher. They may also become so independent that they gradually withdraw from teacher, students and even the school itself. For successful learning there must be an effective and continuing interdependent relationship between students and teacher. However, this interdependence must be controlled and limited in order to promote good education.

4. For successful learning to take place there must be effective, three-way communication. There must be open, free and understanding communication from teachers to student, from student to teacher and from student to student. All communication, in the school, must be free from any pressures and restraints which might interfere with the learning process.

CHARACTERISTICS OF ADULT COSMETOLOGY STUDENTS

Before an adult enrolls in a cosmetology school it is certain that he has run a mental and physical self-analysis. Probably, prior to enrolling, the adult student has carefully considered fatigue, the weather, lack of activity, family responsibilities, social demands and personal economic conditions. The student was forced to overcome many mental doubts and phobias before even coming to the school. Considering all of the obstacles to overcome, it would be fair to assume that the student has a very great initial desire to participate. It is strange, therefore, that this same adult is always a potential drop-out.

The following are some of the characteristics formed in many adult cosmetology students:

1. **Lack Self-Confidence.** Because these students, for the most part, have rarely experienced success in earlier schooling, or in their work, or in their social life, they often feel that they are inadequate, unable to learn or to compete.

   Teacher Action. The cosmetology teacher must understand the importance of helping adult students to achieve some success during the first session and, in fact, every session. Standards of achievement must be set which can realistically be achieved by the various students. Adult students should be permitted to set their own pace in approaching classroom tasks.

2. **Fear of School.** Adult students who have had unpleasant experiences with school many times develop a deep-seated fear of school. They fear ridicule for being slower than other students or being rejected by fellow students for emotional or physical reasons. Associated with the fear of school is the fear of public exposure of being wrong and fear of tests.

   Teacher Action. The teacher must avoid, at all costs, the use of ridicule or sarcasm with any student. It is impossible to overemphasize the importance of the necessity for warm, uncritical acceptance of adult students. By giving praise for work the students have done correctly, rather than emphasizing errors, the teacher can soften the student's supersensitive fear of making mistakes and being exposed to ridicule. "Accentuate the Positive" should be the daily slogan of all teachers of adults.

3. **Weak Motivation.** Motivation of adult cosmetology students is low because of their life history of failure in previous pursuits. They are easily discouraged, and frequently show an attitude of almost complete resignation because of repeated failures. Most adults enrolled in cosmetology schools have one thing in common: They don't have to be in school and may leave at any time. This lack of a compulsory aspect makes the teaching of adults a direct challenge to the cosmetology teacher to motivate and interest such students. This is often true of adult cosmetology students who have built-in biases against schools and studies. If the teaching techniques employed are out-moded or boring, if the classes drag or if the teacher does not attract and maintain the interest of all his students, he may soon find many adult students "dropping-out".

   Teacher Action. It is essential that the teacher recognize the importance of motivation and to bring motivating factors into the learning process. It is motivation which makes the student want to know, to understand, to believe, to act, to gain knowledge or a skill. Professional teachers use many different methods to motivate their students and are constantly on the look-out for new ideas. Some motivation factors are: the need for financial security, the need for a new field of interest, the need for recognition and acceptance, the need for self-esteem and the need for conformity.

4. **Feeling of Helplessness.** A student's thinking processes are blocked and retarded when he doubts his own ability to learn. As a result of these doubts, feelings of anxiety and helplessness are developed. This feeling of helplessness is indicated by acts of hostility, continuous misunderstandings, absence of participation and attention, procrastination and inability to work alone.

Teacher Action. It is important that the teacher recognize the signs of helplessness indicated above. Every effort must then be expended in an effort to build-up a feeling of self-confidence and a development of student ability to learn.

5. **Hostility Toward Authority.** Many adult students have had some unhappy experiences with the representatives of authority, as indicated by a "boss", earlier teachers or some other person symbolizing authority. As a result, any authority figure, in this case the teacher, arouses either hidden or open hostility.

   Teacher Action. The teacher of adults must project himself as a friend and guide rather than as a symbol of authority. This hostility and suspicion cannot be overcome quickly, but with patience and serious effort the student will gradually become reassured and responsive.

6. **Unacceptable Behavior.** Because of earlier hurts and damage, many adult students reveal their resentment and hostility by using unacceptable language or behaving in offensive ways. If this action develops a critical attitude by the teacher, either open or silent, a serious barrier may be set up between the teacher and student. It alienates the student, not only from the teacher, but also from the entire program.

   Teacher Action. The teacher must look for the positive qualities and potentials in adult students. Instead of being repelled by and antagonistic to the shortcomings of such students, the teacher must concentrate on the fact that, in spite of these handicaps, they could develop into successful students and cosmetologists.

7. **"Live from Day to Day" Attitude.** Many adult students have little concept of long range planning. The idea of doing something or learning something now and not receiving any benefits for months to come is incomprehensible to them.

   Teacher Action. These students can only be motivated by immediate results. The student must achieve some success each day. Assign tasks within the students capabilities so that immediate success is evident.

8. **Reticence.** Many adult students find it difficult to express their feelings, discuss their needs or to stand up for their rights. Their silence in answering questions does not necessarily mean that they do not know the answers. In many cases silence means that these students may be shy and reluctant to speak before a group. This silence may indicate that they were hurt in previous experiences of answering or speaking up.

   Teacher Action. It might be wise to break the class up into small groups or to deal with these students individually until such time as they realize that speaking up in the group is not a terrible experience. Many of these students will really open up and talk in small groups.

9. **Need for Respect and Status.** Using the student's first name or nickname tends to arouse antagonism and resentment in adult students. The adult student resents being treated as a child and wants the dignity and respect to which he feels he is entitled.

   Teacher Action. The teacher should use the more formal title of Mr., Mrs., or Miss until such time as confidence and warmth are clearly established.

At some future time a discussion could be developed where each student could indicate how he should like to be addressed.

10. **Tendency to Lose Interest.** Adult students lose interest and often drop out of classes which do not fulfill their needs. When signs of apathy appear the teacher must use all of his teaching skill, patience and understanding to handle the problem. The teacher must discover the cause of the difficulty and take immediate steps to resolve the problem.

    Teacher Action. Many times the teacher can change the situation by steps taken in the classroom. The teacher should also attempt to have a personal discussion with the students and perhaps find a solution. Some of the measures to be considered by the teacher are:

    (a) Survey of the class programs and the study of methods and techniques employed may reveal the weakness.

    (b) Discussion of the immediate and long term objectives of the program in order to involve the students in the program.

    (c) The teacher and students should discuss the standards to be set, exercising great care to make sure that the standards are attainable by the students.

    (d) The teacher may find it necessary to enlist the aid of a school counselor or administrator to solve some of the more difficult situations.

    (e) Private tutoring, by the teacher, very often straightens out the student, eliminates the problems and reverses the possibility of dropping out.

QUALITIES FOR SUCCESSFUL TEACHING OF ADULTS

Adult cosmetology students do not learn as a result of what the teacher does, but rather as a result of what the teacher gets them to do. Teachers must have special characteristics and qualities in order to teach adults successfully. Some of these qualities are:

1. **Flexibility** — The teacher must be flexible enough to be ready to change tactics and methods if the technique employed is not right.

2. **Creativity** — The teacher should be able to introduce new methods or new techniques in development of a subject.

3. **Forward Looking** — The teacher should be able to anticipate results of school activities and impart to students the anticipated and expected results of their efforts.

4. **Perceptivity** — The teacher must be able to see the practical application of student efforts. If the teacher is able to anticipate successful results, then students can be imbued with a feeling of accomplishment and encouraged to proceed toward their objectives.

5. **Understanding** — The teacher must understand the needs and fears of adult students. The teacher must sense when students are in trouble and react to ease the tensions and handle the problems.

6. **Sense of Humor** — The teacher must have the ability to see the funny side of a situation. The teacher's sense of humor can maintain the equilibrium of the classroom and student balance.

7. **Versatility** — Many adult students have a short attention span and require a variety of short tasks or facts to maintain their interest and participation.

8. **Analytical** — The teacher must be able to quickly observe and evaluate the adult students weaknesses, failures and strengths, without the students being aware of the fact that they are being evaluated.

9. **Patient** — Adult students are usually slower to do a job or master some facts. The teacher must not lose patience or even let the student feel that he is delaying the class or is too slow.

10. **Optimistic** — The teacher must always expect that results will improve and must never give up. The teacher must impart this feeling to students and prevent them from becoming discouraged. The teacher must develop the feeling that with time, the students will pick-up the subject matter and attain school and personal objectives.

HINTS FOR TEACHING ADULTS

An important part of the cosmetology teacher's job is to keep students interested and to create and develop a sincere desire to learn and become proficient in the practice of beauty culture. In dealing with adult students, school administrators have found that if teachers do not immediately interest these adults and keep them involved they will drop-out of school. In fact if adults stay in school for the first month or six weeks they will rarely drop-out after that time.

It is, therefore, essential that, from the first day, teachers must develop an interesting and exciting learning atmosphere, if they wish to retain their students.

Following are a few hints to cosmetology teachers of how best to handle and deal with adult students.

1. If the cosmetology training program is to be a truly living and constructive process, the teacher must recognize that individual differences exist among students. No two students learn at the same rate.

The cosmetology teacher with adult students who recognizes this fact and plans the training program accordingly, will help each student to learn as much as he is capable of learning. The teacher will also avoid a great deal of student unhappiness, frustration and perhaps drop-out.

2. Cosmetology teachers must learn quickly that if the training program and its contents are to be meaningful it must be related to deep and important needs and objectives of the adult student. If it is not, the student feels that he is wasting time and leaves the school.

3. Adult students learn best by participating actively, rather than simply hearing or reading words. The teaching program must be planned for maximum student participation, in order to attain measurable success.

4. In dealing with adult students, the successful cosmetology teacher plans for a variance in techniques and methods, which are necessary to capture the particular mood of the class for the best learning experience for the topic at hand. The responsibility of the teacher lies in the careful thought which must be given to the possible types of activities in which the class may be involved, at various points in the class presentation.

This does not mean that the teacher must plan every step and every move in the entire period. However, the teacher must be cognizant of the possible need for a shift in the planned techniques or methods of the presentation. The teacher must be flexible enough to make the necessary changes, as required, to meet the class needs.

5. The teacher must provide for a natural fluidity of movement in the classroom activities. Successful training of adult cosmetology students requires that students be completely involved in the training program. There must be provision made in the planning for a periodic "change of pace" to prevent growing boredom and loss of interest.

6. Interesting and worthwhile adult cosmetology education depends almost entirely on the variety and usefulness, to the student, of the teaching method used. Students can be caught up in the teacher's enthusiasm and become absorbed in every detail of cosmetology knowledge. Or they can yawn, stare out of the window, and get that glassy-eyed look that means absolute boredom. By applying imagination and variety in the methods of presentation, classes can be made to have a never-ending air of growth and excitement which means interested students and good learning.

7. Successful cosmetology teachers with adult students have found that it is important to be friendly and noncritical. In a strict and stern classroom atmosphere adult students wither and retreat. They hide their individual skills and abilities, for fear of ridicule or rejection, because they have experienced this type of treatment before. For success with these students it is necessary that they be constantly encouraged. Praise their successes, minimize their failures, boost their self-respect and give them greater confidence. Above all, be **patient.**

REVIEW

1. **Why does cosmetology offer special advantages to adults seeking a new means of earning a livelihood?**

   They can be trained within a comparatively short time. They can find some means of financial security.

2. **List the eleven ways in which adult students differ.**
   1. Different motivation
   2. Teachers lack authority over adults
   3. Students older
   4. Students have more worldly experience
   5. Adult students demand faster and more visible results
   6. Adult students require careful handling
   7. Require more individualized instruction
   8. Have more outside problems which may interfere
   9. May not learn as rapidly
   10. Vision and hearing not as good
   11. Learning only a part time activity

3. **How do the Rules of Learning and Methods and Techniques of Teaching compare in teaching adults and teenagers?**

   They are basically the same.

4. **Where do the differences exist in the teaching of adults?**

   In the application of methods and techniques and the handling of students.

5. **What are the four basic obstacles to adult learning?**
    1. Irritation
    3. Fear
    2. Confusion
    4. Boredom

6. **List the eight learning areas where adult students differ.**
    1. Lack of concentration
    2. Sometimes limited intelligence
    3. Lack of interest
    4. Health
    5. Bad past-experiences with learning
    6. Slower to remember
    7. Slower imagination
    8. Lack of self-confidence

7. **List the five emotional signs which indicate adult students problems and frustrations.**
    1. Rationalization
    2. Flight
    3. Resignation
    4. Projection of blame
    5. Aggressiveness

8. **What are the four practices which should be followed to develop a good teacher-student relationship?**
    1. Teacher should help student set reasonable, attainable goals.
    2. The teacher should guide the student to help themselves.
    3. Students should be kept informed of programs and course objectives.
    4. Students should be encouraged to evaluate the program and their own progress.

9. **What are the four basic classroom conditions for effective learning?**
    1. Warm, friendly classroom atmosphere
    2. Encourage student imagination and experimentation
    3. Encourage student independence from teacher supports
    4. Effective communication in classroom

10. **List six objections considered by adults before enrolling in a beauty school.**
    1. Fatigue
    2. Weather
    3. Inertia
    4. Family responsibilities
    5. Social demands
    6. Economic conditions

11. **List the 10 special characteristics found in adult beauty culture students.**
    1. Lack of self-confidence
    2. Fear of school
    3. Weak motivation
    4. Feeling of personal helplessness
    5. Hostility toward authority
    6. Unacceptable personal behavior

7. Live from day-to-day attitude
8. Reticence
9. Need for respect and status
10. Tendency to lose interest

12. List the ten qualities required for the successful teaching of adults.

1. Flexibility
2. Creativity
3. Forward looking
4. Perceptivity
5. Understanding
6. Sense of humor
7. Versatility
8. Analytical
9. Patient
10. Optimistic

13. When do most drop-outs take place among adult students?

Within the first month or six weeks.

14. How can a teacher minimize drop-outs?

By developing an interesting and exciting learning atmosphere.

15. List seven hints for handling adult cosmetology students.

1. Provide for individual differences.
2. Relate program to important student needs and objectives.
3. Have students participate actively.
4. Vary techniques and methods.
5. Provide for fluidity of movement in classroom activities.
6. Use a variety of methods to keep student involved.
7. Be friendly and non-critical.

CLASSROOM PROBLEMS IN COSMETOLOGY SCHOOLS

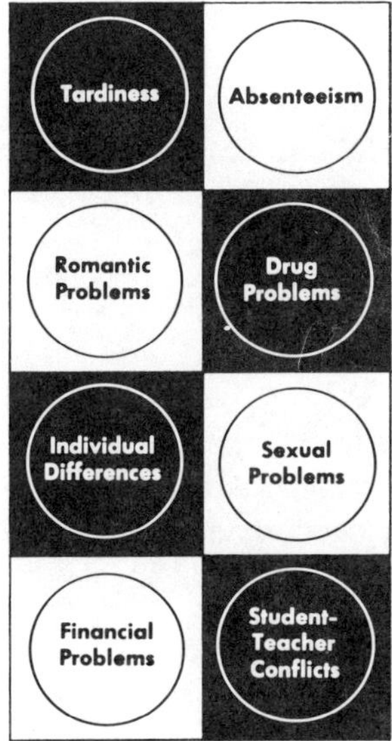

INTRODUCTION

In its most modern and inclusive sense, discipline in the beauty school means preparing students for a useful life in the cosmetology "world of work". The purpose of discipline is to help students acquire theoretical knowledge, technical skills, working habits, professional interests and ethical ideals which are designed for the well-being of himself, his fellow cosmetologists, the entire practice of cosmetology and for society as a whole.

It should be clearly understood that the best results are obtained when students are kept busily engaged in worthwhile learning.

Discipline which is enforced by threats or force serves only to destroy rapport between the teacher and the students. This type of discipline does little to establish any worthwhile training or to develop any realistic habits of self-discipline in the salon after entering the "world of work." The great challenge to the cosmetology teacher lies in intelligent study and control of those elements which may and often do develop into disciplinary problems.

The personal role of the teacher, in the classroom, is of paramount importance in maintaining the equilibrium and emotional balance of his students. By the very nature of his position, the teacher is a parent figure, an object of identification, a target for confidence, aggression, displaced hostility, and a haven for emotional support. Teachers establish and maintain their effectiveness as professionals only as long as they remain warmly human, sensitive to the personal needs of their students and skillful in establishing effective teacher-student relations.

The well-adjusted, mature teacher, who demonstrates his professional competency by establishing a favorable rapport with his students, may exert a very positive influence on their emotional well-being. It is especially important that teachers recognize the fact that in order to do an effective job of teaching, they must first gain a better understanding of the individual student and of his everyday problems.

The cosmetology teacher is faced with the additional perplexing problem of dealing with various age groups (each with its own unique problems) all combined into a single heterogeneous class. It is the responsibility of the teacher to deal with both group and individual problems and still maintain a classroom atmosphere which is conducive to effective teaching and learning.

Individual student problems must be handled judiciously and diplomatically, in order to avoid upsetting the equilibrium of the student and to prevent disruption in the classroom. In an effort to maintain a student-centered and constructively oriented cosmetology training atmosphere, the professional cosmetology teacher makes a special effort to solve or at least to minimize the adverse effects of student problems.

The professional teacher should realize that both the teacher and the student must feel at ease with each other as the first step in the learning pattern. He must develop the appropriate classroom climate before any teaching or learning can take place. Thereafter, as a good teacher, he maintains a position as a sensitive observer, flexible in his own thinking and in his own responses, prepared to react to the great variety of personality and behavioral difficulties which do appear all too frequently.

Considering the foregoing, it is reasonable to assume that there must be a sense of rapport, that is, a relationship between teacher and students marked by harmony and accord. Following are a few ideas to be employed by cosmetology teachers in order to create the proper atmosphere for learning.

1. The teacher must sincerely believe in the cosmetology training he is giving and of its value to the students.

2. The teacher must command the respect of his students. Not the respect born of hard fisted tyranny, but respect earned by professional leadership.

3. The teacher must be thoroughly familiar with the psychology of learning, in order that he may practice the principles of good teaching.

4. The teacher must be willing to do everything possible to foster and encourage the development of each student as a skilled cosmetologist.

5. The teacher must make specific and complete preparation for the total teaching program and for each individual session.

6. The teacher must indoctrinate the students with the importance of each subject to the long and short term objectives of the teaching program.

7. The teacher must make certain that the physical facilities of the classroom as well as the psychological atmosphere are conducive to good learning.

8. The teacher must employ a variety of activities and methods in order to maintain student interest and motivation.

In spite of the fact that all elements and student needs have been taken into consideration and provided for, day-to-day problems are sure to appear. Following are just a few of such problems and one possible way of handling them. It should be noted that each teacher may have his own way of handling such difficulties which may be equal to or even more effective than those presented.

TARDINESS

One perplexing situation often facing the cosmetology teacher is the problem of habitual tardiness. This is a classroom condition where one or two students are consistently late in coming to school.

While this may seem to be a rather innocuous and harmless practice it may lead to very serious classroom problems. If this situation is permitted to continue, it could lead to a serious disruption in classroom control and a serious weakening in student morale.

No student should be permitted to disrupt a lesson or interrupt the continuity of the teaching program by arriving late. It can be very distracting and annoying to a teacher, who is trying hard to present subject matter in an interesting and informative manner, to have his trend of thought or projection broken or interrupted by a tardy student.

The effect upon the rest of the class can be truly destructive. Class morale can be adversely influenced by the actions of habitual late students. Students begin to wonder and ask questions as to whether special privileges and considerations are being extended to one or two students. If these students are permitted to come late why not others? Why not skip classes completely? Thus, a finely organized and smoothly functioning class can become completely demoralized.

Continued lateness is most detrimental to the welfare of the offending students. These students soon develop very poor habits of punctuality which will inevitably hurt them in the beauty salon. In spite of the fact that they obviously feel that they can safely miss part of the teacher's presentation, they often miss important subject matter to their own learning detriment.

This continuous tardiness often reveals a great deal about the student's attitude toward the teacher. It is an indication of a negative reaction toward the teacher and even shows a disrespectful attitude, which no teacher should be required to tolerate.

In the case of adult students, continuous tardiness usually shows an "I don't care," attitude which may, unless reversed, lead to the student finally dropping out of school.

Possible Solutions

A private discussion with a habitually tardy student may do a great deal to remedy the situation.

It is advisable to impress upon the student the importance of punctuality in the beauty salon. It is essential that the teacher emphasize the necessity of keeping appointments and developing good patron relations, in order to achieve success as a cosmetologist.

Discuss the importance of each member of the salon staff in accepting his share of the responsibility for developing a smoothly functional, professional cosmetology operation. Indicate that the irresponsibility of one member of the staff reflects on the entire staff.

This sense of personal responsibility must be developed in the schools as an essential part of the training program. Habits of punctuality must be developed in the school.

In all fairness, it is wise that the teacher analyze his own performance to see whether or not he is a contributing factor to the problem of tardiness. The teacher, of course, must serve as an example to the entire class by, at all times, being punctual himself.

The teacher must ask himself:

1. Whether his presentation is so dull and uninteresting that the student is seeking any excuse to miss as much as possible.

2. Whether he has failed to impress upon the students the importance of the subject matter in achieving his short and long range goals.

3. Whether he has failed to properly motivate the student as to the importance of the material presented.

Take Positive Action

The teacher, however, must also take some positive action to minimize the problem of consistent student tardiness. The following suggestions may help to alleviate this problem:

1. Try to build some special interest into the subject matter to be covered each day.

2. Develop some student motivating factors so that they recognize the importance of each lesson.

3. Try to build some excitement into each day's lesson, so that students look forward eagerly to each class.

4. Try to make the start of each lesson an important and interesting experience.

5. Do not interrupt or repeat material for the benefit of late students.

Summary

The teacher should bear in mind that open communications with the student may be the key to the solution of the tardiness problem. A complete understanding and a frank discussion often results in a satisfactory ending to the difficulty.

In the most extreme cases of tardiness, where the student resists all of the teacher's efforts, there may be only one solution, that of dismissal. No school administrator wants to dismiss a student, however, it may be necessary to do so in order to protect the attitude and morale of the entire class. It should be understood, however, that dismissal is the final action when all other efforts have failed.

ABSENTEEISM

A school problem which is very similar to that of habitual tardiness is that of chronic absenteeism.

This problem, if allowed to continue, could result in the complete destruction of the student's continuity of learning. It impairs the student's ability and opportunity to acquire necessary cosmetology knowledge and/or technical skills.

The development of erratic attendance habits inevitably result in the formation of very poor working habits in the salon. This type of activity "builds in" almost certain failure in the cosmetology "world of work."

In dealing with absenteeism, teachers must be especially alert to prevent the creation of a classroom situation which unfairly affects other students. This situation is created when absentees interrupt the continuity of the learning program by trying to make-up lost work.

Teachers could and should make a positive effort, in the orientation of the students, to anticipate the problem of absenteeism. On the very first day of school students should be indoctrinated and strongly impressed with the importance of good attendance habits. Perhaps this may have some positive effect to minimize or even prevent the occurrence of chronic absenteeism.

Chronic Absenteeism

Studies of the problem of chronic absenteeism have indicated that there are many different reasons which create this condition. Some of these reasons are student motivated and some of them are caused by the teacher or the school.

The most common causes of chronic absenteeism are:

A. **Student Created:**
   1. Lack of interest in the subject of cosmetology.
   2. Personal health problems of the student.
   3. A completely irresponsible student attitude.
   4. Family problems interfering with proper schooling.
   5. Financial problems.
   6. Student fatigue or boredom.
   7. Outside activities which interfere with school attendance.
   8. Change of interest.
   9. Student laziness.
   10. Student discouraged by difficulty in keeping up with work.

B. **Teacher-School Created:**
   1. Teacher makes class presentation dull and uninteresting.
   2. Lack of teacher cooperation and coordination which tends to confuse and discourage students.
   3. Teacher failure to motivate students.
   4. Disorganized teaching — lacking in reason and continuity.
   5. Creation of a tense, nervous classroom atmosphere.
   6. Lack of teacher enthusiasm.
   7. Lack of teacher control, inadequate supervision.
   8. Dull and dreary classrooms which are not conducive to good learning.
   9. Lack of a planned schedule of training.
   10. Teacher assignment of too many housekeeping chores, unrelated to learning cosmetology.

Possible Solutions

The first essential in trying to resolve a problem of continued absenteeism is to have a private conference with the offending student. At this meeting the teacher must exert every personal effort to gain the confidence of the student. If this is accomplished the problem and the reasons for it may be revealed and a possible solution developed.

The teacher may be completely surprised by the revelation that he or the school have been creating the problem. Once the facts of school or teacher failure are revealed, immediate steps can be taken to improve the situation. Not only the absentee student will benefit but the entire teaching/learning program could be improved for the benefit of all.

With reference to student oriented problems the teacher may have a more difficult situation. The important thing, at this moment, is to identify or isolate the problem. Solutions are much easier when a complete understanding of the matter is developed.

The teacher should explain to the student the importance of each lesson in achieving his short and his long range goals. He (the teacher) must exert every effort to motivate the student and develop a sincere desire for learning cosmetology. He should emphasize the fact that the study of cosmetology offers the opportunity of creating a lifetime career.

A student with any kind of a health problem must be advised to see his personal physician without delay. The health problem is of extreme importance and must be followed-up by both teacher and administration.

The student with outside, family or financial problems presents totally different conditions. The teacher must obtain the complete confidence of the student before any attempt at advising him is made.

If he has financial problems, arrange a conference with the Director of the school. Perhaps some Student Aid program can be arranged to meet his needs. It might even be possible to arrange for part-time employment in order that the financial burden be eased.

The handling of other personal problems must be done on a completely individual basis. No general rules can be set down for each crisis. They must be dealt with discreetly, avoiding any embarrassment to the student, always maintaining his dignity and self-esteem. A sincere effort by the teacher may help to change an absentee student into one who is interested, motivated and sincere.

When all teacher and administrative efforts have failed, it might be wise to encourage the student to find some other area of endeavor which might be more to his interest and liking.

PROBLEMS WITH ROMANTIC STUDENTS

It may very well be that "All the World Loves A Lover." But, this axiom certainly does not apply in the classroom.

Students who have been bitten by the "love bug" are usually more of an annoyance than they are a serious problem. The student "lovers" are often so involved and concerned with each other that they are oblivious to those around them. However, they could create a situation and present a problem, harmful to the rest of the class, as well as to themselves, and which is detrimental to educational progress.

This delicate situation must be handled with tact and extreme care. The teacher's first concern is the welfare of the entire class; however, he cannot make the "lovers" a target for the ridicule and mockery of fellow students. It is also obvious that the teacher cannot permit the situation to continue if it is disrupting the entire teacher-learning pattern.

The teacher must also proceed very cautiously because drastic action could "martyrize" the "lovers," arouse student sympathy and make the teacher appear to be an unfeeling villain. Any attempt to embarrass the offending students could "boomerang" and destroy the teacher/student rapport with the rest of the class.

Possible Solutions

The first procedure the teacher should follow is to try to solve the situation without any open, aggressive action. If at all possible, the "lovers" should be separated into different classes, classrooms and clinic sessions.

If this action is possible, it may solve the problem quietly and efficiently. It would provide both students with a better learning situation. It would also relieve the class of the annoyance or embarrassment of being subjected to their distracting activities.

If it is not possible to place the two students in different classes, it is advisable to, at least, seat them in different sections of the classroom.

However, if the teacher's most discreet and diplomatic efforts to separate the two students are ineffective, it will become necessary to call them into a private conference.

This private meeting should be scheduled at a time which does not interfere with the class, which is convenient to the parties, and is not embarrassing to the students.

Discuss with the students, as diplomatically as possible, the problems which their antics are creating. Indicate that you, the teacher, are, personally, very much in favor of their romance. However, the school was not the place for their romantic affair. Explain that their activities were:

a) unfair to their classmates, because they were a distracting influence and upset the decorum of the class;

b) unfair to each other, because they made their own learning situation very diffiicult, in fact, almost intolerable; and

c) unfair to themselves, because they were jeopardizing their future happiness and well-being by destroying their opportunity to prepare themselves for successful future careers.

This conference should solve the problem and influence the students' future classroom conduct.

STUDENTS WITH SEXUAL PROBLEMS

One of the most difficult, most sensitive and yet most annoying problems for a teacher to deal with, is that of students with sexual problems.

Cosmetology students, as a rule, are old enough to be subjected to all of the problems of sexual maturity. They are also, for the most part, adult enough to handle them personally and without school entanglements. However, occasionally a problem with sexually involved students is forced upon the teacher, regardless of how reluctant he may be to deal with it.

Students with sexual problems require very special and very careful handling. Neither the teacher nor the school can afford to ignore the problem, hoping it will solve itself with time, because if it is known to the teacher, it is no secret to other students.

It can become the subject of much student gossip and in turn lead to classroom disruption and demoralization.

The school cannot refuse to become involved because the very fact that the implicated student or students are in attendance affects the reputation of the school.

The problem must be faced and dealt with, but with great sensitivity and delicacy.

Under no circumstance should the teacher ever bring the matter up in the classroom. An accusation could bring an infuriated parent or guardian to the school. It might even lead to a lawsuit against the school. Also, it could completely demoralize and destroy the students involved and disrupt the entire class.

Tact, sensitivity and discretion are absolutely essential in resolving this type of problem.

Possible Solutions

The teacher has several options open for dealing with the involved students. No solution is completely satisfactory, however, as educators and counselors, teachers must make every effort to advise, counsel and guide all students.

The first option open is to try the practice of separation. If possible separate the offending students, keeping them in separate classrooms, separate clinic areas and even different hours.

If this does not work a private meeting with the students becomes mandatory. First point out to the students how unfair their actions are to themselves and to their fellow students. Try to prevail upon them to exercise good sense, good manners and mature judgment. Explain that their actions reflect adversely upon themselves and upon the reputation of the school.

Insist that they must keep their personal activities and morals completely separate from the school.

Finally, if all other efforts fail, it may be necessary to ask the students to resign. If this fails, expel the students from the school.

STUDENTS WITH HOME PROBLEMS

It is unreasonable to expect that students with serious problems involving their families or their personal relations with their families will be able to function with maximum interest and efficiency.

Cosmetology teachers sometimes notice that a student who has usually been completely cooperative and deeply involved suddenly seems to lose interest and become discouraged . The student appears to have become demoralized and despondent. There is a complete loss of concentration and his thoughts seem to be far away from the class work. Such students seem to be emotionally upset and apt to create a scene at the slightest provocation.

The competent teacher realizes that something important is amiss with this usually capable student and his actions could be a real test of his own professionalism. If the teacher is to be helpful, he must first discover the reasons for the student's conduct before even attempting to find a solution to the problems.

The student must be handled with great sensitivity and sympathetic understanding. The teacher must be extremely careful not to give the impression that he is "snooping" into the student's personal life. However, he could diplomatically encourage the student to confide in him and relate his problems.

Many times, under these circumstances, the student will tell the teacher of the personal home problem that is disturbing him so much that it makes it difficult for him to concentrate on his work.

At this time the teacher must exercise great patience and kindness. Often he can be helpful simply by listening attentively and sympathetically. On occasion, the teacher can try to help the student to isolate or identify the problem. It is quite probable that clearly identifying the source of the trouble can suggest a reasonable solution.

However, few teachers are really qualified to give advice about personal problems. After helping the student to isolate and identify the problem, it is advisable to refer him to trained and qualified advisers. There are a number of such qualified individuals to whom the student could be referred; among them being, the student's religious adviser, the student's physician, or (if one is available) a trained counselor in the school.

Whatever action is taken, the teacher must never give advice he is not qualified to give. He must avoid, at all times, any semblance of "snooping" or "digging" into the student's personal life.

STUDENTS WITH FINANCIAL PROBLEMS

In spite of the fact that a number of financial aid programs are available to cosmetology students, we sometimes find students with severe financial difficulties.

These problems often reveal themselves on the "barometers" indicating student troubles.

1. A student, usually alert and deeply involved, suddenly finds it difficult to concentrate on school work.
2. A steady, competent student seems to become demoralized and discouraged.
3. An able, well-adjusted student begins to talk about "dropping-out."
4. A normally quiet student becomes fretful and unusually irritable.
5. A student seems to be lost in a morass of deep thought, far removed from immediate classroom work.
6. A good student suddenly seems to lose the ability to perform properly, and, for no apparent reason, his work standards fall off and become of unacceptable quality.

The foregoing are only a few of the signs which may indicate that trouble is brewing and that the student is in some kind of difficulty.

Possible Solutions

The professional teacher does not disregard the signs and leave the student to "sink or swim" on his own. He arranges a private conference with the student, in an effort to find out exactly what is wrong.

At this conference, the teacher's first action must be to establish a relationship of understanding, trust and confidence with the student. If the student then responds to the teacher's sincere concern and sympathy, and tells of his financial troubles, the teacher is at least aware of the problem. He, the teacher, should listen very intently and carefully and try to determine the exact nature and seriousness of the problem.

Sometimes the problem is very temporary and can be alleviated by pointing out how to "tighten up" on current outlays and expenditures. Sometimes helping the student to organize and develop a proper budget may solve the entire matter to the student's complete satisfaction.

However, at times the problem is so severe that it threatens the student's ability to continue in school. The student requires more than sympathy and temporary assistance. The student desperately needs permanent help if he is to stay in school.

Under these conditions, the best course is to arrange a conference with the Director of the school. He is, or should be, thoroughly familiar with the many State and Federal Student Financial Aid Programs. Cosmetology students have available to them a number of such educational assistance plans.

The conference with the Director should identify some plan or plans which could solve the student's financial problem and enable him to continue in school. With the cooperation of all parties, the Director, the teacher and the student, the selected plan should be implemented without delay. The necessary documents or applications for financial aid should be prepared and submitted as soon as possible.

Although, at times, the temptation may be very great, the teacher should, under no circumstances, lend any money to the student. Such action, at best, can only be temporary help and does not solve the problem. However, it does destroy the objective relationship established between a student and the teacher and destroys a proper teacher-learning atmosphere.

INDIVIDUAL DIFFERENCES

Cosmetology teachers are constantly faced with the problem of trying to teach students with varying backgrounds and various differences in ability, interest and emotional reaction. Progressive activity and real participation cannot be obtained from students, unless provision is made to accommodate these individual differences. No teacher can, realistically, expect that every student will progress at the same speed, and with the same success, in the learning program.

Although the teacher's classroom presentation is usually directed toward the average student, learning problems develop as a result of individual student differences. While the term "individual differences" may relate to many areas of a physical, emotional or mental nature, a teacher is primarily interested in those differences which affect the rate of learning. These may include differences in emotional reaction, differences in interest, and differences in learning ability. The most successful teachers are those who try to reach individual students in accordance with their needs.

While individual students all try equally hard, they may show very different degrees of progress. A good teacher appreciates both honest effort and high achievement, and therefore expends extra effort to bring along slower students.

Slow Learners

Though there seems to be much misunderstanding about the term "slow learner," it is sufficient to say that these students take longer to grasp the material being taught. It is quite possible that slow learners grasp the ideas, concepts and directions completely, once they learn them. However, they perform at a much slower pace and their learning takes longer.

Many students are trying desperately to achieve some sense of identity, self-worth and accomplishment. Such students, if not encouraged and provided with the opportunity to learn, soon feel bewildered, frustrated and discouraged. Their reaction could very well be a complete loss of interest, emotional upset and actually dropping out of school. The competent, cosmetology teacher plans carefully to provide for the proper training of those students who are unable to keep up with the rest of the class.

Possible Solutions

The keys for dealing with slow learners effectively are: patience, understanding and a simple, direct classroom presentation.

Sometimes by using audio-visual aids on an individual instructional basis, the student can learn the required subject-matter while the rest of the class goes ahead. Cosmetology is the sort of field which especially lends itself to this type of teaching, because such a large part of the time is spent in practice and application.

The teacher might also try a variety of different methods of presentation in the hope that the students would better understand. Slow learners, as a rule, require more of the teacher's time for assistance and guidance. However, this additional time pays dividends in the form of student progress and achievement.

The Use of Workbooks

The workbook can be of great value in providing slow learners with a means of keeping pace with the class. As a study and learning guide, the workbook encourages students to help themselves under the supervision of the teacher. Workbook exercises and practice lessons can be studied and performed at home, thus giving a slower student the additional time he may need.

It might also be wise for the teacher to carefully study the individual student's problem, to see whether or not some simple outside problem or physical handicap is the cause of the student's problem. Perhaps some fairly simple adjustment, such as glasses, can accomplish great changes in the student's work, attitude and personality.

Above all, it must be remembered that slow learners require much more encouragement, more guidance, more help and especially a patient, cooperative teacher.

Gifted Students

At the opposite pole from the slower learner, in the cosmetology educational spectrum, we find the gifted students. These are those very fortunate students who easily and quickly grasp all forms of learning and can move ahead much faster than the average.

The problem for the teacher is to discover new ways and ideas to challenge these students in order that they fulfill their potential. If no provision is made for this type of individual difference, the students very soon get bored, lose interest and create disciplinary problems.

Possible Solutions

The teacher's first concern, in working with a gifted student, is to avoid any procedure which will retard his progress. The teacher should plan, with the student, individual goals, assignments, problems, deadlines and methods of evaluating progress. The student can be kept interested by "enrichment" projects of his own, such as special research or advanced cosmetology techniques.

It might even be possible to enlist the aid of gifted students in working with and assisting slower learners.

Normal or Average Students

Very often the student who is most neglected and receives the least teacher guidance is the, so called, **average student.** The teacher is so intent and so occupied with the need for providing for the gifted students and guiding the slower students that the "average student" is completely overlooked.

This type of teacher activity, or rather lack of it, can have a very frustrating and discouraging effect. Even "normal" students require guidance and encouragement. When this is lacking it can have a truly devastating effect on students. They become discouraged, they lose their initiative and very often lose their desire for learning.

In some cases "normal" students deliberately or subconsciously begin to fall behind in their work in order to attract some of the teacher's attention. Average or normal students also begin to lose interest in their work and begin to lose their motivation for learning.

Possible Solutions

The professional teacher knows that while slow students require more attention and gifted students require special challenges, the average student must also be provided for. The average student is entitled to and should receive a fair share of the teacher's time, efforts and guidance.

Summary

Providing for individual differences is a practical and progressive way of teaching. It includes recognizing and respecting each student's worth and his ability. It also includes a procedure for encouraging each student to do his best and obtain the maximum benefits from the teaching-learning situation, in accordance with his own ability.

DISRUPTIVE STUDENTS

Classroom control studies indicate that only 3% of all students really cause disciplinary problems. However, this relatively small number of students can disrupt and disorganize the learning process of the entire class.

A good, professional teacher with a dynamic personality and a pleasing manner can often develop a nearly ideal classroom situation, regardless of other factors. However, a teacher lacking in forcefulness, or with an irritable and negative manner, can create an unwholesome, unhappy and tense classroom atmosphere, which is ripe for disruptive incidents.

The development of an effective climate for learning is one of the primary duties of the cosmetology teacher. It is truly a frustrating experience to have a single student disrupt and disturb this climate, in spite of the efforts being expended to create a professional, relaxed environment which is conducive to good learning.

It is the responsibility of the teacher to see to it that every student is contributing to the learning atmosphere. The teacher should never permit one student to deprive the others of the valuable training to which they are entitled, by disrupting the class.

Cosmetology students bring into the classroom a wide range of problems from outside sources; from their homes, from their friends and even from their own physical condition. These problems may be entirely unrelated to the teacher, to the class or to the study of cosmetology. Yet, they may be unintentionally aggravated by the teacher's actions or by some student incident, and suddenly, a serious problem may develop in the classroom.

Harmony in the classroom rests largely on mutual respect and understanding. It is, therefore, advisable that teachers try to understand the disruptive student and discover the reason for his actions. By isolating and identifying the cause or reason for some unusual conduct problem, its solution is often indicated.

Possible Solutions

The first thing the teacher should do is have a private meeting with the disruptive student. A personal discussion may clear-up many misunderstandings or identify certain personal, unrelated problems.

1. Just by discussing his actions the teacher may make the student realize the unfairness of his actions with relation to his fellow students.

2. The teacher might point out that one sign of adult behavior is to handle strictly personal problems without disrupting and disturbing innocent, uninvolved people.

3. The student may be troubled by certain difficulties which can best be handled by the school administration; such things as arranging financial aid or personal guidance.

4. The student may also be affected by school related problems.

    a) If he does not understand the work or is having difficulty in keeping-up, try to arrange for special visual aids, devote more time in individualized training, to help the student with his learning problem. Perhaps arrange for one of the very good students to help him over the rough spots.

    b) If the student finds the work too easy, has too much time on his hands and therefore is thoroughly bored and restless, the teacher must arrange a program to combat this situation. The teacher must plan, together with the student, to keep him busily occupied with creative and constructive cosmetology work. He should be kept so busy that he doesn't have time to disrupt the class.

    c) If the student is completely disinterested, dislikes cosmetology and is totally unresponsive, it might be advisable to turn him over to the school Director for further handling.

Above all, the teacher must remember that he is dealing with individual human beings, each subject to personal and individual weaknesses and personal idiosyncrasies.

STUDENTS LIVING AWAY FROM HOME

Many cosmetology students are required to live away from home in order to attend school. For many of them this experience is the first time they have lived completely without parental guidance. This situation could be, and often is, a time for serious adjustment in the lives of these students.

At times the condition of living "on their own," plus the adjustment to a new school situation can create serious emotional problems for students. Students become depressed with severe cases of anxiety. Unless these conditions are extremely severe, this homesickness, this condition of anxiety and depression will not last too long and is not too dangerous. The best way a teacher can help students under these conditions is to be friendly, thoughtful and reassuring. At times, permitting the student to "talk it out" and being sympathetic and kind is all that is necessary.

Sometimes a student living away from home casts off all restraints and decides to really "cut loose." The student sheds all signs of parental guidance and develops a style of living which is his own. Such a student, unless he is restrained, can get involved in all kinds of trouble such as drugs, drinking, sex and bad associates. This student is heading straight for failure, not only in school but in his entire lifestyle.

A teacher who becomes aware of such a problem cannot disregard it under the guise that these activities are conducted outside of school and the student is creating his own life. It is the responsibility of cosmetology teachers, not only to teach beauty culture, but to try to mold character and good citizenship.

Possible Solutions

The teacher should have a private talk with the student and indicate that living away from home offers the opportunity for personal growth, the development of character and maturity. The discussion could include the qualities of good citizenship and the possibilities of creating a useful and constructive life for himself. He should indicate that one sign of maturity, of being an adult, is the ability to live within the bounds of decency and self-restraint.

Living away from home is not a license for unrestrained freedom and the casting off of responsibility. Living away gives the student the opportunity to achieve and earn his freedom through proper and adult social behavior. Just as in all life cycles, there can be no real freedom without responsibility. Uncontrolled and unrestrained activities lead not to freedom but to trouble and chaos.

The teacher should make it clear that promiscuous living is not the only way to enjoyment. He could point out and direct the student to a life-style which would permit him to achieve his objectives of successful training in cosmetology and still be able to enjoy his life.

The important signs of maturity of students living away from home is the ability to live within the bounds of decency and self-restraint.

If the student persists in his new life-style, and strictly as a last resort, the teacher should turn the problem over to the school's Director. Perhaps the Director will have a greater influence on the student and bring the entire problem to a satisfactory conclusion.

THE DRUG PROBLEM

A fairly recent and, in many respects, the most serious and perplexing of all problems facing the cosmetology teacher and the schools today, is that of students taking drugs.

The use of drugs has, unfortunately, spread rapidly to students in all parts of the country. It has become an accepted fact of life that from 30 to 50 percent of all teenage students, either are at present, or have had in the past, some experience with smoking "pot" or taking some form of drugs.

Whatever the reason for starting their contact with drugs, these students are now in schools, presenting a truly awesome problem to teachers and to the school administration.

The student's involvement with drugs actually presents a four dimensional dilemma:

1. The student is jeopardizing himself, his health and his future.
2. The danger of influencing other students to experiment with drugs is very real and frightening.
3. The student is violating the law and is subject to arrest and creation of a police record.
4. The damage to the image and reputation of the school may possibly destroy its future. Parents, hearing of drug use by students of a particular school of beauty culture, would be reluctant to send their teen-age sons or daughters to that school.

The question facing the teacher is also two-fold in nature. If the student does not disrupt or disturb the class, does the teacher have either a legal or a moral right to take action against the suspected student? If the teacher is to report the student, to whom should he report? To the school Director? To the student's parents? To the police?

The teacher must consider that if he makes an official report, and the student is a drug user, a possible criminal record could result for the student. If the teacher is mistaken, and the student is not a drug user, the school could be liable to a serious lawsuit. With these considerations in mind, teachers are slow and hesitant to take any official action against suspected drug using students, unless they disturb the class.

Possible Solutions

Because the student use of drugs is a comparatively recent problem, teachers are completely uncertain as to how to cope with the problem. No guidelines have, as yet, been established for dealing with drug taking students. If the student is not disturbing anyone, the tendency is to ignore the situation rather than to venture into an unknown area.

However, those individuals who are experts in the area of student drug use, do offer some advice.

They advise that if a student is deeply involved with drugs, he (the student) will be unable to cope with the problems, pressures, and tensions involved in the learning process. Since they are unable to cope, they will definitely drop out of school. Therefore, any student (believed to be using drugs) who is able to maintain a productive position in the school, keeps up with other students, and shows progress in learning cosmetology, is not too deeply involved. These students should not be pressured in any way, because, chances are very good that the student will pass through this period and leave the drug scene.

Studies have shown that expelling students at this time, turns many of them completely into the use of drugs. Placing the student in a position where he could have a police record or record of expulsion for drug use, could place a stigma on the student, which could completely destroy his future.

The drug problem is too serious, both from a medical and from a legal point of view, to be handled by the teacher. No cosmetology teacher is qualified to give either medical or legal advice. Therefore, if the teacher discovers, or believes, that a student is taking drugs, the entire problem should be turned over, without delay, to the Director of the school for further action.

The Director, being made aware of the situation, should immediately deal with the problem through the student's parents or guardian. He should be very careful and diplomatic in presenting the problem and suggesting a course of action. He should indicate that the student was not acting normally or properly. The Director should suggest that the student be immediately examined by the family physician.

For additional information and material on the Drug Problem, write to: United States Department of Health, Education & Welfare, Washington, D.C.

PROBLEM OF THE WANDERING STUDENT

Teachers may often be disturbed and a classroom completely disorganized by students who wander in and out of class, at will. No teacher can afford to overlook the situation because, not only is the offending student affected, but other students may be hurt, educationally. In fact, if other students start to emulate this action, classroom control deteriorates rapidly.

Immediate action is required by the teacher before the situation progresses into an educationally intolerable condition.

Students usually do not leave a classroom unnecessarily if they are properly motivated and interested in the subject matter being taught.

The problem with "wandering" students very often lies with the teacher. If the classroom presentation is really interesting and dynamic, students will not look for diversions elsewhere.

A teacher should ask himself:

1. Have I made the lesson truly worthwhile?

2. Have I expended every effort to make the presentation interesting?

3. Have I closely identified the subject matter with the student's short and long term objectives?

4. Have I made an effort to make it educationally unprofitable for a student or students to seek avenues of escape from class?

When teachers find that they are having difficulties in holding students, it might be very wise to analyze and review their own attitudes, their own activities and their own teaching enthusiasm, or lack of it. They may be surprised to find that many of their problems, with students, have their origin within themselves.

At times it becomes necessary for the teacher to take immediate steps to protect the classroom morale and decorum. It might also be necessary to protect a student from his own carelessness and neglect.

When the "wandering" problem involves only one particular student, it is essential to isolate and identify the possible causes for this condition. A private conference with the student is essential. Such a meeting may help to develop the reason for the student's actions and might even indicate a solution.

It is important to establish whether the student is really interested in a career in cosmetology. If not, both the student and the teacher are wasting a great deal of time, energy and money by having him continue in school.

If the student is sincerely interested, the teacher should make it very clear that continued "wandering" in and out of the class cannot be tolerated. The student should be made to understand that such action serves to impede and interfere with the learning process.

The meeting may establish the possibility that the student has a health problem. In that event, the student should be strongly urged to consult with a doctor. If the student fails to see a doctor, it may be necessary to discuss the problem with the school's director or even with the student's parents or guardian.

If the class "wandering" continues, it may become necessary to demand a doctor's statement indicating some unusual or abnormal physical condition. The statement should also indicate that the student is receiving proper medical care.

In any event, continuous wandering in and out of the classroom cannot be tolerated. The situation must be brought out into the open and stopped before classroom discipline is completely demoralized.

STUDENT-TEACHER CONFLICTS

Every teacher likes to feel that all of his students admire, like and respect him. Sometimes, however, a student will react unfavorably to the teacher on a purely personal basis.

The teacher who enjoys a good rapport with his students will be quick to notice when a particular student seems to be angry and antagonistic. In spite of all preventive measures taken, in spite of all efforts to avoid provoking the student, a feeling of antagonism exists which can lead to severe disciplinary problems.

Every unwholesome student condition must be handled in some way. Failure to deal with it could cause it to become so serious that it would upset the entire classroom environment and lead to completely disrupting conditions.

Of course the chances for a student-teacher conflict to develop are greatly reduced if the teacher is mature and possesses an even and controlled temperament. However, there are times that, in spite of the teacher's best efforts, student-teacher conflicts do arise.

Often, discovering the exact reason for the difficulty in such an interpersonal condition is so very difficult as to almost be impossible to determine. Nevertheless, the truly concerned teacher wants to know why the student reacts the way he does. There is no doubt that some very careful diagnosis of the student's behavior problem must be undertaken.

Sometimes the teacher must go through a soul-searching process to see what he may have said or done to cause the student's reactions. This should involve a careful review and analysis of his own (the teacher's) past and present relations with the student and his activities.

It might even involve a real or imagined slight insult or an unfortunate experience with an earlier teacher, causing the student to resent and oppose all teachers. Whatever its cause, isolating and identifying the problem may be a long step toward its solution.

Possible Solutions

A quiet, serious conference with the student, in which the teacher asks well directed questions, may reveal the reasons for his behavior. Often just exposing the reasons for the student's actions leads to his realization of the unreasonableness of his behavior and the possible very serious results. The open and frank discussion at a teacher-student conference is usually the most effective way of correcting this faulty and dangerous situation. It is also possible that, if the student is given the opportunity to explain, what seems to be almost inexcusable behavior may turn out to be entirely understandable and plausible.

Of course, if the student persists in his antagonistic and rebellious attitude, further action may be necessary.

If it is possible, it might be best to assign the student to another class and teacher. However, in most cosmetology schools, this may not be possible.

If reassignment is not possible, unless the student or his attitude is disturbing the rest of the class, as intelligent human beings they may be required to continue as they are. Both the teacher and the student will find it necessary to call upon their own patience and maturity to maintain themselves as intelligent human beings.

Every professional teacher tries to handle all classroom problems himself. However, at times it becomes impossible to resolve a problem without outside help. If the teacher finds that the student, in spite of all efforts, still continues in his attitude and disrupts the teaching-learning process, it may be necessary to enlist the aid of the chool Director.

If even this fails, no course is left open but to arrange a conference with the student's parents or guardian and enlist their aid.

The final and least desirable action, used only as a last resort, is to dismiss the student.

STUDENTS WHO FEEL INSECURE AND INFERIOR

The student who feels ignored, neglected, insecure and inferior, as a rule, will naturally and normally react against these threats to his personal security. These feelings, when revealed, are often outward signs of deeply rooted emotional problems and tensions.

Perhaps the student's economic condition makes him feel inferior to others. Perhaps he is deficient in his social relationships with his fellow students. Perhaps he is a slow learner and is unable to keep up with other students. There is almost no end to the possibilities for causing this feeling of failure and the creation of poor relationships and unhappy attitudes. This situation will inevitably be reflected in his classroom behavior and in his educational progress.

Every student experiences frustrations at times. The real problems arise, however, with those students who experience it to a marked degree. In their inability to solve their problems by normal means, these students often develop deep-seated, emotional feelings of insecurity and resignation. Such students often recede into lonely isolation from other students and from a frustrating world. They actually withdraw from a reality which they find too painful to resist, too harsh to accept and too complex to deal with by themselves.

Most cosmetology teachers, unless they have received detailed training in psychology and in specialized behavior problems, are unable to deal with individual problems of this type. However, a teacher who is thoughtful, dedicated and understanding usually tries to make some effort to help.

Possible Solutions

The teacher must explore every possible reason for the student's classroom behavior which could stem even indirectly from some social maladjustment either in or out of school. Often discovering the reasons for this maladjustment may also indicate the possible means for correcting it.

It is the responsibility of the teacher to make him (the student) feel that he is looked upon as an important, worthwhile individual, capable of achieving success on an equal basis with all other students. The teacher and, indeed, the entire school administration should make the student feel welcome and comfortable within the teaching-learning atmosphere. It is essential to try to make the student achieve some real sense of identity, self-worth and self-respect.

The sincerely compassionate teacher, who is thoughtful and understanding, can help to dispel some of this feeling of insecurity and inadequacy. The teacher can help to reassure the student by praising his efforts and accomplishments. No matter how slight the student's accomplishment, a few words of praise and commendation can help to restore a shattered ego and help to rebuild his confidence.

The teacher who will take the time to praise some small accomplishment, speak words of encouragement frequently, and give students special individual help, where required, reveals himself to be a truly professional educator.

SUMMARY

In a well-disciplined classroom the prevailing atmosphere is one of friendliness and good will. Students are expected to be honest, industrious, cooperative and deeply involved in the training program.

The primary objective of discipline, in the beauty school, is to make efficient cosmetology training possible. A smoothly functioning cosmetology training program has a number of specific objectives in maintaining classroom discipline. Following are a few of the primary objectives:

1. To stimulate and encourage self-activity of students.

2. To initiate and develop resourcefulness in students.

3. To develop habits of cooperation with others.

4. To encourage careful analysis and thorough evaluation.

5. To train students to acquire knowledge and skills which will enable them to function efficiently in the beauty salon.

It would be almost impossible to guess which student will cause some disciplinary problem in the classroom at any given time. Usually a number of factors are involved when trouble starts. No one can tell who will develop into a villain or who will become the victim on any given day.

There are countless numbers of classroom problems which may arise to disrupt a teaching program. Some have been discussed in this chapter, but many new ones are constantly developing. Even though the teacher does everything in his power to create favorable learning conditions, disciplinary problems will still occur from time to time.

It is imperative that every classroom problem be dealt with without undue delay. No student situation should be allowed to develop until it disrupts the learning patterns of the entire class.

How to handle any specific student problem at any particular time is almost an impossible question to answer. Each case is different because the students are different, the classroom situations are different, the causal factors are different, and the probable results are different. Two apparently similar cases of student disciplinary activities, identical or seemingly identical, usually have no real similarity except for the overt action itself.

No list of suggestions for the handling of student behavior problems can be more than a group of reasonable proposals, based on similar situations and the experience with them. Nevertheless, the practical suggestions offered may well be borne in mind, by the cosmetology teacher, when considering specific disciplinary situations.

An alert and observant teacher can spot many behavior problems before they occur. It is far better to deal with them at once, before they can develop and disrupt instruction.

Some general suggestions may be made for teacher guidance in dealing with classroom problems. The following problem handling suggestions are offered for consideration.

1. The most important and effective single act is the private conference with the student.

2. Use and apply good common sense and mature judgment in dealing with all student problems.

3. Avoid sarcasm and ridicule. To humiliate a student before others, by using sarcasm and ridicule, is most unwise and unprofessional. It can only make the situation worse.

4. Win the confidence of the student.

5. Recognize and respect individual differences and individual characteristics and emotional conditions.

6. Always employ positive rather than negative methods in handling problems.

7. Use courtesy and tact in dealing with students.

8. Carefully consider student motives and causes for particular actions.

9. Handle every situation without delay.

10. Maintain a good sense of humor.

It is essential that every teacher remember that "Prevention is much better than correction." If a teacher recognizes a problem brewing, handle it immediately and avoid much greater difficulties later.

REVIEW PROBLEMS IN COSMETOLOGY SCHOOLS

Short Answer Questions

1. **What is the prevailing atmosphere of the well-disciplined classroom?**
   The prevailing atmosphere is one of friendliness and goodwill.

2. **What is the primary objective of discipline in the beauty school?**
   To make efficient cosmetology training possible.

3. **What are the five primary objectives of a smooth-functioning training program?**
   1. To encourage and stimulate self-activity.
   2. To initiate and develop resourcefulness.
   3. To develop habits of cooperation.
   4. To encourage careful analysis and evaluation.
   5. To train students to acquire knowledge and skills in cosmetology.

4. **Why must every classroom problem be dealt with without undue delay?**
   It should not be allowed to develop to the point where it disrupts the learning patterns of the entire class.

5. **Why is it almost impossible to set specific rules on how to handle any specific student problem?**
   Each case is different. The students, classroom situations, and causal factors are different, making the probable results different.

6. **List ten problem-handling suggestions.**
   1. The most important act is a private conference.
   2. Use and apply good common sense and mature judgment in dealing with problems.
   3. Avoid sarcasm and ridicule.
   4. Win the confidence of the student.
   5. Recognize and respect individual differences.
   6. Employ positive methods.
   7. Use courtesy and tact.
   8. Consider student motives and causes.
   9. Handle every situation without delay.
   10. Maintain a good sense of humor.

CHAPTER 15

TEACHER EVALUATION

EVALUATION

The teacher is the key factor in helping cosmetology students to achieve their goals. Whether or not the school has the finest training equipment, an abundance of audio-visual aids, or an ultra-modern building does not decide the quality of success of training. The one individual who works with students on a regular day-to-day basis is the person who is most likely to inspire their confidence and to whom they will reveal their innermost feelings, hopes and ambitions. The teacher is the person to whom students turn for advice and guidance in:

1. Establishing realistic cosmetology goals.
2. Finding a job after completion of the program.
3. Solving personal problems which may be blocking their efforts to learn or even to continue in school.

The most important key to the success of a teaching program is the teacher.

For many hundreds of years, students have been won by the magic of the teacher's smile, the strength of the teacher's encouragement, and the wisdom of the teacher's advice. The competent teacher keeps the class together, keeps it moving steadily toward its objectives, and helps to find or develop the means to satisfaction and success in the learning process.

Teaching techniques alone can never enable a cosmetology teacher to do a thorough and effective job. If the teacher really wants to help students with their problems and try to direct their learning, he must show a sincere and friendly interest. The teacher must instill confidence and gain the honest respect of the students.

While no teacher reaches absolute perfection, the professional teacher constantly learns as he teaches. Each teaching/learning experience serves to help the alert teacher to handle the next one more adequately and efficiently.

How do you think you measure up to the many-sided challenges of teaching cosmetology students? Your flexibility, interest, cooperation and creativity are pretty good indexes to your probabilities of teaching success.

Following is a checklist to help you rate yourself. It might be wise to rate and evaluate yourself just as you might rate and evaluate a student in whom you are interested. Many areas of teaching strengths and weaknesses may be indicated for your consideration.

HOW DO YOU RATE YOURSELF AS A TEACHER?

TEACHER'S SELF-EVALUATION CHECKLIST

	Yes	No	Don't Know	Sometimes
Personal Qualities — Communication Skills				
1. Do you maintain a friendly but businesslike atmosphere in the classroom?				
2. Do you avoid sitting down while teaching?				
3. Do you maintain a direct rapport with your students?				
4. Do you concentrate your attention on the entire class and not on one or two students?				
5. Do you maintain your speaking voice at a level to be heard clearly in every part of the room?				
6. Do you avoid speaking in a monotonous drone, but vary the pitch, volume and tempo of your speech?				
7. Do you avoid making unnecessary tonal sounds when you speak? (i.e., "uhs," "ahs," "ohs," etc.)				
8. Do you maintain the speed of your speech at a tempo that best reaches your class and stimulates responses?				
9. Are you exact and definite in your presentation and avoid generalization?				
10. Are you especially careful to use proper grammar and pronunciation in your speech?				
11. Do you give your students your complete attention, listen carefully to what they say and respect their comments and questions?				
12. Do you avoid using annoying personal mannerisms such as toying with personal objects, cracking your knuckles, twirling a key or lavalier, etc.?				
13. Do you keep completely informed on your subject matter and maintain it at an up-to-date level?				
14. Do you organize your material properly to maintain the best teaching pattern?				
15. Do you make careful preparation for each teaching session?				
16. Do you candidly admit to your class that you do not know the answer to a particular question?				
17. Do you spend your time and effort to look up material on a subject or question which you could not answer and then report your findings to your class?				

	Yes	No	Don't Know	Sometimes
Classroom Attitude of Teacher				
18. Do you get real pleasure out of teaching?				
19. Do you develop and clearly show a real enthusiasm through the entire teaching program?				
20. Do you make every subject area seem essential and important to the entire course?				
21. Does teaching stimulate and inspire you to increase your own knowledge and organized thinking of the subject?				
22. Do you try to develop in your students a proper professional attitude toward their work responsibilities as well as knowledge and technical skill of the subject material?				
23. Do you have a personal, professional interest in each student?				
24. Are you fair and impartial in your dealings with the entire student body?				
25. Do you stimulate your students to apply their own experiences in relation to the subject?				
26. Do you inspire enough enthusiasm and interest so that students tend to remain after class and ask questions or discuss the subjects?				
27. Do fewer than 20% of your students drop out and fail to complete the subject?				
28. Are most of your students stimulated to take an active part in the class discussions rather than the relative few?				
29. To all appearances, do your students feel at ease and relaxed and interested in their work?				
30. Have you inspired your students so that they apply what they learned in class and voluntarily seek further knowledge outside?				
Teaching Techniques				
31. Are you punctual in starting each class?				
32. Do you continue the teaching procedure up to the very end of the time period?				
33. Do you briefly review or make reference to the previous lesson in order to orient your students as to the continuity of the subject matter?				
34. Do you summarize the material covered and make reference to the next step at the end of each lesson?				

	Yes	No	Don't Know	Sometimes
35. Are your assignments to your class clear and definite?				
36. Do you keep your students occupied with practical, worth-while projects?				
37. Do you make frequent use of the chalkboard and other teaching aids in presenting your subject?				
38. Do you stimulate your students to think for themselves?				
39. Do you create an interesting, harmonious and cooperative classroom atmosphere?				
40. Do you encourage classroom discussions, enlisting all your students, to stimulate student response and self-expression?				
41. Do you make maximum use of available sound and visual aids?				
42. Do you keep your students interested by associating class-room training with actual practice in the field?				
43. Do you exercise care that you do not talk over the heads of your students or do not talk down to them?				
44. Are you able to cope with a situation where the students do not like the subject taught but must attend your classes and are disinterested and restless?				
45. Do you make a conscious effort to know the names of all your students?				
46. Do you try to get the students to know each other?				
47. After several meetings, do you address your students by name thus making them feel that you take a personal interest?				
48. Are you careful to avoid directing all of your attention to either the smartest or the weakest members of the class?				
49. Do you objectively base your evaluation of a student on several criteria, being careful to be completely fair and not base your judgment on a single item?				
50. Do you suggest to your students other sources for further study or devices which will aid them in further improve-ment after completing the subject?				

EVALUATION TABLE

Scoring

1. Each "Yes" answer counts 3
2. Each "Sometimes" answer counts 2
3. Each "Don't Know" answer counts 1
4. Each "No" answer counts 0

Tabulating

To arrive at your correct score

1. Add your total score   2. Multiply total score by 2

3. Divide new total by 3

Analysis of Evaluation

OVER 90 — Outstanding — Exceptional teaching ability

80 - 90 — Excellent   **70 - 79** — Good   **65 - 69** — Fair

64 or under — Would indicate that you require additional teacher-training

CONCLUSION

Cosmetology education cannot rise above the level of its teachers. The trend in teacher training, or the lack of such training, in the cosmetology field is such as to give the thoughtful individual cause for much concern. This is a real problem in education which cannot be brushed lightly aside without serious consideration. How well trained are cosmetology teachers? Is their own education, experience, and training such as to qualify them to be entrusted with the task of molding the future of the professional cosmetologist?

Today we are faced with a new era in educational thinking. The last few years have brought much disillusionment. Education has been brought up sharply and is forced to take greater cognizance of the true values education should seek to achieve. Cosmetology students are no longer accepted at face value but must prove the adequacy and thoroughness of their training before they are accepted as artisans. The constantly rising standards demanded by the public, the state boards and salon owners have made it mandatory that the product of cosmetology schools be properly prepared. Such training is only possible if the teaching staff itself is capable of meeting this challenge.

This manual was prepared to assist cosmetology teachers to properly prepare themselves to meet the demands of modern education. First-hand knowledge and understanding of many teaching, learning and management areas are required of today's teacher in order that he be able to function properly.

There is no easy, guaranteed road to becoming a successful cosmetology teacher. The mere fact that an instructor reads this text does not insure his acquiring great instructional ability. The reading of this text will not automatically create a qualified instructor. However, success as an instructor is dependent upon the application of the concepts, precepts and techniques set forth herein.

We sincerely hope that we have awakened in the teacher a desire to pursue this study in still greater detail and to widen his ability, knowledge and understanding of his position as a **Professional Teacher.**

REVIEW TEST ITEMS

FOR INSTRUCTORS

INTRODUCTION

This section is intended as a comprehensive review of essential information concerning the fundamentals of teaching cosmetology.

Not only will these basic principles serve as a guide for planning, carrying out and evaluating learning activities, but they will help the instructor to solve actual problems relating to the art of teaching, classroom management, and student-teacher relationship.

Instructors-in-training will appreciate this timely review as a thorough preparation for State Board examinations. Experienced instructors will welcome the practical advice as a means of improving their professional work.

MULTIPLE CHOICE EXAMINATION

(Answers will be found on page 200)

DIRECTIONS: *Carefully read each statement. Circle the letter which correctly completes the meaning of each statement.*

1. Cosmetology instructors should employ teaching methods which:
   a) they are used to.
   b) patrons want.
   c) the school has adopted.
   d) students want to use.

2. To correct errors, instructors should:
   a) talk to one student about another.
   b) correct student in front of the patron so that everyone can hear.
   c) discuss errors with entire class without mentioning names.
   d) expel student for making errors.

3. In grading papers, the instructor should:
   a) use an answer key.
   b) let students grade paper.
   c) look up answers.
   d) depend on memory.

4. Students will learn more from demonstrations by:
   a) practicing two days later.
   b) doing it their own way.
   c) immediate and repeated practice.
   d) developing short-cuts in their own work.

5. Special training in methods of presenting beauty culture knowledge and skills to others is:
   a) necessary.
   b) optional.
   c) elective.
   d) unnecessary.

6. State Board members are appointed by the:
   a) legislature.
   b) Governor.
   c) hairdressers' association.
   d) beauty school owners.

7. Basic practical instruction in cosmetology should always be given under the supervision of a:
   a) student teacher.
   b) senior student.
   c) licensed operator.
   d) qualified instructor.

8. Slow learners can best be helped in their studies by:
   a) ignoring them and permitting them to move at their own pace.
   b) allowing them to fall behind the rest of the class.
   c) providing them with workbook assignments and individual help.
   d) permitting them to do as they please.

9. When a student has difficulty with a patron, the instructor should:
   a) ignore the student.
   b) come to student's assistance.
   c) **refuse to help the student.**
   d) **reprimand the student.**

10. In presenting a practical demonstration, the instructor should:
    a) first explain the step-by-step procedure to orient the students.
    b) talk about the way "not" to do it.
    c) stand so students can't see.
    d) talk about what took place the day before.

11. Cosmetology instructors must:
    a) never change their way of teaching.
    b) restrict teaching to the textbook.
    c) apply new techniques along with basic foundations.
    d) use the methods that are easiest.

12. In teaching, you strive to:
    a) have the student acquire speed not perfection.
    b) teach the student just enough to get by.
    c) impart knowledge, understanding and skills.
    d) have students develop shortcuts.

13. If a student loses interest, who is usually at fault?
    a) student.
    b) school.
    c) teacher.
    d) parents.

14. A student has completed his school training and is ready to take the State Board exam. If you are doubtful about his passing, it is advisable to:
    a) say, "I know you won't pass, but you may as well try."
    b) tell him some untruth about the State Board.
    c) give him encouragement.
    d) try to persuade the student to take further training.

15. Cosmetology students with more ability should be:
    a) held back with the class.
    b) given prizes for their work.
    c) allowed to progress more rapidly.
    d) discouraged from moving ahead.

16. Beauty culture knowledge is more meaningful and more easily learned if it is based on:
    a) only related information.
    b) only practical experience.
    c) both science and practice.
    d) only on human anatomy.

17. When a student returns to class after missing a lesson, the instructor should permit him to:
    a) catch up, as soon as possible, with the aid of the textbook and workbook.
    b) study the missed lesson at some future date.
    c) proceed without bothering with work missed.
    d) cancel all new work until he has caught up with work missed.

18. If an instructor fails to pass the State Board teacher's exam, he should:
    a) accuse the Board of being unfair.
    b) review his training to discover his weaknesses.
    c) return to being an operator.
    d) leave the field of cosmetology.

19. Which of the following best indicates a lack of capacity for learning?
    a) lack of interest.
    b) having a cold.
    c) failure in exam.
    d) age.

20. Which of the following is conducive to effective learning?
    a) intent to learn.
    b) parental encouragement.
    c) utilizing basic data.
    d) a, b and c are all correct.

21. Instructors can best give encouragement, guidance and individual instruction when the practical classes are:
    a) 30-40 students.
    b) disorderly.
    c) 15-20 students.
    d) being rushed.

22. Students of large classes can best receive individual help if the instructor:
    a) punishes students more often.
    b) employs efficient classroom management.
    c) teaches only simple subjects.
    d) neglects the bright students.

23. To achieve good classroom supervision, an instructor must:
    a) speak loudly at all times.
    b) leave the students alone more often.
    c) avoid speaking to individual students.
    d) be aware of each student's progress.

24. Units of instruction and steps in procedure should be:
    a) taught rapidly.
    b) difficult to teach.
    c) taught in the order they are to be used.
    d) eliminated because of the confusion they caused.

25. An instructor will make more progress toward better education if he:
    a) follows a definite plan of instruction.
    b) does not have a curriculum.
    c) teaches off the cuff.
    d) stays late after class.

26. When introducing a new lesson to students, the instructor should:
    a) make the lesson seem more difficult than it really is.
    b) avoid answering any questions.
    c) give a clear statement as to its purpose.
    d) be sure that the introduction is lengthy.

27. A system for collecting and distributing supplies could result in:
    a) creating confusion.
    b) a lack of property control.
    c) a great saving in time and supplies.
    d) a waste of time.

28. Most instructors tend to agree that students:
    a) vary in their ability to learn.
    b) do not vary in their power to learn.
    c) have no desire to learn.
    d) cannot increase their ability to learn.

29. If an instructor refers to previous topics through reviews and tests, he will:
    a) confuse the students.
    b) co-ordinate his lessons.
    c) lose student interest.
    d) annoy the bright students.

30. Students engaged in the same type of work should be:
    a) kept at it longer.
    b) left unsupervised.
    c) grouped whenever possible.
    d) separated whenever possible.

31. When an instructor is to present a lecture or demonstration, he should:
    a) obtain supplies as needed.
    b) provide in advance, the necessary supplies and equipment.
    c) avoid student participation.
    d) ask a student to get the supplies for him.

32. The primary objective of a new student performing practical work is:
    a) speed.
    b) pleasure.
    c) keeping busy.
    d) quality.

33. Once students have achieved quality in their practice work, the next objective should be:
    a) a change of subject.
    b) a short vacation.
    c) speed.
    d) change class.

34. The effectiveness of a teaching method can be confirmed if:
   a) half of the students can pass a test.
   b) students show dislike for the lesson.
   c) it results in less work for the instructor.
   d) it effectively carries out the aims of the lesson.

35. For a demonstration to be effective, it must be:
   a) well planned.
   b) of long duration.
   c) concerned with an interesting topic.
   d) original.

36. After a demonstration, there should be a:
   a) lengthy follow-up lecture.
   b) question and answer period.
   c) change of topic.
   d) 30 minute break.

37. Carefully observe students as they practice because:
   a) they will be overworked.
   b) repetition causes errors.
   c) it is very interesting.
   d) repetition of errors create bad work habits.

38. Use individual testing during a drill period to select those students who require:
   a) no attention.
   b) additional instruction or practice.
   c) a change in subject.
   d) more testing.

39. Tests should be followed by correction of mistakes and:
   a) punishment.
   b) additional homework.
   c) new material.
   d) instruction in weak points.

40. A test following drill work can tell the instructor whether or not:
   a) the drill produced the desired results.
   b) the students like the work.
   c) the students will ever succeed.
   d) the textbook was studied.

41. A test can be used effectively as a:
   a) course outline.
   b) review exercise.
   c) lesson plan.
   d) tool for punishment.

42. Frequent testing helps to:
   a) eliminate poor students.
   b) locate students' difficulties.
   c) annoy students.
   d) make students enthusiastic.

43. Whenever matters of instruction are concerned a teacher should express:
   a) sarcasm.
   b) interest.
   c) familiarity.
   d) boredom.

44. Criticism of a student's work should be done:
   a) once a day.
   b) before the class.
   c) after graduation.
   d) privately.

45. Praise for a student's good work should be done:
   a) before the entire class.
   b) privately.
   c) one month later.
   d) after graduation.

46. The function of a school is to:
   a) enforce discipline.
   b) make all students alike.
   c) improve the knowledge and ability of each student.
   d) serve as a social center.

47. A student's instruction can be considered adequate when:
   a) the required number of hours have been accomplished.
   b) the student has a good attendance record.
   c) the student can render proficient services in beauty culture.
   d) the student excels in one area of beauty culture work.

48. The lecture method of instruction employs the use of:
   a) verbal explanations.
   b) manual practice.
   c) physical demonstrations.
   d) practical testing.

49. Good teachers change their lesson plans:
   a) several times each term.
   b) only when instructed to do so.
   c) as conditions warrant.
   d) when students dislike them.

50. Failure to maintain classroom discipline is a sign of:
   a) good class management.
   b) active teacher interest.
   c) advanced teaching technique.
   d) poor class management.

51. A teacher should not start or resume instruction until:
   a) all the students want to.
   b) all students are attentive.
   c) at least half of the students are listening.
   d) attendance is perfect.

52. A good way for the teacher to solve the discipline problem is to:
   a) be sarcastic.
   b) make threats.
   c) raise his voice.
   d) keep students busy.

53. Lesson plans should provide for individual differences in students':
   a) height.
   b) personality.
   c) attitude.
   d) learning ability.

54. Science and practical exercises should be kept:
   a) far below the students' ability to learn.
   b) within the students' ability to learn.
   c) just beyond students' abilities.
   d) until the end of the term.

55. Visual aids should be used:
   a) when the instructor is tired.
   b) when entertainment is desired.
   c) as effective teaching tools.
   d) when no lesson has been prepared.

56. What percentage of initial learning is gained through the sense of sight?
   a) 50%
   b) 60%
   c) 75%
   d) 85%

57. Habits can be formed more easily when:
   a) repetition is made pleasant.
   b) repetition is avoided.
   c) repetition is made unpleasant.
   d) the work is constantly changed.

58. When giving a science test, the student should be advised:
   a) three weeks in advance.
   b) just prior to giving the exam.
   c) one week in advance.
   d) one month in advance.

59. For additional information on beauty culture, teachers should recommend that students attend:
   a) another basic school.
   b) trade shows.
   c) gossip sessions in the rest room.
   d) a business school.

60. An important step in preparing students for a group lesson is to:
  a) make them fear the teacher.
  b) put the class at ease.
  c) exaggerate the difficulties of the lesson.
  d) give a quick test.

61. When introducing a new lesson, an instructor should:
  a) avoid using visual aids.
  b) teach by lecture only.
  c) disregard past student experience.
  d) review briefly the last lesson.

62. Student rules for classroom conduct should be:
  a) very numerous.
  b) few and practical.
  c) overlooked once a week.
  d) put aside until needed.

63. Familiarity can be avoided if students address the teacher:
  a) by his first name.
  b) by his nickname.
  c) as Miss, Mrs. or Mr. .... (last name).
  d) however they please.

64. If the instructor's last name is difficult to pronounce:
  a) let the students struggle with it.
  b) use Miss or Mr. followed by her or his first name.
  c) use a nickname.
  d) have it legally changed.

65. When questioning students in the classroom, avoid:
  a) the direct method.
  b) the overhead method.
  c) asking questions in seating rotation.
  d) individual responses.

66. The purpose of oral questioning is:
  a) to obtain attention.
  b) to stimulate thinking.
  c) to test learning and teaching.
  d) a, b, c, inclusive.

67. When using oral questions, as part of the teaching pattern, the instructor should:
  a) be sure that the questions are clearly worded.
  b) use long, involved questions.
  c) use questions which can be answered "Yes" or "No."
  d) use questions with several sub-themes.

68. The objective of the practice method of teaching is to:
  a) develop manual skills.
  b) stimulate student discussions.
  c) present a lesson in science.
  d) demonstrate the use of visual aids.

69. An important reason for including the workbook in classroom and home-work assignment is to:
  a) keep the students busily occupied.
  b) help students to consume time.
  c) learn and review essential information.
  d) keep students out of trouble.

70. To receive the most benefit from their studies, students should:
  a) memorize the textbook assignment word-for-word.
  b) coordinate the study of textbook and workbook.
  c) write out the textbook assignment word-for-word.
  d) read the textbook assignment three times.

71. Instruction sheets are important teaching aids; however, instructors are cautioned to:
  a) avoid their excessive use.
  b) discontinue lectures.
  c) avoid revising his material.
  d) discontinue demonstrations.

72. If students do not seem to learn at first, they should be:
   a) eliminated from the school.
   b) given individual attention.
   c) transferred to another school.
   d) reprimanded before other students.

73. In preparation for teaching each day, instructors should:
   a) ask students what subjects they would like to discuss.
   b) never give a homework assignment.
   c) plan their lessons.
   d) read several good books on teaching.

74. A good lesson plan in cosmetology should:
   a) proceed from the simple to the complex.
   b) proceed from the most difficult to the easiest.
   c) be very hard, just as life is.
   d) require the least amount of student participation.

75. The purpose of educational psychology is to:
   a) study the behavior of all organisms.
   b) select subject matter and determine its objective.
   c) cure mentally ill students.
   d) provide a scientific basis for teaching.

76. In most beauty schools, the procedures are adapted to:
   a) the better students.
   b) the poorer students.
   c) the bright students.
   d) the average students.

77. Knowledge of success or progress in learning generally:
   a) is a spur to greater achievement.
   b) makes a student lazy.
   c) results in discouragement.
   d) has no effect on learning.

78. Which training method is likely to be most effective in developing a specific manual skill?
   a) well-planned lectures.
   b) repeated practice.
   c) appropriate visual aids.
   d) interesting demonstrations.

79. In teaching students correct job skills, the instructor should know that:
   a) students differ in the amount they can learn in a given time.
   b) learning should be the same for all if the instruction is the same for all.
   c) students learn faster by group instruction than by individual instruction.
   d) students over 30 years of age learn at a faster rate than students under that age.

80. In influencing the rate of learning, rewarding students for good work:
   a) tends to give only temporary results.
   b) is of relatively little value unless combined with punishment.
   c) is more effective than punishment.
   d) gives less predictable results than punishment.

81. The biggest loss as a result of forgetting, takes place:
   a) immediately after learning, if not applied.
   b) after the first attempt at recognition.
   c) after the first attempt at recall.
   d) after a period of disuse.

82. Audio-visual aids are most effective as teaching devices when:
   a) they are used spontaneously.
   b) they are varied to fit different lessons.
   c) the same aid is used over and over until students are familiar with it.
   d) they are used to relieve the instructor of the necessity of personal instruction.

83. According to modern studies, which of the following is **not true** about the ability to learn?
   a) learning ability is at its height in the early twenties.
   b) learning ability increases with age until the time of senility.
   c) learning ability tapers off a little starting in the fifties.
   d) in later years, it is difficult for the average person to learn anything not connected with lifetime experiences.

84. Students who are learning cosmetology frequently encounter difficulty in their studies when they:
   a) do not enjoy hairdressing.
   b) want to learn their own way.
   c) are nervous and lack confidence.
   d) know that when they learn they will have more to do.

85. Which of the following expressions would be best when starting to give constructive criticism?
   a) you know that you can do better than this.
   b) if you keep on like this, you will never learn beauty culture.
   c) this is pretty good, but I'll show you how to do it better.
   d) this is partly right; now take it back and correct it.

86. In class, a student becomes upset because of inability to solve a problem. What action is best for the instructor to take?
   a) give a different type problem which the student may be able to solve.
   b) minimize the importance of finding a solution to the problem.
   c) encourage other students to contribute to the solution.
   d) provide hints which would lead the student to a solution of the problem.

87. Since physical health affects learning efficiency, one should:
   a) do most of the studying in the evening.
   b) study when tired and depressed.
   c) study when not feeling well.
   d) get an adequate amount of rest and exercise.

88. The most important thing in forming good study habits is:
   a) infrequent practice.
   b) knowing the nature of habits.
   c) regular practice and study.
   d) to be uninterested.

89. It is good educational practice to:
   a) permit students to do as they please.
   b) read the textbook aloud in class.
   c) have students copy the entire textbook.
   d) employ efficiently both the textbook and the workbook.

90. The student's interest in cosmetology is largely:
   a) the responsibility of the student.
   b) a matter of the student's own background.
   c) dependent upon the teacher's enthusiasm.
   d) dependent upon dull lectures.

91. One of the better ways to remember basic principles is to:
   a) be sure to understand what is said and written.
   b) record what the teacher says.
   c) read an advanced textbook.
   d) memorize a statement in a textbook.

92. When faced with a difficult situation, the instructor should:
   a) ignore it.
   b) place the blame on others.
   c) try to solve the problem.
   d) forget it.

93. School grades may serve a constructive purpose if they are used as:
   a) an end in themselves.
   b) a means of embarrassing students.
   c) a means to stimulate other interests.
   d) a means to evaluate progress towards a goal.

94. The use of a reprimand or censure, as a means of motivation to learning:
   a) is more effective with slow learners.
   b) is more successful when it is deserved.
   c) is more successful when it is not deserved.
   d) usually works best when it is used abundantly.

95. Teaching success depends to a great extent upon:
   a) the involuntary nervous system.
   b) receptive students.
   c) the heart and lungs.
   d) nose and ears.

96. Drill, as an approach to learning, should:
   a) be varied and meaningful.
   b) be avoided.
   c) be monotonous.
   d) be routinized.

97. Which of the following probably has the **least influence** as a factor in learning?
   a) age.
   b) sex.
   c) intelligence.
   d) guidance.

98. Students may be helped to develop good study habits by applying themselves:
   a) completely to textbook study.
   b) completely to workbook study.
   c) to a combination of the textbook and workbook.
   d) completely to notebook study.

99. In dealing with student behavior problems, the instructor should:
   a) decrease the feeling of personal worth.
   b) make the student feel less secure.
   c) treat the reasons for the behavior problems rather than the action itself.
   d) treat the behavior acts rather than the reasons for such actions.

100. When learning skills, it is particularly advantageous to:
   a) space periods of practice.
   b) hold long practice sessions.
   c) practice at intervals of a week.
   d) practice only when highly motivated.

TRUE-FALSE EXERCISE

(Answers will be found on page 200)

DIRECTIONS: *Read carefully each statement. Some are true; others are false. If you believe the statement is true, draw a circle around the letter (T); if you believe the statement is false, draw a circle around the letter (F).*

1. An instructor should keep up-to-date in teaching methods. .... T   F

2. An instructor's examination must have validity and reliability in order to have value. .... T   F

3. Every instructor owes loyalty to the school in which he is teaching. T   F

4. When the school director and the instructor disagree, the instructor should take the problems to the State Board. .... T   F

5. A good instructor does not need to respect the laws of learning. T   F

6. Sympathetic understanding and patience should be practiced by the instructor at all times. .... T   F

7. You must learn to control yourself and master your emotions before you can guide others. .... T   F

8. All teaching requires some degree of planning. .... T   F

9. Slow learners can best be helped, in their studies, by ignoring them and permitting them to move at their own pace. .... T   F

10. Student enthusiasm will vary according to the degree of interest in a particular subject. .... T   F

11. Aptitude tests should **not** be used as the exclusive device for the acceptance or rejection of students for training in cosmetology. ..... T   F

12. Audio-visual aids are most effective as teaching devices when they are varied to fit different lessons. .... T   F

13. An important reason for using the workbook in both classroom and homework assignments is to learn and review essential information. T   F

14. An instructor must be able to supplement oral instructions with various visual aids. .... T   F

15. The size of the class is important in the teaching and learning process. .... T   F

16. An instructor should assume a superior attitude with students. T   F

17. An instructor need not concern himself with the proper maintenance of equipment. .... T   F

18. It is the duty of an instructor to carry out all safety measures at all times. .... T   F

19. School sanitation and compliance with the State Board rules and regulations are the instructor's responsibility. .... T   F

20. Physical health is as important to an instructor as it is to a professional cosmetologist. .... T   F

21. Instructors should be completely familiar with the state laws pertaining to their profession. .... T   F

22. All lessons must be in the form of demonstrations and be followed
with practice. .... T   F

23. Teaching is helping others to learn through planned activities. .... T   F

24. Progressive learning is built on previous knowledge arranged in
a sequential order. .... T   F

25. If a group of students completely understand a demonstration, it
would indicate that the instructor did a good job. .... T   F

26. A cosmetology instructor has no obligation to the student after
graduation. .... T   F

27. Student participation is necessary to all learning. .... T   F

28. A test helps both the instructor and the student to determine if the
objective of the lesson has been achieved. .... T   F

29. Textbooks serve as the complete source of knowledge without
supplementary information. .... T   F

30. Public speaking and speech training are important aids to teach-
ing abilities. .... T   F

31. Slow learners can best be helped in their studies by providing them
with workbook assignments and individual help. .... T   F

32. Repetition is important in learning. .... T   F

33. An instructor should be qualified to teach all subjects relating to
beauty culture. .... T   F

34. Environment is one factor which influences the individual's ability
to learn. .... T   F

35. Deeper and more lasting impressions are obtained when more than
one sense organ conveys the message. .... T   F

36. All lessons should be conducted in the same manner in order that
students do not become confused. .... T   F

37. The beginning of all learning is derived from the impressions
received from the senses. .... T   F

38. While giving practical instruction to the student, stressing correct
posture is part of the lesson. .... T   F

39. Developing the student's skill is one of the instructor's objectives. T   F

40. Gossip is to be encouraged because it is an emotional release. ...... T   F

41. Learning can be drilled into a student who continues to have a
negative attitude. .... T   F

42. "If a student hasn't learned, the instructor hasn't taught." .... T   F

43. A neat personal appearance and good hygienic habits are two
"musts" for cosmetology instructors. .... T   F

44. Audio-visual aids are most effective as teaching devices when
they are used to relieve the teacher of the necessity of personal
instruction. .... T   F

45. Lesson plans are the instructor's guideposts to a good lesson. .... T   F

46. An instructor tries to help students accomplish the aims and goals
of the beauty culture course, as fast as they are able to progress. T   F

47. Style shows, conventions, and manufacturers' demonstrations are beneficial to both student and instructor. .... T   F

48. Sympathetic understanding and praise for the efforts of slow learners will encourage them to greater efforts. .... T   F

49. An instructor should train students to advise patrons as to the care of a contagious disease. .... T   F

50. An instructor should instill in the student the motto, "Clean as you work." .... T   F

51. Being an expert hairdresser qualifies one to teach the subject. ...... T   F

52. It is good educational practice to employ both the textbook and workbook. .... T   F

53. Preparing a student for State Board examination is the sole purpose of the instructor. .... T   F

54. Students should practice on patrons immediately following their instructor's **first** demonstration. .... T   F

55. The best classroom atmosphere results from the imposed authority of the instructor. .... T   F

56. Instructors should recognize that variability in a student's performance is normal. .... T   F

57. State Board failure of students may be a direct reflection on the instruction that has been given. .... T   F

58. Instructors can motivate the student's desire to learn. .... T   F

59. Some students learn best by reading, some by listening, and some by observing. .... T   F

60. If a student is in a state of learning readiness, the instructor does not need to employ continuous motivation. .... T   F

61. Emotional disturbances of students may hamper or retard their learning. .... T   F

62. Emotional stability is a necessary trait for the successful cosmetologist. .... T   F

63. Some students must stay in school longer than the required time in order to become competent .... T   F

64. All students could become beauty operators with the same quality of skills if they have had the same instructor. .... T   F

65. Students who lack emotional stability in school will usually show the same emotional instability on the job. .... T   F

66. Only an interest in beauty culture is necessary to make a successful beautician. .... T   F

67. Attitudes are traits that can be developed in the student. .... T   F

68. When students repeatedly exhibit undesirable attitudes, they should be dismissed from school. .... T   F

69. Adult students should be discouraged by the school because they are more difficult to teach. .... T   F

70. Safety practices should be taught in a beauty salon, not in a school. .... T   F

71. A good instructor perfects one method of teaching and sticks to it.   T   F

72. A student's questions or suggestions may indicate that the student is in a state of readiness to learn. .... T F

73. If an instructor gives a good demonstration, he should not repeat it until there is a new class. .... T F

74. Instruction sheets explaining the demonstration should be given to students so that the practice will be in proper order. .... T F

75. The objective of the practice method of teaching is to demonstrate the use of visual aids. .... T F

76. Only the first practice should be supervised. .... T F

77. Students who have difficulty should receive individual help. .... T F

78. An instructor's attitude may promote or retard the student's progress. .... T F

79. Firmness and strict supervision are necessary for the lazy student. T F

80. Perfection should be expected when students perform their first practice. .... T F

81. A written test should be spontaneous and be a surprise to the student. .... T F

82. The instructor should correct and assist the student during a testing period. .... T F

83. Trade terms in cosmetology are considered as part of related knowledge. .... T F

84. A test should be constructed in such a manner that it would be fair to only a few students. .... T F

85. Facial expressions of the examiner may at times reveal to the students whether they have answered correctly. .... T F

86. Learning is accelerated by well planned and prepared visual aids. T F

87. All lessons should include a demonstration. .... T F

88. Cosmetology instructors should develop a plan book as an aid to good teaching. .... T F

89. Lesson plans should be revised periodically as required. .... T F

90. An unrevised cosmetology textbook is usually up-to-date-in every detail. .... T F

91. Textbooks should contain correct information which can be relied upon. .... T F

92. Cosmetology students can improve learning by direct participation. .... T F

93. All motion pictures are excellent training aids. .... T F

94. An instructor should always preview slides or filmstrips before showing them to the students. .... T F

95. An instructor who is a skilled photographer and takes pictures in the school may add interest to his presentation. .... T F

96. Students may be helped to develop good study habits by using a combination of the textbook and workbook. .... T F

97. Cosmetology instructors should always demonstrate on patrons because they like that special attention. .... T F

98. Comments of the patrons should be taken seriously because they reflect upon the teaching that is done in the school. .... T F

99. Instructors should attend workshops because in this way they learn new methods and keep abreast with the times. .... T F

100. A student instructor may take charge of the school for a short while when the licensed instructor goes for lunch. .... T F

DIRECTIONS: *Place the correct word in spaces provided in sentences below.*

COMPLETION EXERCISE NUMBER 1

instructors	habit	file	individual
skills	trait	single	fast
administer	point	slow	plan

1. A beauty school is only as good as the .... it employs.

2. An instructor should keep a .... of all lesson plans.

3. One main objective of teaching beauty culture is helping the students develop ....

4. Do not expect a student to grasp all the points in a .... lesson.

5. Individual help and workbook assignments are methods employed to assist .... learners.

6. Teachers should give .... instruction to the slow learner.

7. An attitude is a .... that can be developed.

8. In scoring a performance test, use a .... system rather than a pass-fail evaluation.

9. Plan your work and work your ....

10. The main function of the State Cosmetology Board is to .... the law.

COMPLETION EXERCISE NUMBER 2

challenging	individual	references	method
blueprint	sanitary	training	practice
intellectual	dull	testing	lowest

1. Students who have difficulty should receive .... help.

2. .... rules are set up by the State Boards of Cosmetology.

3. Beauty culture trade magazines are good .... for the instructor.

4. A demonstration is almost useless unless the student can follow it with ....

5. A good teacher should give instructions geared to the .... level of the class.

6. A process of evaluating students' knowledge is called ....

7. A good instructor will use every .... possible to obtain results.

8. An instructor's plan book is a .... to teaching.

9. Special .... is required to present knowledge and skills to others.

10. To stimulate learning, present .... problems.

COMPLETION EXERCISE NUMBER 3

eyes	good	lesson	validity
lasting	patron	motivate	objectives
ears	beauty	bad	dismissed

1. .... plans are the instructor's guideposts.

2. A good test must have .... and reliability.

3. It is important for the instructor to make a good impression to the class because first impressions are ....

4. 85% of all learning is derived from the impressions received through the ....

5. A good instructor will try to .... students.

6. In a lesson plan, stress its ....

7. Teaching a new student is easier than teaching one who has already developed a .... habit.

8. A .... may serve as a live model in instructor demonstrations.

9. Students who continually disrupt the class or fail to follow the school rules should be ....

10. Cosmetology instructors must abide by state laws governing .... schools.

COMPLETION EXERCISE NUMBER 4

state	participation	skills	problems
silent	passiveness	attitudes	live
plan	mannequin	appraised	patience

1. .... can only be learned by doing.

2. Instructors should help maladjusted students overcome specific ....

3. Cosmetology schools must be licensed by their .... Board.

4. .... can either help or hinder a learning situation in a classroom.

5. The practice of manicuring is best performed on .... subjects.

6. A bulletin board is also known as a .... instructor.

7. An instructor's .... book is as necessary to teaching as the blueprint is to building a house.

8. Understanding and .... should be part of a good student-instructor relationship.

9. Each phase of a student's practice should be ....

10. Student .... is a necessary part of all learning.

COMPLETION EXERCISE NUMBER 5

Governor	practical	slowly	curriculum
student	workbook	fast	increases
progressive	encouragement	readiness	decreases

1. When demonstrating, speak .... and make the work clearly visible to the student.

2. In testing students, use .... written or oral examinations.

3. Praise and .... should be given students when they try.

4. When a student returns to class, after missing a lesson, the instructor should permit him to catch up as soon as possible, with the aid of the textbook and ....

5. State Board members are usually appointed by the ....

6. Testing is the method of determining the ability of both instructor and ....

7. The instructor's greatest challenge is to get the student in a state of ....

8. Learning based on previous knowledge is called .... learning.

9. An entire course of activities is called the ....

10. Repetition .... learning.

COMPLETION EXERCISE NUMBER 6

workbook	desire	ridicule	complicated
loyalty	motivated	patience	audio-visual
reference	study	instruction	simple

1. Learning does not take place unless there is a ....

2. Sympathetic understanding and .... should be practiced until they become part of teaching.

3. An .... sheet gives definite directions for performing skilled operations.

4. Students are .... faster when they see the materials assembled for a demonstration.

5. When using oral or written questions, as part of the teaching pattern, the instructor should avoid .... questions.

6. Important teaching aids which can be employed to help students learn and review essential information are the .... and textbook.

7. Both the textbook and the workbook help to develop good .... habits.

8. Above all else, cosmetology instructors owe their school, employer and students .... and respect.

9. An instructor should not .... a student at any time.

10. .... aids play an important role in a teaching program.

COMPLETION EXERCISE NUMBER 7

theory	techniques	same	record
example	required	curriculum	oral
lasting	beginning	temporary	additional

1. In a beauty school, all instructors should use the .... cosmetology textbook.

2. Instructors should follow the .... of the school in which they teach.

3. The general phases of beauty culture training are .... and practice.

4. Instructors should set a good .... for their students to follow.

5. It is important to keep a .... of services rendered in a beauty school.

6. Accomplishing a task by repetition establishes a .... skill.

7. Complicated statements should be avoided when using .... questions.

8. When students practice on each other, ... learning takes place.

9. Demonstrations should be used when teaching new .... to students.

10. Cosmetology students should be .... to be well-groomed.

COMPLETION EXERCISE NUMBER 8

immediately	mental	instructor	habitual
workbook	physical	sight	safety
hearing	lecture	professional	readiness

1. The .... is the most influential factor in cosmetology education.

2. Verbal explanations constitute an important element in the .... method of instruction.

3. The sense of .... is probably the most useful sense in learning.

4. The sense of .... rates second as the sense enabling effective learning.

5. Beauty culture basically consists of mastering manual skills co-ordinated with .... direction.

6. Continuous practice of a skill will produce actions which are automatic or ....

7. A student should practice .... after a demonstration.

8. Students should strive to establish .... and sanitary habits.

9. An important teaching aid, employed both in the classroom and for home-work assignments, to help students learn essential information, is the ....

10. Students learn best when they are in a state of ....

COMPLETION EXERCISE NUMBER 9

motivate	not	more	interesting
art	always	fear	boring
counseled	group	progress	attitude

1. The task of the instructor is to make students want to learn, or to .... them.

2. .... and worry are great retarders of learning.

3. Cosmetology is both a science and an .... requiring manual skills.

4. Students should be .... to seek some other training if their abilities do not seem compatible to beauty culture.

5. Aptitude tests should .... be used as a rejection device, unless other factors indicate it also.

6. .... teaching may be used in an introduction to a lesson.

7. Students with more ability should be allowed to .... rather than be kept with the slower students.

8. Practicing a skill that can be done in a routine manner can be very .... to a student.

9. An .... is a trait that can be developed.

10. Older students may require .... study periods to master the theory.

COMPLETION EXERCISE NUMBER 10

answer key	all	self-appraisal	allowed
capable	progress	various	few
instructors	improve	limit	skills

1. Instructors should be required to .... their skills and keep abreast with the new techniques.

2. Instructors should try .... methods and techniques in their teaching.

3. Alert instructors observe their students' progress as a means of ....

4. Any attitude that inhibits learning should not be .... in the classroom.

5. Emotionally disturbed students do not usually make .... hair-dressers.

6. When school problems are discussed and changes planned, the .... should be consulted and serve in an advisory capacity.

7. A school curriculum includes .... of the activities which influence students in their growth and development.

8. Students having more ability should be allowed to .... more rapidly.

9. In grading exam papers, the instructor should use an ....

10. Instructors strive to impart knowledge, understanding and .... to others.

Multiple Choice Test Items

1—c	21—c	41—b	61—d	81—d
2—c	22—b	42—b	62—b	82—b
3—a	23—d	43—b	63—c	83—b
4—c	24—c	44—d	64—b	84—c
5—a	25—a	45—a	65—c	85—c
6—b	26—c	46—c	66—d	86—d
7—d	27—c	47—c	67—a	87—d
8—c	28—a	48—a	68—a	88—c
9—b	29—b	49—c	69—c	89—d
10—a	30—c	50—d	70—b	90—c
11—c	31—b	51—b	71—a	91—a
12—c	32—d	52—d	72—b	92—c
13—c	33—c	53—d	73—c	93—d
14—d	34—d	54—b	74—a	94—b
15—c	35—a	55—c	75—d	95—b
16—c	36—b	56—d	76—d	96—a
17—a	37—d	57—a	77—a	97—b
18—b	38—b	58—c	78—b	98—c
19—a	39—d	59—b	79—a	99—c
20—d	40—a	60—b	80—c	100—a

True-False Items

1—T	21—T	41—F	61—T	81—F
2—T	22—F	42—T	62—T	82—F
3—T	23—T	43—T	63—T	83—T
4—F	24—T	44—F	64—F	84—F
5—F	25—T	45—T	65—T	85—T
6—T	26—F	46—T	66—F	86—T
7—T	27—T	47—T	67—T	87—F
8—T	28—T	48—T	68—T	88—T
9—F	29—F	49—F	69—F	89—T
10—T	30—T	50—T	70—F	90—F
11—T	31—T	51—F	71—F	91—T
12—T	32—T	52—T	72—T	92—T
13—T	33—T	53—F	73—F	93—F
14—T	34—T	54—F	74—T	94—T
15—T	35—T	55—T	75—F	95—T
16—F	36—F	56—T	76—F	96—T
17—F	37—T	57—T	77—T	97—F
18—T	38—T	58—T	78—T	98—T
19—T	39—T	59—T	79—T	99—T
20—T	40—F	60—F	80—F	100—F

Completion Items

Exercise 1

1—instructors
2—file
3—skills
4—single
5—slow
6—individual
7—trait
8—point
9—plan
10—administer

Exercise 2

1—individual
2—sanitary
3—references
4—practice
5—intellectual
6—testing
7—method
8—blueprint
9—training
10—challenging

Exercise 3

1—lesson
2—validity
3—lasting
4—eyes
5—motivate
6—objectives
7—bad
8—patron
9—dismissed
10—beauty

Exercise 4

1—skills
2—problems
3—State
4—attitudes
5—live
6—silent
7—plan
8—patience
9—appraised
10—participation

Exercise 5

1—slowly
2—practical
3—encouragement
4—workbook
5—Governor
6—student
7—readiness
8—progressive
9—curriculum
10—increases

Exercise 6

1—desire
2—patience
3—instruction
4—motivated
5—complicated
6—workbook
7—study
8—loyalty
9—ridicule
10—audio-visual

Completion Items (continued)

Exercise 7	Exercise 8	Exercise 9	Exercise 10
1—same	1—instructor	1—motivate	1—improve
2—curriculum	2—lecture	2—fear	2—various
3—theory	3—sight	3—art	3—self-appraisal
4—example	4—hearing	4—counseled	4—allowed
5—record	5—mental	5—not	5—capable
6—lasting	6—habitual	6—group	6—instructors
7—oral	7—immediately	7—progress	7—all
8—additional	8—safety	8—boring	8—progress
9—techniques	9—workbook	9—attitude	9—answer key
10—required	10—readiness	10—more	10—skills

GLOSSARY

ability: skill, power to do or act in special ways; cleverness; aptitude.

absorb: to interest very much; to take in or receive and assimilate knowledge.

absorbing: to be extremely interesting.

accomplishment: an achievement; success in completing some act or art; acquiring some skill or art.

achieve: to bring to a successful end; to accomplish.

achievement: act of bringing something to a successful conclusion.

adjunct: a word or phrase modifying or qualifying another word or phrase; something that is added that is less important or not necessary but helpful.

aggressive: very forceful; energetic; driving; a disposition to dominate; bold, self-confidence in expression of opinion.

aims: purposes; intentions; ultimate objectives.

allergy: unusual sensitiveness to a particular substance.

alleviate: to make something easier to endure or to accept.

ambiguity: a word or expression the meaning of which is uncertain and is capable of being understood in two or more ways.

ambiguous: capable of being understood in two or more ways; of uncertain meaning.

ambition: strong desire for fame, honor or position.

analysis: examination of parts of something to find their essential features.

analytical: examining something (e.g., a teaching program) to study and evaluate its merits.

annex: to join or add to a larger thing; a supplementary branch to a school.

antagonistic: to be actively opposed; counteracting.

anticipate: to foresee and deal with something in advance; to expect something to happen; to expect certain actions or reactions and to take certain precautions in anticipation.

anxiety: uneasiness; concern over an impending or anticipated event.

applicable: capable of being put to practical use.

application: the act of putting to practical use; continuing effort.

appreciate: to recognize the worth or quality of something; to be thankful for.

appreciation: a sympathetic understanding of the worth or quality of something.

aptitude: a quickness to understand; a natural tendency, ability or capacity for learning.

archaic: no longer in general use; old fashioned; out of use.

arrange: to put in proper order.

art: a branch of learning that depends more on special practice than on general principles; some special kind of skill or practical application of a skill.

articulate: speak distinctly; spoken in distinct syllables or words.

aspect: one side, part or view of a subject; outlook.

assignment: a specific task or amount of work given to one, or to a group, to perform.

assimilate: digest or absorb; to take in.

assume: to take for granted; to suppose.

assurance: making sure or certain; a positive statement inspiring confidence.

assure: to make sure or certain; to make safe against loss; to insure.

atmosphere: surrounding influences; the general air or morale of a classroom.

attain: to accomplish; to succeed in coming to or arriving at a desired conclusion.

attainable: achievable.

attitude: the manner displayed toward a person, thing or emotion.

audio-visual: teaching aids which are designed to appeal to both the senses of sight and hearing.

avocation: a minor occupation; something that takes one away from his/her regular calling.

axiomatic: a self-evident truth; an established principle.

basic: fundamental; forming the base of an object, idea or plan.

bore: to tire by annoying repetition; to weary, fatigue; a dull, tiresome person.

boredom: the state of being wearied or annoyed by a dull, tiresome person or condition.

career: a way of earning a living; an occupation or profession; a general course of action or progress.

character: the special thing or quality which makes one person different from others; all qualities or features possessed by a person; the special way that a person feels, thinks and acts.

colloquial: word or phrase used in everyday informal talk, but not in formal speech or writing.

communication: the process of exchanging information; the method or means of expressing ideas effectively in speech or writing, or by some other means.

complexity: an involved or intricate quality or condition.

comprehension: the act or ability to understand the meaning of; understanding.

comprehensive: understanding; wide or extensive understanding.

concentration: close attention; paying very close attention.

concept: a general notion or idea.

conducive: the act, condition or quality tending to promote or assist.

conference: a meeting of a class of students and teacher to discuss a particular subject.

confidence: a firm belief in yourself and your abilities.

conjunction: the act of joining together; combination.

construct: to put together the parts of something in their proper place and order.

constructive: helpful; tending to build up.

contact: condition of touching; to get in touch with someone.

context: the parts before and after a word or a sentence which influence its meaning.

continuity: the state or quality of being continuous; connecting comments or statements between the parts of a program which make it a complete body of subject matter.

contrive: to invent, design or plan.

cooperative: willing to work together with others.

coordination: the act of joining words, phrases, clauses or ideas of equal importance.

course of study: a complete and detailed breakdown of the general subjects, listed in the curriculum, into their specific component parts.

course outline: a comprehensive and organized series of class sessions covering the entire curriculum as a coordinated and cohesive unit.

create: to make by giving a new character, function or status to a thing or an idea.

creative: having the power to invent, produce or to bring into being.

critic: a person who expresses a judgment or opinion of the faults and/or merits of any matter, book, play, etc.

critique: an act of criticizing, a careful analysis of the merits, strengths and/or weaknesses of any matter, book, play, etc.

curriculum: a body of selected subjects, phrased in general terms, which is designed to stimulate the development of cosmetologists, to acquaint them with necessary knowledge, to develop in them the fundamental skills and to make clear to them the interrelationships of all phases of cosmetology.

dedication: the act of devoting oneself wholly or earnestly to the achievement of a predesigned goal.

defect: the lack of something essential to completeness; a fault or a blemish.

deliberate: thinking out slowly and carefully in deciding a course of action.

depict: to represent by drawing, painting or describing.

detrimental: harmful; injurious; damaging.

dexterity: manual skill and ease in using the hands.

diagnosis: a careful study of the facts about something to find out its essential features or faults.

difference: the condition of having a different opinion; a disagreement.

digest: to understand and absorb mentally; to make something part of one's thoughts; to condense and arrange according to some system.

dignity: self-respecting character or manner.

discipline: training of the mind or character; the trained condition of order and obedience.

discussion: the process of going over the reasons for and against a particular theme.

distract: to divert one's attention from any point toward another point.

distraction: a disturbance of thought or a confusion of mind which draws away the mind or attention.

diversify: to produce variety or to engage in a number of different operations.

education: development in knowledge, skill, or ability by teaching, training, study or experience.

effect, law of: a law of learning which indicates that interest cannot be aroused unless we justify, to our students, the experience or material about to be presented to them.

effective: a course of action which produces a desired effect.

efficiency: ability to produce desired results without waste of time and energy.

element: one of the parts of which any object, plan or program is made up.

elimination: the process of removing something from consideration.

emphasis: special force; importance or effect given to particular syllables, words, phrases or ideas.

emphasize: to give special force or stress to.

enthusiasm: eager interest or zeal; eagerness or fervor.

environment: all of the surrounding conditions and influences that affect the development of a living thing; act or fact of surrounding.

essentials: necessary elements or qualities needed to make a thing what it is.

ethics: standards of right and wrong.

evaluate: to fix or find the value of something.

executive: the ability to carry out or manage an operation.

exercise, law of: the law of learning which indicates that the students' reactions and ability to perform effectively will determine their understanding and retention.

facets: any of the definite or distinguishable parts which make up a subject or a course.

factor: an element, condition or quality which helps to bring about a result.

fervor: great warmth of feeling; intense emotion.

fetish (fetich): a fixation; an object or idea regarded or followed with unreasonable or extravagant trust or devotion.

flexibility: easily adapted to various purposes; easily managed or willing to yield to influence or persuasion.

format: general arrangement, makeup and basic plan of a lesson.

gestures: motions of the body or parts of the body to express or emphasize ideas or emotions.

grooming: making neat and tidy; to take care of one's appearance.

heterogeneous: made up of unlike, dissimilar elements or individuals; mixed.

homogeneous: composed of similar elements or individuals; alike.

hostility: the state or quality of being in opposition; antagonistic.

image: a mental picture of something; conception; impression.

impression: an effect produced on the mind or senses by some force or influence.

incentive: the motive or stimulus for a course of action.

indoctrinate: to teach a doctrine, belief or principle to someone.

inducement: any argument, reason or fact that persuades or influences the mind.

inept: unsuitable; unfit; foolish.

inert: lacking in the power of moving or of active resistance to motion; inactive, sluggish.

inertia: lack of a desire to move, exert any energy or effort.

initiative: the readiness and ability to be the one to start a course of action or a program.

innovative: to make changes; to bring in something new or new ways of doing things.

inspire: to put thought, feeling, life or force into a class or students.

instinct: a natural feeling, tendency, knowledge or power.

instruction: teaching; knowledge; education.

instructional unit: a unit of knowledge or information which is the teaching and learning objective of the class session.

instructor: a teacher.

intensity, law of: the law of learning which indicates that teaching is most successful when it is applied through as many senses as possible.

interpretation: bringing out the meaning of certain facts; an explanation.

irrelevant: off the subject; not to the point at issue.

lecture: an informative talk given before a class.

lesson plan: a "blue print" of the teaching-learning situation containing important guidelines to direct the teacher's activities throughout the lesson.

logic: reason; the science of correct reasoning; the system of principles underlying any art or science.

logical: to be expected because of what has gone before.

manipulate: to manage or deal with a situation or thing.

mannequin: a model of the human head used by cosmetologists.

mannerism: manner or style of behavior.

manners: personal behavior; a way of acting.

mature: to become fully grown or developed.

maturity: the state or quality of being fully-grown or fully developed.

maximize: to make the most of something.

method: a form of procedure; the manner in which the teacher proceeds to achieve the desired educational objective.

minimize: to make the least of something.

monotone: to speak in a single tone without inflections, emphasis or in an unvaried key.

monotony: the uniformity of tone or sound; any persistent sameness or want of variety.

morale: a mental condition which influences one's courage, confidence, or enthusiasm.

motivate: to furnish with a motive; to give impetus, to incite or impel a student to study.

motivation: a method, idea or force which furnishes a student with the impetus, incitement or incentive to study.

narration: to recite the details of a story or statement; the act of telling in detail; a form of composition which relates an event or story.

objective: existing outside of the mind as an actual object and not merely in the mind as an idea; actions are objective, ideas are subjective.

objectives: the aims; the goals or objects to be achieved.

objectivity: the state or quality of being independent of the mind or feelings; of being real and actual.

occupation: the business or trade one follows to earn a living.

occupational: pertaining to an occupation.

oral test: an examination which is conducted verbally, the questions are asked by the spoken word and answers are given in the same manner.

participate: to take part in or share in.

participation: the act or fact of sharing or partaking.

perception: the act or process of the mind which makes known an external object; becoming aware of something through the senses.

perceptivity: the power of the mind which makes known an external object; the power of the mind to attain awareness or understanding.

performance test (practical test): an examination in which the examinee is required to actually execute, manually, a number of technical operations requested by the examiner. The quality of his (the examinee's) actual completion of these operations is evaluated by the examiner.

personality: the extent to which individuals develop habits and skills which interest and please other people.

plateau: used figuratively to a period in the development of a person's learning characterized by a relative absence of progress.

poise: general composure, balance and stability; ease and dignity of manner.

practical: engaged in actual practice or work; having to do with actual practice rather than thought or theory.

practice: the working at or following of an occupation; an action done many times over to perfect a skill.

preliminary: serving as an introduction; going before the main part.

prerequisite: a condition or program required beforehand as a condition for something following.

presentation: something that is being presented.

primacy, law of: the law of learning which indicates that learning the right way the first time is easiest for the student.

principle: a fundamental truth or motivating force upon which other acts are based.

procedure: the method or manner of proceeding in some course of action.

process: a particular method of doing something.

professional: engaged in a specified occupation as a means of a livelihood; having a great deal of experience and skill in a specified role.

progressive: some system or program which is marked by progress.

project: to send forth one's thoughts or imagination; a unit of work involving constructive thought and action in connection with learning.

projection: the process of presenting one's thoughts and ideas to others.

quality: the basic nature, character or characteristics which may make an object good or bad.

range: the limits of possible variations of amount or degree.

rapport: harmonious relation; relation; agreement; harmony.

reaction: a response to a stimulus or influence; a return or opposing action.

readiness, law of: the law of learning which requires that the willingness, desire and interest to learn be present on the part of the student.

realistic: practical rather than visionary; tendency to face facts.

recall: to take back; to cancel; to revoke.

redundancy: something which uses an excessive number of words to express a single thought.

redundant: more than enough; excessive; overabundant; wordy; superfluous.

reference: the directing of attention to a person or thing.

related: to have some connection or relation to.

relevant: relating to the matter in hand; to the point; pertinent or applicable.

repetition: the act of saying or doing the same thing over and over again.

reticence: the trait of being silent or secretive; the condition of being restrained in expression, presentation or appearance.

ridicule: words or actions intended to express contempt and excite laughter.

routine: a regular, more or less unvarying procedure; the customary way to perform.

sarcasm: a taunting, sneering, cutting or jeering remark.

schedule: a list of times of recurring events; a list, catalog or inventory of details.

science: systematized knowledge derived from observation, study and experimentation, carried on in order to determine the nature or principles of what is being studied.

segment: a piece; one of the parts into which a body, plan or idea is divided.

sensory: connected with the reception and transmission of sense impressions; of the senses.

standard: something established for use as a basis of comparison in measuring or judging quality; anything recognized as correct.

static: not moving or progressing.

stimulate: to excite or animate to action or more vigorous action.

stimulating: exciting or rousing to action or more vigorous action.

subjective: existing in the mind; personal; existing in the thoughts and feelings of the individual.

subjectively: existence in the mind only.

subject matter: the material presented for consideration; course of instruction.

summary: a short or condensed statement or abstract of the substance of a fuller and more complete statement.

systematic: organized, set or arranged in such form as to develop a unified and organic whole.

tact: ability to say and do the right things; skill in dealing with people or handling difficult situations.

tactic: arrangement or system.

teach: to direct learning; to give instruction.

technical: of or pertaining to the special facts of a science, art or skill.

technique: the method or procedure in carrying out a scientific or mechanical operation.

tempo: the rate of activity.

theoretical: planned or worked out in the mind—not from experience.

theory: that branch of an art, science or vocation consisting of a knowledge of its principles and method rather than its practice.

transparencies: a visual teaching aid which makes a picture visible on a screen when light shines through it.

valid: something correctly derived from the application of accepted principles of performance; conclusions which are supported by facts or authority.

ventilation: the act or process of circulating air in a room; a system or means of supplying fresh air.

versatility: the quality of being capable of embracing a variety of subjects, fields or skills.

vocation: a career or occupation or trade.

vocational: pertaining to an occupation or trade.

vocational training: training for a career, occupation, or trade.

written test: an examination which is based strictly on written questions and the examinees answers are also in written form.

zeal: ardor; fervor; eager interest and enthusiasm

Recommended List of Reference and Library Books

STANDARD TEACHER'S GUIDE FOR BEAUTY CULTURE
—by S.C. Thorpe.

Intended to aid teachers in planning and presenting the theory and operations of cosmetology. Instructional units for both theory and practice.

COSMETOLOGY TEACHER'S MANUAL
—by Ruth Bok.

If you are an experienced teacher who has not had formal training, or if you are a student intent on becoming a beauty culture instructor, "Cosmetology Teacher's Manual" should be No. 1 on your required reading list.

COSMETOLOGY TEACHERS' EXAM REVIEW
—by Ruth Bok.

Need help in improving your classroom instruction or in qualifying for an instructor's license? This book provides practice and review in the principles of effective teaching, classroom management, pupil-teacher relationships, and business law. It contains over 400 test items (essay, true or false, completion and multiple choice) together with answers. A special section is devoted to practical exams for teacher's license.

325 TEACHING HINTS FOR PROFESSIONAL COSMETOLOGY INSTRUCTION
—by Jacob J. Yahm.

A compact presentation of the duties and responsibilities of cosmetology instructors. A book you will refer to again and again for suggestions on how to conduct various phases of your teaching and training program.

HUMAN ANATOMY AND PHYSIOLOGY
—by Dr. King and Dr. Showers.

This book for beginning students reflects the latest advances in anatomy and physiology.

COSMETOLOGY TEACHER-TRAINING MANUAL
—by Jacob J. Yahm.

This manual offers to cosmetology teachers and to teachers-in-training a complete, illustrated study of new techniques in the field of cosmetology education. It is designed to meet the needs of schools that train cosmetology teachers and also of practicing teachers eager for more understanding and knowledge of the most modern teaching procedures. The book presents the latest theories, methods and programs for elevating the standards of cosmetology education.

PSYCHOLOGY AND LIFE
—by Floyd L. Ruch, professor of psychology.

An understanding of psychology underlies effective teaching. This book, which describes the mental and behavioral characteristics of individuals and groups, will be useful to all teachers.

TEXTBOOK OF ANATOMY AND PHYSIOLOGY
—by Kimber, Gray, Stackpole and Leavell.

Latest revised edition. Clearly organized and fully illustrated, each chapter stresses the interlocking relationship between structure and function. A summary outline follows each chapter.

WEBSTER'S NEW COLLEGIATE DICTIONARY.

A complete dictionary arranged in a new format. Presents clear, concise, easy to understand definitions, pronunciations, derivations, synonyms and illustrations. Includes a pronouncing gazetteer, a biographical section and many special features.

TECNICAS MODERNAS DEL PEINADO (Standard Textbook of Cosmetology).

Spanish edition of the popular English title. A practical course on the scientific fundamentals of beauty culture for students and practicing cosmetologists.

PERFORMANCE (COMPETENCY) BASED TRAINING FOR COSMETOLOGY
—by Jacob J. Yahm.

This manual includes performance and learning objectives with recommended testing. Designed to be used in conjunction with all basic cosmetology textbooks. Encased in an 8½" x 11" 3-ring binder, it can be used as is, or separated and placed within lesson plan sets.

BASIC LESSON PLANS FOR THE COSMETOLOGY TEACHER.

This is a completely new set, consisting of 220 detailed lesson plans keyed to the completely revised 1981 edition of the "Standard Textbook of Cosmetology." Closely following the new text and breaking down each chapter into manageable lessons, the entire contents are presented in one 3-ring binder. Each detailed lesson follows the most popular lesson plan outline used by modern educators, and each lesson objective is clearly stated in behavioral terms. Lessons include the materials and facilities needed, suggested visual aids, step-by-step procedures for the presentation of each lesson, motivational devices, leading questions, and student assignments. Persons involved in curriculum and course planning can use this set of lesson plans as a guide in developing a comprehensive course of study.

NEW GOULD'S (Large) MEDICAL DICTIONARY.

76,000 words, 1528 pages. All leading educators use this king-size dictionary for reference.

CHEMISTRY IN YOUR BEAUTY SHOP.

A book on the chemistry involved in the most common phases of beauty culture, such as cold waving, shampooing, hair dyes and tints, etc. Written to help the beautician understand the "why" of each operation as well as the "how."

THE ENCYCLOPEDIA OF HAIRCUTTING
—by Charles Ross.

This internationally known hair design expert has created a comprehensive book describing over twenty different hairstyles. The Encyclopedia connects classic, contemporary and modern haircutting so that understanding one method makes the learning of the next one easier. Each method is explained fully, with diagrams, photographs and step-by-step procedure charts included to make the material readily understood. Every instrument and all techniques of haircutting are described and explained in this book.

6,000 YEARS OF HAIRSTYLING
—by M. Louis.

An encyclopedia of hairdressing that traces the history of hair fashions in a clear and logical manner, this book is both interesting and informative.

WIGS (A Complete Guide for the Profession)
—by Sally Cooney & Charlotte Harper.

Styling, coloring, cutting, blocking, cleaning, and conditioning are but a few of the areas covered in this practical, easy-to-use handbook on wigs. The authors also offer detailed information on sanitation, sterilization, salesmanship, and business management, and even include an indispensable glossary of wig terms. This is a vitally important book for the operator-in-training, the practicing beautician, and the salon manager or owner.

BEAUTICIAN'S GUIDE TO BEAUTY, CHARM AND POISE.

The first book of its kind ever to be published. Will help your students to achieve confidence, charm and poise. The Government, several years ago, conducted a survey which showed that women who have had training in charm and poise earn far more than other women of comparable business background. A charm course (in school or at home) can help your students be more successful and eventually earn more money.

HAIR STRUCTURE AND CHEMISTRY SIMPLIFIED
—by A.H. Powitt, B.Sc., A.S.T.C. (Applied Biology).

Profusely illustrated, using numerous photos made with the new scanning electron microscope. Pertinent, factual and easy to read. Two-color printing throughout. Coordinated with existing instructional aids: "Lectures in Hair Structure and Chemistry," "Exam Reviews in Hair Structure and Chemistry," and audio-visual aids describing hair structure and chemistry, including overhead projector transparencies, slides and flip charts.

VISUAL AIDS

AV INSTRUCTIONAL MEDIA AND METHODS.

This book was written to assist prospective and practicing teachers in becoming acquainted with the broad range and interrelated uses of many different kinds of educational media, techniques and devices.

AV INSTRUCTIONAL TECHNOLOGY MANUAL FOR INDEPENDENT STUDY.

This manual provides exercises that give you active learning experiences in the practical problems of choosing, using and inventing instructional materials, and in operating audio-visual equipment.

VISUAL AIDS PROJECTOR TABLE.

Protect your investment with the best in video tables—Heavy gauge steel, tubular chrome legs, 2" ball casters, electrical assembly and lockable cabinet. 30" W x 40" H x 20" D—Weight 90 lbs. 5-Year warranty against defects and workmanship.

ADJUSTABLE AV TABLE.

The finest AV table money can buy. The solution to all your problems—adjustable to any height—welded steel construction. Weight—42 lbs. 5-Year warranty against defects and workmanship.

NOTE: Other models available—write for information.

NOTES:

**For Complete List
of Cosmetology Books and Visual Aids**
write to

Milady Publishing Corporation
3839 White Plains Road
Bronx, New York 10467